THE FEATHER THIEF

THE
FEATHER
THIEF

Beauty, Obsession, and the
Natural History Heist of the Century

KIRK WALLACE JOHNSON

VIKING

VIKING

An imprint of Penguin Random House LLC
375 Hudson Street
New York, New York 10014
penguin.com

Illustration Credits

Page 1: *(left)*: From *Alfred Russel Wallace: Letters and Reminiscences* by James Marchant (1916); *(top right)*: Courtesy of the Linnean Society of London; *(bottom right)*: Courtesy of the Field Museum of Natural History Bird Collection. **Page 2:** *(top)*: Flickr/Francesco Veronesi; *(bottom)*: Flickr/Matthias Appel. **Page 3:** *(top)*: iStock/Uwe-Bergwitz; *(bottom)*: © Tim Laman, used with permission. **Page 4:** *(top left)*: *Harper's Bazaar*; *(bottom)*: From *Our Vanishing Wild Life* by William T. Hornaday (1913). **Page 5:** *(top right)*: From *Our Vanishing Wild Life* by William T. Hornaday (1913); *(bottom)*: Photograph by H.B. Thrasher, Courtesy of the U.S. Fish and Wildlife Service Museum/Archives at National Conservation Training Center. **Pages 6 and 7:** From *The Salmon Fly: How to Dress it and How to Use it* by George M. Kelson (1895). **Page 8:** *(top)*: From *The Salmon Fly: How to Dress it and How to Use it* by George M. Kelson (1895); *(bottom)*: Courtesy of Spencer Seim. **Page 9:** *(top, middle, and bottom)*: Courtesy of Edward Muzeroll. **Page 10:** *(top)*: Photo © Gerald Massey, licensed for reuse under Creative Commons License; *(bottom)*: Courtesy of the Natural History Museum, London. **Page 11:** *(top)*: Courtesy of Dr. John R. Hutchinson; *(bottom)*: Courtesy of the Natural History Museum, London. **Page 12:** *(top)*: Courtesy of the Natural History Museum, London; *(bottom)*: Courtesy of Anonymous. **Page 13:** *(top and bottom)*: Courtesy of the Hertfordshire Constabulary. **Page 14:** *(top)*: Courtesy of the Hertfordshire Constabulary; *(bottom)*: Courtesy of Press Association Images. **Page 15:** *(top and bottom)*: Courtesy of Robert Delisle. **Page 16:** *(top left)*: From *The Rod and the Line* by Hewitt Wheatley (1849); *(top right)*: Courtesy of Anonymous; *(bottom)*: Courtesy of David Stenström.

ISBN: 9781101981610 (hardcover)
9781101981627 (e-book)
9780525559092 (EXP)

Printed in the United States of America
1 3 5 7 9 10 8 6 4 2

Set in Sabon LT Std
Designed by Cassandra Garruzzo

For Marie-Josée:
C'était tout noir et blanc
avant que tu aies volé et atterri
dans mon arbre

Man is seldom content to witness beauty.
He must possess it.

Grand Chief Sir Michael Somare,
Prime Minister of Papua New Guinea
1979

CONTENTS

III. TRUTH AND CONSEQUENCES

A section of illustrations follows page 212.

THE FEATHER THIEF

PROLOGUE

B y the time Edwin Rist stepped off the train onto the platform at Tring, forty miles north of London, it was already quite late. The residents of the sleepy town had finished their suppers; the little ones were in bed. As he began the long walk into town, the Midland line glided off into darkness.

A few hours earlier Edwin had performed in the Royal Academy of Music's "London Soundscapes," a celebration of Haydn, Handel, and Mendelssohn. Before the concert, he'd packed a pair of latex gloves, a miniature LED flashlight, a wire cutter, and a diamond-blade glass cutter in a large rolling suitcase, and stowed it in his concert hall locker. He bore a passing resemblance to a lanky Pete Townshend: intense eyes, prominent nose, and a mop of hair, although instead of shredding a Fender, Edwin played the flute.

There was a new moon that evening, making the already-gloomy stretch of road even darker. For nearly an hour, he dragged his suitcase through the mud and gravel skirting the road, under gnarly old trees strangled with ivy. Turlhanger's Wood slept to the north, Chestnut Wood to the south, fallow fields and the occasional copse in between.

A car blasted by, its headlights blinding. Adrenaline coursing, he knew he was getting close.

The entrance to the market town of Tring is guarded by a sixteenth-century pub called the Robin Hood. A few roads beyond, nestled between the old Tring Brewery and an HSBC branch, lies the entrance to Public Footpath 37. Known to locals as Bank Alley, the footpath isn't more than eight feet wide and is framed by seven-foot-high brick walls.

Edwin slipped into the alley, into total darkness. He groped his way along until he was standing directly behind the building he'd spent months casing.

All that separated him from it was the wall. Capped with three rusted strands of barbed wire, it might have thwarted his plans were it not for the wire cutter. After clearing an opening, he lifted the suitcase to the ledge, hoisted himself up, and glanced anxiously about. No sign of the guard. There was a space of several feet between his perch on the wall and the building's nearest window, forming a small ravine. If he fell, he could injure himself—or worse, make a clamor that would summon security. But he'd known this part wouldn't be easy.

Crouched on top of the wall, he reached toward the window with the glass cutter and began to grind it along the pane. Cutting glass was harder than he had anticipated, though, and as he struggled to carve an opening, the glass cutter slipped from his hand and fell into the ravine. His mind raced. Was this a sign? He was thinking about bailing on the whole crazy scheme when that voice, the one that had urged him onward these past months, shouted *Wait a minute! You can't give up now. You've come all this way!*

He crawled back down and picked up a rock. Steadying himself atop the wall, he peered around in search of guards before bashing the window out, wedging his suitcase through the shard-strewn opening, and climbing into the British Natural History Museum.

Unaware that he had just tripped an alarm in the security guard's office, Edwin pulled out the LED light, which cast a faint glow in front of him as he made his way down the hallways toward the vault, just as he'd rehearsed in his mind.

He wheeled his suitcase quietly through corridor after corridor, drawing ever closer to the most beautiful things he had ever seen. If he pulled this off, they would bring him fame, wealth, and prestige. They would solve his problems. He deserved them.

He entered the vault, its hundreds of large white steel cabinets standing in rows like sentries, and got to work. He pulled out the first drawer, catching a waft of mothballs. Quivering beneath his fingertips were a dozen Red-ruffed Fruitcrows, gathered by naturalists and biologists over hundreds of years from the forests and jungles of South America and fastidiously preserved by generations of curators for the benefit of future research. Their coppery-orange feathers glimmered despite the faint light. Each bird, maybe a foot and a half from beak to tail, lay on its back in funerary repose, eye sockets filled with cotton, feet folded close against the body. Tied around their legs were biodata labels: faded, handwritten records of the date, altitude, latitude, and longitude of their capture, along with other vital details.

He unzipped the suitcase and began filling it with the birds, emptying one drawer after another. The *occidentalis* subspecies that he snatched by the handful had been gathered a century earlier from the Quindío Andes region of western Colombia. He didn't know exactly how many he'd be able to fit into his suitcase, but he managed forty-seven of the museum's forty-eight male specimens before wheeling his bag on to the next cabinet.

Down in the security office, the guard was fixated on a small television screen. Engrossed in a soccer match, he hadn't yet noticed the alarm indicator blinking on a nearby panel.

Edwin opened the next cabinet to reveal dozens of Resplendent Quetzal skins gathered in the 1880s from the Chiriquí cloud forests of western Panama, a species now threatened by widespread deforestation and protected by international treaties. At nearly four feet in length, the birds were particularly difficult to stuff into his suitcase, but he maneuvered thirty-nine of them inside by gently curling their sweeping tails into tight coils.

Moving down the corridor, he swung open the doors of another cabinet, this one housing species of the Cotinga birds of South and Central America. He swiped fourteen one-hundred-year-old skins of the Lovely Cotinga, a small turquoise bird with a reddish-purple breast endemic to Central America, before relieving the museum of thirty-seven specimens of the Purple-breasted Cotinga, twenty-one skins of the Spangled Cotinga, and another ten skins of the endangered Banded Cotinga, of which as few as 250 mature individuals are estimated to be alive today.

The Galápagos island finches and mockingbirds gathered by Charles Darwin in 1835 during the voyage of the HMS *Beagle*— which had been instrumental in developing his theory of evolution through natural selection—were resting in nearby drawers. Among the museum's most valuable holdings were skeletons and skins of extinct birds, including the Dodo, the Great Auk, and the Passenger Pigeon, along with an elephant-folio edition of John James Audubon's *The Birds of America*. Overall, the museum houses one of the world's largest collection of ornithological specimens: 750,000 bird skins, 15,000 skeletons, 17,000 birds preserved in spirit, 4,000 nests, and 400,000 sets of eggs, gathered over the centuries from the world's most remote forests, mountainsides, jungles, and swamps.

But Edwin hadn't broken into the museum for a drab-colored finch. He had lost track of how long he'd been in the vault when he finally wheeled his suitcase to a stop before a large cabinet. A small plaque indicated its contents: PARADISAEIDAE. Thirty-seven King Birds of Paradise, swiped in seconds. Twenty-four Magnificent Riflebirds. Twelve Superb Birds of Paradise. Four Blue Birds of Paradise. Seventeen Flame Bowerbirds. These flawless specimens, gathered against almost impossible odds from virgin forests of New Guinea and the Malay Archipelago 150 years earlier, went into Edwin's bag, their tags bearing the name of a self-taught naturalist whose breakthrough had given Darwin the scare of his life: A. R. WALLACE.

The guard glanced at the CCTV feed, an array of shots of the parking lot and the museum campus. He began his round, pacing the hallways, checking the doors, scanning for anything awry.

Edwin had long since lost count of the number of birds that passed through his hands. He had originally planned to choose only the best of each species, but in the excitement of the plunder, he grabbed and stuffed until his suitcase could hold no more.

The guard stepped outside to begin a perimeter check, glancing up at the windows and beaming his flashlight on the section abutting the brick wall of Bank Alley.

Edwin stood before the broken window, now framed with shards of glass. So far everything had gone according to plan, with the exception of the missing glass cutter. All that remained was to climb back out of the window without slicing himself open, and melt into the anonymity of the street.

———

I was waist-high in the Red River, which slices through the Sangre de Cristo Mountains just north of Taos, New Mexico, when I first heard the name Edwin Rist. My fly-line was midcast, hovering energetically over the current behind me, ready to shoot forward in pursuit of the golden-bellied trout that Spencer Seim, my fly-fishing guide, had assured me was hiding behind a car-size boulder in the middle of the stream. Spencer could sense fish behind logs, through the white froth of fast currents, in the blackness of deep pools, and in the chaos of swirling eddies. He was certain that a fourteen-incher was fanning a foot below the surface, waiting for the perfect fly if I could cast it right.

"He broke into a museum to steal *what?*"

Distracted by what I'd just heard, I blew the cast, slapping the line against the water and sending any trout below darting off. "Dead birds?" Until that moment, we'd spoken only in hushed tones so as not to scare off the fish, approaching each hole as deftly as possible, mindful of the sun and where it might throw our shadows, but I couldn't contain my disbelief. I'd just heard one of the strangest stories of my life, and Spencer was only at the beginning of it.

Normally, nothing could break my concentration on the river. When I wasn't fishing, I'd count the weeks and the days until I could pull on a pair of waders and slosh into the water. I'd leave my cell phone in the trunk of the car to buzz until its battery died, keep a fistful of almonds in my pocket to ward off hunger, and drink from the stream when thirsty. On good days, I'd spend eight straight hours working my way up a river without seeing another human being. It was the only thing that brought calm amid the storm of stress that had become my life.

Seven years earlier, while on vacation from my job coordinating the reconstruction of the Iraqi city of Fallujah for USAID, I sleep-walked out of a window in a PTSD-triggered fugue state and nearly died. I was left with broken wrists, a shattered jaw, broken nose, and a cracked skull, with scores of stitches across my face, to say nothing of a newfound fear of sleep and the tricks my brain might play on me during the night.

During my recovery, I realized that many of my Iraqi colleagues—translators, civil engineers, teachers, and doctors—were being hunted and killed by their own countrymen because they had "collaborated" with the United States. I spoke out on their behalf in an op-ed in the *Los Angeles Times*, naïvely thinking that someone in power would swiftly fix things by granting them visas. I hadn't anticipated the thousands of e-mails that would soon flood in from Iraqis imploring me for help. I was unemployed, sleeping on a futon in my aunt's basement. I didn't know the first thing about helping refugees, but I started a list to track the names of everyone who wrote to me.

Within months, I launched a nonprofit organization, the List Project. Over the coming several years, I wrestled with the White House, cajoled senators, rallied volunteers, and begged for donations to keep my staff paid. Though we managed to bring thousands of refugees to safety in the United States over the years, it was clear that we would never be able to help everyone. For every victory, there were fifty cases stalled in a federal bureaucracy that treated these interpreters, the moment they fled Iraq, as potential terrorists. By the fall of 2011, as the official end to the war was drawing near, I felt trapped in a cage of my own creation. There were still tens of thousands of Iraqis and Afghans running for their lives. It could take a decade, maybe even several, to get them out, but I never managed to raise enough funds for more than a year down the road. Once the war was "over" in the minds of the American public, it would only be harder.

Whenever I felt like giving up, I'd get another desperate appeal from a former Iraqi colleague and grow ashamed of my weakness. But the truth was, I was exhausted. Ever since the accident, I couldn't fall asleep without distracting myself, so I queued up an endless sequence of the most boring shows I could find on Netflix. Every morning I woke to a new tide of refugee petitions.

Unexpectedly, fly-fishing became a kind of release. Out on the river, there were no journalists to call or donors to beseech, just currents and insects to study and rising trout to tempt. Time took on an unusual quality: five hours would pass in what felt like thirty minutes. After a day in my waders, I would close my eyes and see faint outlines of fish fanning dreamily upstream as I drifted into a deep sleep.

It was such an act of escapism that had deposited me on that mountain stream in northern New Mexico. I'd hopped into my beat-up Sebring convertible and driven from Boston to Taos to work on a book about my experiences in Iraq at a small artists' colony in town. Writer's block rolled in on the first day. I didn't have a book deal; I had never written a book before; and my narcoleptic literary agent was ignoring my increasingly anxious requests for guidance. Meanwhile the list of refugees kept growing. I had just turned thirty-one and didn't know why the hell I was in Taos, much less what I was supposed to do next. When my stress peaked, I searched for someone to show me around the local rivers.

I met Spencer at dawn at a gas station just off State Highway 522. He was leaning against his tan 4Runner, its BIG LEBOWSKI bumper sticker faintly visible beneath the mud: "Not on the rug, man."

In his late thirties, Spencer kept his sideburns long and his hair short. He had an infectious laugh and, like the best guides, an easy way of conversing. We hit it off immediately. As we worked the river, he refined my cast and went on at length about the life cycle of the various insects in the area. There wasn't a scrub or mineral or bird or bug the former Eagle Scout couldn't identify, and he seemed to know every trout on a personal basis. *Caught that bastard last month on the same rig, can't believe he fell for it again!*

When I snagged a fly in a juniper tree on the riverbank, I winced. I'd already spent a small fortune on trout flies—little bits of elk hair, rabbit fur, and rooster hackle feathers threaded around a tiny hook, made to mimic a wide range of aquatic insects in order to fool the fish into biting.

Spencer just laughed. "Shoot, I tied all these myself!" He flipped open his fly box to reveal hundreds of tiny floaters, spinners, streamers, nymphs, emerges, stimulators, parachutes, and terrestrials. He had locally themed flies like the San Juan worm and the *Breaking Bad*-inspired crystal meth egg. He deployed subtle variations in thread color or hook size to match the insect hatches in each river or stream he fished. The flies he carried in May were different from those he used in August.

Sensing my curiosity, he opened up a separate fly box and pulled

out one of the most strangely beautiful things I'd ever seen: a Jock
Scott salmon fly, which, he explained, had been tied according to a
150-year-old recipe. It bore the feathers of a dozen different birds,
flashing crimson and canary yellow, turquoise and setting-sun orange as he turned it this way and that. It was finished with a dizzy-
ing spiral of gold thread around the hook shank, and it was capped
with an eyelet made from the gut of silkworms.

"What the hell is *that*?!"

"This here's a Victorian salmon fly. Calls for some of the rarest
feathers in the world."

"Where do you get them from?"

"There's a little community of us online that tie 'em," he said.

"Do you *fish* with these things?" I asked.

"Not really. Most guys that tie have no idea how to fish. It's
more of an art form."

We pushed upstream, crouching low as we approached a fishy-
looking stretch. The hobby seemed strange, searching for rare feathers to tie a fly you don't know how to cast.

"You think *that's* strange—you should look up this kid Edwin
Rist! He's one of the best tiers on the planet. Broke into the British
Museum of Natural History just to get birds for these flies."

I don't know if it was Edwin's Victorian-sounding name, the
sheer weirdness of the story, or the fact that I was in desperate need
of a new direction in life, but I became obsessed with the crime
within moments. For the rest of the afternoon, as Spencer did his
best to get fish on my line, I was unable to focus on anything except
learning about what happened that night in Tring.

But the more I found out, the greater the mystery grew, and with
it, my own compulsion to solve it. Little did I know, my pursuit of
justice would mean journeying deep into the feather underground,
a world of fanatical fly-tiers and plume peddlers, cokeheads and big
game hunters, ex-detectives and shady dentists. From the lies and
threats, rumors and half-truths, revelations and frustrations, I came

to understand something about the devilish relationship between man and nature and his unrelenting desire to lay claim to its beauty, whatever the cost.

It would be five consuming years before I finally discovered what happened to the lost birds of Tring.

I.

DEAD BIRDS
AND RICH MEN

1

THE TRIALS OF ALFRED
RUSSEL WALLACE

Alfred Russel Wallace stood on the quarterdeck of a burning ship, seven hundred miles off the coast of Bermuda, the planks heating beneath his feet, yellow smoke curling up through the cracks. Sweat and sea spray clung to him as the balsam and rubber boiled and hissed below deck. He sensed the flames would soon burst through. The crew of the *Helen* raced frantically around him, heaving belongings and supplies into the two small lifeboats that were being lowered down the ship's flank.

The lifeboats had been baking in the sun above deck for so long that the wood had contracted; water began to seep in as soon as they hit the ocean. The cook bolted off in search of corks to plug the gaps, while panicked crewmen searched for oars and a rudder. Captain John Turner hurriedly bagged up his chronometer and nautical charts as his men lowered casks filled with raw pork and bread and water into the boats. They had no idea how long they might drift before being rescued—if they were to be rescued at all. Thousands of miles of sea spread in every direction.

Four years of being soaked to the bone beneath the ceaseless downpour of the Amazonian rain forest, with malaria, dysentery, and yellow fever tugging at his mortal coil—and the element that would bring Wallace's mission to ruin was not water but fire. It must have seemed a terrible dream: the small menagerie of monkeys and parrots he'd painstakingly shielded from the damp cold were now sprung from their cages, scurrying and flapping away from the flames to the bowsprit that poked like a needle nose from the prow of the 235-ton *Helen*.

Wallace stood there, squinting through wire-rimmed glasses at the panicked birds as chaos engulfed him. He was so depleted of vitality, leeched by vampire bats and inflamed by the chigoe fleas that had burrowed under his toenails to deposit their eggs, that he wasn't thinking clearly. All his notebooks, containing years' worth of research on the wildlife along the ink-black Rio Negro, were in his cabin.

As the fire danced toward the parrots, below deck it lapped at the edges of cartons filled with the true bounty of his expedition into the Amazon: the skins of nearly ten thousand birds, each meticulously preserved. There were river tortoises, pinned butter-flies, bottled ants and beetles, skeletons of anteaters and manatees, sheaves of drawings illustrating the transformation of strange, unknown insects, and an herbarium of Brazilian fauna that included a fifty-foot leaf of the Jupaté palm. The notebooks, skins, and spec-imens represented a career-establishing body of research. He'd left England an unknown land surveyor with only a few years of formal education, and now, at the age of twenty-nine, he was on the brink of a triumphant return as a bona fide naturalist, with hundreds of unidentified species to name. If the flames were not extinguished, he would return a nobody.

The eighth of nine children, Wallace was born in 1823 in the Welsh village of Llanbadoc on the west bank of the River Usk, which ribbons south from the Black Mountains of Mid-Wales into the estuary of the Severn River. Thirteen years earlier Charles Darwin had been born on the banks of the Severn, ninety miles north, but it would be decades before the two men's lives collided in one of the most astonishing coincidences in scientific history.

After a series of foolish investments by his father put tuition beyond reach, Wallace was withdrawn from school at thirteen and sent off to his older brother to work as a surveyor's apprentice. The arrival of the steam engine, which precipitated a railway boom that saw thousands of miles of tracks laid across the British Isles, meant that surveyors were in high demand. While other boys his age translated Virgil and studied algebra, surveying turned the countryside into a classroom for young Wallace, who scampered through valleys and forests, learning the principles of trigonometry as he helped map out future train routes. As the earth was carved open, he had his first lessons in geology as vanished species like belemnites—fossilized sixty-six million years ago—were revealed in the deep history of the earth. The precocious boy devoured introductory works on mechanics and optics and located the satellites of Jupiter through a telescope he'd fashioned out of a paper tube, an opera glass, and an optician's lens.

Wallace's informal education happened in the midst of a great back-to-nature movement, the result of a century of industrialization and urbanization. Crammed in sooty, squalid cities, people began longing for the rustic idyll of their ancestors, but a trip over rutted roads to the coasts or distant stretches of the British Isles was uncomfortable and prohibitively expensive. It wasn't until the arrival of the trains that Britain's overworked city dwellers were finally able to escape. Embracing the biblical proverb that "idle hands are the devil's workshop," the Victorians promoted natural history collecting as the ideal form of recreation, and stalls at train stations were packed with popular magazines and books on building a private collection.

Mosses and seaweeds were pressed and dried; corals, seashells, and sea anemones were dredged up and bottled. Hats were designed with special compartments for storing specimens gathered on a stroll. Microscopes became more powerful and affordable, exacerbating the frenzy: what was once common and unremarkable to the naked eye—a backyard leaf or a beetle—suddenly revealed an intricate beauty under the lens. Crazes spread like fire: the French led the way with conchlyomania, with conch shells fetching obscene prices. Pteridomania followed, as the British obsessively uprooted ferns from every corner of the isles for their fern albums. There was status in owning something rare, and parlor room vitrines laden with natural curios became "regarded as one of the essential furnishings of every member of the leisured classes with claims to be considered cultivated," according to the historian D. E. Allen.

When young Wallace overheard a wealthy governess in Hertford brag to her friends about finding a rare plant known as the Monotropa, his curiosity was piqued. He was unaware that systematic botany was a science, or "that there was any kind of . . . order in the endless variety of plants and animals." He soon discovered an insatiable need to classify, to know the names of everything living within the planes of his surveying maps. He snipped specimens of flowers and dried them back in the room he shared with his brother. He started a herbarium and graduated to entomology, flipping stones to see what wriggled underneath, trapping beetles in little glass jars.

In his early twenties, after reading Charles Darwin's *Voyage of the Beagle*, Wallace began to dream of an expedition of his own. Having already cataloged every creeping and flowering thing he could find in England, he was eager for new species to examine. When the railway bubble burst and surveying work dried up, he began searching for an unexplored part of the world that might help him unlock the greatest scientific mysteries of the day: How did new species form? Why did others, like those he had found while surveying, die off? Was it such a crazy thought that he might set sail for South America in the footsteps of Darwin?

Throughout 1846, he corresponded about the prospect of a voyage with a young entomologist he'd befriended named Henry Bates. After a visit to the insect room at the British Museum, Wallace told Bates that he had been underwhelmed by the number of beetles and butterflies he'd been permitted to examine: "I should like to take some one family to study thoroughly, principally with a view to the theory of the origin of species. By that means I am strongly of opinion that some definite results might be arrived at."

Their minds settled on a destination following the publication that year of *A Voyage Up the River Amazon*, by an American entomologist named William Henry Edwards, who opened with a tantalizing preface: "Promising indeed to lovers of the marvelous is that land . . . where the mightiest of rivers roll majestically through primeval forests of boundless extent, concealing, yet bringing forth, the most beautiful and varied forms of animals and vegetable existence; where Peruvian gold has tempted, and Amazonian women have repulsed, the unprincipled adventurer; and where Jesuit missionaries, and luckless traders, have fallen victims to cannibal Indians and epicurean anacondas."

They would start at the Brazilian port city of Pará and work their way into the Amazon, shipping specimens back to London throughout their expedition. Samuel Stevens, their specimen agent, would fund their way by selling off "duplicate" skins and insects to museums and collectors. In the week before their departure to northern Brazil, Wallace traveled to the Bates estate in Leicester to learn how to shoot and skin birds.

———

On April 20, 1848, Wallace and Bates boarded the HMS *Mischief* for a twenty-nine-day voyage to Pará, most of which Wallace spent doubled over in his berth with seasickness. From there, they ventured into the heart of the Amazon, netting butterflies and shooting rapids in crude canoes. They ate alligators, monkeys, turtles, and ants, and they sucked the juice from fresh pineapples. In a letter to Stevens, Wallace recalled the constant threat of jaguars, bloodsucking vampire bats, and deadly serpents: "at every step I almost expected to feel a cold gliding body under my feet, or deadly fangs in my leg."

Two years and a thousand miles into the journey, Wallace and Bates decided to part ways: unless they started collecting unique specimens, they were, in effect, competing with each other. Wallace would head up the Rio Negro, while Bates headed toward the Andes. Periodically, Wallace sent boxes of specimens downriver, intending for them to be shipped by intermediaries to London.

In 1851 Wallace was stricken with yellow fever for several months. He struggled to prepare doses of quinine and cream of tartar water. "While in that apathetic state," he wrote, "I was constantly half-thinking, half-dreaming, of all my past life and future hopes, and that they were perhaps all doomed to end here on the Rio Negro." In 1852 he decided to cut short his voyage by a year.

He loaded the canoe that would take him back to Pará with crates of preserved specimens and makeshift cages containing thirty-four live animals: monkeys, parrots, toucans, parakeets, and a white-crested pheasant. At stops along the way, he was startled to discover that many of his previous shipments had been held up by customs officials as suspected contraband. He paid a small fortune to liberate them and loaded them onto the *Helen*, which set sail on the twelfth of July, four years after he had first arrived in Brazil.

Now, ten thousand bird skins, eggs, plants, fish, and beetles, more than enough to establish him as a leading naturalist and burnish a lifetime of research, were cooking in the belly of the *Helen*, seven hundred miles east of Bermuda. There was still hope that the fire might be extinguished, as Captain Turner's men jettisoned cargo and hacked away at the planks, pushing desperately against suffocating plumes of smoke in search of the hissing heart of the blaze. Down in the cabin, the smoke was so thick that each man could manage only a few swings of the ax before fleeing for fresh air.

When the captain finally gave the order to abandon ship, the crew descended down the thick-braided ropes mooring the leaky lifeboats to the *Helen*. Wallace finally sprang into action, hurrying down to his cabin, "now suffocatingly hot and full of smoke," to see what might be saved. He grabbed a watch and some drawings he'd made of fish and palm varieties. He felt "a kind of apathy," perhaps a result of shock and physical depletion, and failed to take his notebooks, full of observations he'd risked his life many times over to gather. All the bird skins, plants, insects, and other specimens trapped in the cargo hold were gone.

As the emaciated Wallace began to lower himself from the *Helen*, his grip slipped from the rope, flaying his palms as he tumbled into the half-submerged lifeboat. The salt water burned at his flesh as he began to bail.

Most of the parrots and monkeys were asphyxiated on the deck, but a few survivors were still huddled on the bowsprit. Wallace tried to coax them into the lifeboat, but when the bowsprit finally caught fire, all but one of his parrots flew into the flames. The last parrot tumbled into the sea after the rope it was perched upon went up in flames.

From the lifeboats, Wallace and the crew watched the fire consume the *Helen*, the frenzy of evacuating replaced by the monotony of bailing. Every now and then, they pushed back flaming wreckage that drifted close enough to pose a danger. When the sails, which had the effect of steadying the ship, finally caught fire, the vessel capsized and splintered, presenting "a magnificent and awful sight as it rolled over . . . the whole cargo forming a fuming mass at the bottom."

They waited for rescue as the sun set. Their intention was to stick as close to the ship as possible without getting burned for as long as the flames gave off light: if they were lucky, a passing ship would see the fire and come to their rescue. Whenever Wallace shut his eyes and began to drift off, he almost immediately jerked awake under the red glare of the *Helen*, searching vainly for signs of salvation.

By morning, the ship was a charred husk. Mercifully, the wooden planks of the lifeboats had become swollen enough to seal off the leaks. Captain Turner surveyed his charts. Under favorable conditions, they might reach Bermuda in a week. With no other ships in sight, the dilapidated flotilla hoisted sail and headed for land.

They sailed west, through squalls and storms, rationing a dwindling supply of water and raw pork. After ten days, hands and faces skinned by the sun, they crossed paths with a lumber ship en route to England. That night, in comfort aboard the *Jordeson*, Wallace's survival instincts gave way to a profound sense of grief. "It was now, when the danger appeared past, that I began to feel fully the greatness of my loss," he wrote to a friend. "How many times, when almost overcome . . . had I crawled into the forest and been rewarded by some unknown and beautiful species!"

But he was soon wrenched back into survival mode. The *Jordeson*—one of the slowest ships in the world, averaging two knots under good conditions—was dangerously overloaded and underprovisioned. By the time the English port of Deal was sighted, the crew had been reduced to eating rats. Eighty days after emerging triumphantly from the mouth of the Amazon with a small museum's worth of specimens, Wallace descended from the half-sunk ship threadbare, drenched, hungry, and empty-handed, his ankles so swollen he could barely walk.

In the wake of the disaster, a bedridden Wallace took stock of what he had to show for his years in the Amazon. A handful of drawings of tropical fish and palm trees. His watch. Of all the things to save from the fire! Wallace never managed to explain his thought process in the fateful final moments aboard the *Helen*.

Samuel Stevens had taken out a £200 insurance policy—roughly $30,000 today—on the specimen collection in the event of its destruction, but the money was little consolation. There was no way to file a claim on lost scientific insights, not to mention stories for a book of his own, in the spirit of Darwin.

What was he to do? To tackle the origin of species, he would need new specimens, which required another expedition. But his resources were limited, his body depleted, and his reputation nonexistent. By the middle of the nineteenth century, the terra incognita that had once hazily marked unexplored forests and islands was rapidly vanishing from maps. The gunships of the British navy, now dominant, sailed into ports and harbors to seize virgin territories and pry colonies from senescent empires such as the Dutch and Portuguese. More often than not, they traveled with a naturalist on board. Darwin's Cambridge professor had recommended him for the voyage of the HMS *Beagle*, a navy ship tasked with opening up much of South America's west coast and the Galápagos Islands, and his father covered all incidental expenses over the five-year journey. The botanist J. D. Hooker, Darwin's close friend, boarded the HMS *Erebus* in 1839 for a four-year expedition in the Antarctic, and then the HMS *Sidon* for several years in the Himalayas and India. These were men of Royal Societies, from great families with deep pockets, and they were naming hundreds of new species each year. Wallace didn't have any Cambridge dons to recommend him for berths on upcoming expeditions.

If Wallace was to leave his mark, he had little time to wallow. As soon as he regained his health, he began to write his way into the hallowed rooms of London's scientific societies, drawing upon his recollections and the few sketches he'd saved. Only five weeks after his return, he read a paper on Amazonian butterflies before the Entomological Society. He went to the Zoological Society with a presentation on the monkeys of the Amazon, theorizing that when a great ocean once covering the region receded, three rivers—the Amazon, the Rio Madeira, and the Rio Negro—had divided the land into four parts. The "great divisions" that resulted explained the variation and distribution of the twenty-one species of monkeys he'd observed there.

Wallace didn't have an answer to the origin of species, but he knew that geography was an essential instrument in the search. He railed against the sloppy way in which other naturalists recorded geographical data: "In the various works on natural history and in our museums, we have generally but the vaguest statements of locality. S. America, Brazil, Guiana, Peru, are among the most common; and if we have 'River Amazon' or 'Quito' attached to a specimen . . . we have nothing to tell us whether the one came from the north or south of the Amazon." Without precise information on the range of different species, it would be impossible to know how or why species diverged. The tags, in his view, were nearly as important as the specimens to which they were attached.

In the months after returning, Wallace became a fixture at London's scientific societies, but his true priority was selecting the site of his next adventure. A return to the Amazon, though, was pointless—his friend Bates was still there building a massive collection and by now was so far ahead of him that it would defeat the purpose. It hardly made sense to retread Darwin's route, and Alexander von Humboldt had already summited the mountains of Central America, Cuba, and Colombia. Wallace needed to find a gap in the record, a stretch of the map that hadn't yet been combed over by a rival naturalist.

After reading a description of "a new world" with an "animal kingdom unlike that of all other countries," Wallace settled on the Malay Archipelago, which had yet to be explored by a natural historian. In June 1853, with his reputation growing, Wallace took a proposal to Sir Roderick Murchison, president of the Royal Geographical Society, describing an itinerary as ambitious as it was protracted: Borneo, the Philippines, the Indonesian island of Sulawesi, Timor, the Moluccas, and New Guinea. Wallace planned to spend a year or two in each location—an expedition that could easily demand a dozen years. Murchison agreed to find Wallace passage on the next ship traveling toward the region and to broker valuable introductions to colonial authorities.

In preparation, Wallace frequented the insect and bird rooms at the British Museum of Natural History in London, lugging along his copy of Prince Lucien Bonaparte's *Conspectus generum avium*, an eight-hundred-page volume that described every known species of bird up to 1850, and making meticulous notes in its margins. He soon realized the museum had an incomplete collection of the strangest and most beautiful birds on the planet: the Birds of Paradise.

The Birds of Paradise occupied a perch in the Western public's imagination worthy of their mythical name. The first skins, brought to Europe by Magellan's crew as a gift for the king of Spain in 1522, were missing their feet—such was the skinning practice of early Bird of Paradise hunters—leading Carolus Linnaeus, the father of modern taxonomy, to name the species *Paradisaea apoda*: the "footless Bird of Paradise." Many Europeans thus believed that the birds were inhabitants of a heavenly realm, always turning toward the sun, feeding on ambrosia and never descending to earth until their death. They thought females laid their eggs on the back of her mate, incubating them as they soared through the clouds. The Malayans called them *manuk dewata*, "God's birds"; the Portuguese referred to them as *passaros de col,* "birds of the sun." Linnaeus described nine species that had never been spotted since, known to the traders in the archipelago as *burong coati,* "dead birds."

Pope Clement VII owned a pair of the heavenly skins. Young King Charles I, posing for his portrait in 1610, stood confidently next to a hat bedecked with a stuffed Bird of Paradise. Rembrandt, Rubens, and Bruegel the Elder captured their undulating plumes in oil on canvas. Entranced as the West was by these supposedly celestial beings, no trained naturalist had ever observed them in the wild.

———

On March 4, 1854, eighteen months after his calamitous return from South America, Wallace boarded a Peninsular & Oriental steamer that ferried him through the Strait of Gibraltar, past the citadels of Malta to Alexandria, where he boarded a barge that traveled up the Nile to Cairo, where he loaded his gear onto horse-drawn wagons caravanning across the eastern desert toward Suez. The *Bengal*, a 123-foot cargo barque, took him the next leg, stopping in Yemen, Sri Lanka, and the "richly wooded shores" of the Strait of Malacca before depositing him in Singapore.

Within a month of arriving, Wallace sent nearly a thousand beetles from more than seven hundred species to Stevens. To gather such a haul, he kept a grueling schedule. Each morning he was up at five-thirty to analyze and store the insects collected the previous day. Guns and ammunition were readied, and insect nets were repaired. He'd have breakfast at eight, then head into the jungle for four or five hours of collecting, after which he would return home to kill and pin insects until four p.m., when dinner was served. Every night before bed, he'd spend an hour or two recording specimens in his registry.

The British Museum was buying up nearly everything Wallace sent home. Stevens, wanting more of anything that could be captured and sold, asked if he might speed up his collecting by also heading out at night, triggering an irate reply: "Certainly not . . . night work may be very well for amateurs, but not for the man who works twelve hours every day at his collection."

Gathering specimens was taxing, but protecting them against the constant threat of scavengers was maddening. Small black ants routinely "took possession" of his house, spiraling down papery tunnels onto his work desk and carrying off insects from under his nose. Bluebottle flies arrived by the swarm and deposited masses of eggs in his bird skins: unless they were swiftly cleaned, the eggs would hatch into maggots and feast on the bird. But his greatest enemies were the lean, hungry dogs pacing outside: if he left a bird he was in the midst of skinning for an instant, "it was sure to be carried off." Wallace hung bird skins from the rafters to dry, but if he left a stepladder too close, the dogs would climb up and make off with his most cherished specimens.

The passage of time also presented a unique danger. For centuries, taxidermists had struggled to determine the best method to preserve birds for future research. They'd tried pickling them, drowning them in spirits, bathing them in ammonia, shellacking them, and even baking them in ovens, but each of these techniques led to the ruination of the skin or damaged the beauty of the feathers. It was only in the previous few decades that naturalists had perfected the art of skinning birds, by making a fine incision from the belly to the anus, stripping out their guts, scooping their brains out with a quill, cutting out the roots of the ears, extracting their eyeballs and replacing them with cotton, and applying a coating of arsenical soap to the skin. By the middle of the nineteenth century, guidebooks with ghastly tips abounded: fashion a noose out of a pocket handkerchief to strangle maimed birds, use No. 8 shot when hunting birds smaller than Pigeons, No. 5 for those of "greater hulk," and knock a wounded and aggressive Heron firmly on the head with a walking stick in order to subdue it. Tendons should be cut from the feet of larger birds of prey. Grebes should be skinned from the back instead of the gut. Toucans' tongues should be left in their skulls. Instead of being sliced open, Hummingbirds could be dried over a stove and packed with camphor.

Losing a poorly preserved bird skin to insects or a mangy dog was nearly as bad as seeing them go up in flames. To help with the quotidian tasks of specimen collecting, Wallace had brought along a sixteen-year-old named Charles Allen. Early in their expedition, he happily informed his mother that Charles "can now shoot pretty well. . . . He will soon be very useful, if I can cure him of his incorrigible carelessness." But within a year, Wallace had lost all patience and begged his sister to find a replacement: "I could not be troubled with another like him for any consideration whatever. . . . If he puts up a bird, the head is on one side, there is a great lump of cotton on one side of the neck like a wen, the feet are twisted soles uppermost, or something else. In everything it is the same, what ought to be straight is crooked."

After eighteen months, Wallace and young Allen parted ways. For his specimens to survive into posterity, he recruited a young Malay assistant named Ali, whose attention to detail was a welcome change. In the first two years of his voyage, Wallace sailed from Singapore to Malacca, Borneo, Bali, Lombok, and Makassar, gathering some thirty thousand specimens, six thousand of which were distinct species. Perhaps mindful of the lessons of the *Helen*, he routinely dispatched crates of skins to Stevens. The Peninsular & Oriental's "Overland" route was the swiftest but costliest: seven thousand miles by sea to Suez, a sweltering caravan to Alexandria, and a steamer to London—a journey of seventy-seven days. Otherwise he sent his cases on a four-month voyage stowed aboard ships sailing around the Cape of Good Hope.

Nearly three years into his expedition, though, he had yet to see the Birds of Paradise.

In December 1856, when a half-Dutch-half-Malay captain told Wallace of a place where the coveted birds might be caught, Wallace and Ali eagerly set sail on a ramshackle prau for a tiny cluster of islets a thousand miles to the east known as the Aru Islands. Before him lay roving bands of pirates, impassable jungles of towering mahogany and nutmeg, malaria and venom, and thousands of unknown species to discover. Fluttering somewhere in its depths were the elusive Birds of Paradise and one of the greatest scientific breakthroughs in history.

———

As the prau inched east across the Flores and Banda Seas, Wallace took stock of his supplies: a pair of shotguns, a bag of shot, and a hunting knife. His specimen boxes were stacked neatly in the corner of his bamboo hut tethered to the prow's deck, along with a pouch of tobacco and a collection of small knives and beads to use as payment to local bird and insect hunters. In bottles and pouches, he carried arsenic, pepper, and alum for preserving specimens, and hundreds of labels, upon which were printed the words COLLECTED BY A. R. WALLACE. Drawing ever closer to the Birds of the Gods, he measured his food stock in periods of time: a three-month supply of sugar, eight months' worth of butter, nine months of coffee, and a year of tea.

Time was the key to understanding how Aru and the nearby island of New Guinea first produced the mysterious Birds of Paradise. One hundred forty million years ago, a supercontinent in the southern hemisphere known as Gondwana began to break apart. After forty-six million years, the Australian Plate separated and began drifting north. For eighty million years, as the Australian Plate slowly drifted into tropical waters, a wide range of birds winged throughout the continent, among them the common ancestor of both Birds of Paradise and crows and jays of the family Corvidae. Twenty million years ago the crowlike Birds of Paradise began to diversify. Two and a half million years before Wallace first approached the islands, the landmass of New Guinea, the second largest island in the world behind Greenland, emerged from the ocean just off the northern coast of Australia. Colliding tectonic plates drove up a spine of mountains that continue to grow faster than anywhere else on earth. Over the next million years of Ice Age, sea levels rose and fell and rose again. Every time the water receded, a land bridge appeared between Australia and New Guinea, allowing plants and animals and birds to cross between the two. But when the water rose, the birds left on New Guinea were once again isolated.

There were no civets or cats hunting them on the remote islands. No monkeys or squirrels with which to compete for fruit and nuts. For millions of years, there were no humans to cut their trees down or hunt them for their feathers. Without natural predators, the males had no need to develop armament for self-defense. Similarly, they had no need to blend into their surroundings, and there was no harm in standing out. The abundance of fruit, isolation, and safety provided by these islands created the perfect conditions for what would become known as runaway selection—over millions of years, the Birds of Paradise developed extravagant plumage and elaborate dancing rituals on meticulously prepared dance floors, all in the ostentatious pursuit of the ultimate goal: sex.

When Wallace finally arrived at Aru, he searched for locals who could guide him into the jungles but came up against an unexpected problem: the river channels veining the islands were plagued by pirates known to seize everything from a boat, even a man's clothes. They burned villages and took women and children as slaves. No matter how many beads Wallace had to offer, the residents of Aru weren't lining up to help him search for some birds. Eventually he found someone to paddle him through a mangrove up a small river to the two-hut village of Wanumbai, where he traded a knife for a room in a crude hut that he shared with twelve other people. Two cooking fires were burning away in the middle of the room when he stepped in.

He was so close, he could hear the distinctive *wawk-wawk wawk-wawks* of the birds echoing from the treetops in the early morning hours. Eager to lay eyes on them, he waded through muck and heat, hounded by mosquitos. By night, he was besieged with sand flies, which left little circular welts on his limbs. In the tropical haze, they swarmed his legs until they became too swollen and ulcerated for him to walk, forcing him to convalesce in his hut.

Though he'd traveled thousands of miles across deserts and oceans to finally see Birds of Paradise in the wild, he was hobbled in the final yards by minuscule sand flies—revenge, he joked, for all the thousands of insects he'd caught and pinned. "To be kept prisoner in such an unknown country as Aru, where rare and beautiful creatures are to be found in every forest ramble . . . is a punishment too severe," he complained in his journal.

Wallace put his beads and blades to work, offering a bounty for anyone who could bring him a living Bird of Paradise. Ali, his assistant, set off with indigenous hunters, armed with blunt-tipped arrows and tiny snares devised to capture the birds without damaging their plumage.

When Ali emerged from the forest clutching a King Bird of Paradise, Wallace rejoiced. The small bird had an otherworldly beauty: an "intense cinnabar red" body, a "rich orange" head, "deep metallic green" spots above the eyes, a bright yellow beak, a pure white breast, and cobalt blue legs. From its tail emerged two wiry feathers that spiraled tightly into two glittering emerald coins. "These two ornaments," Wallace wrote, "are altogether unique, not occurring on any other species . . . known to exist upon the earth."

He was overcome: "I thought of the long ages of the past, during which the successive generations of this little creature had run their course—year by year being born, and living and dying amid these dark and gloomy woods, with no intelligent eye to gaze upon their loveliness; to all appearance such a wanton waste of beauty."

As he marveled on their extraordinary evolutionary journey, his thoughts turned worriedly toward the future. "It seems sad, that on the one hand such exquisite creatures should live out their lives and exhibit their charms only in these wild inhospitable regions . . . while on the other hand, should civilized man ever reach these distant lands . . . we may be sure that he will so disturb the nicely-balanced relations of organic and inorganic nature as to cause the disappearance, and finally the extinction, of these very beings

whose wonderful structure and beauty he alone is fitted to appreciate and enjoy.

"This consideration," he concluded, "must surely tell us that all
living things were *not* made for man."

Before departing Aru, he witnessed a "dancing-party" of the Greater Bird of Paradise, the particular species first brought to Europe as
footless skins by Magellan's surviving crewmembers over three
centuries earlier and displayed on a hat like a trophy by King Charles
I. High in the widespread canopy, twenty coffee-colored males with
yellow heads and emerald throats stretched their wings and necks
before elevating a wispy fan of gold-orange plumes overhead. En
masse they began to vibrate their feathers, hopping from branch to
branch, turning the treetop into a kind of thrumming "golden glory,"
all for the discerning eyes of the drab-colored females perched nearby.

As he stood in awe beneath dozens of pulsing golden fans, Wallace became the first naturalist ever to observe the mating ritual of
the Greater Bird of Paradise, unaware of the scope of destruction to
come. The "civilized man" he feared was already gnawing at the
edge of those virgin forests. In ports throughout the archipelago,
commercial hunters and traders exchanged sacks of the dead birds
with outstretched plumes, slaughtered at the peak of mating season
to feed a marketplace that was taking root in the West.

After twenty million years, their predators were on their way.

———

For the next five years, Wallace spent months at a time in intense
privation in the tropical depths of the Malay Archipelago, crammed
into shacks, methodically netting, bagging, bottling, skinning, la-
beling, and studying the minutest variations between specimens.

He had set up a home base on the small island of Ternate, seven
hundred miles north of Aru, renting a forty-square-foot house on
the outskirts of the island's main town. After exhausting expedi-

tions, he luxuriated in the comfort of his hut, with verandas on either side framed with palms, a deep well with pure, cold water, and a nearby grove of durian and mango trees. He planted a small garden of pumpkins and onion and was reinvigorated by the steady supply of fish and meat.

But at the start of 1858, he found himself again stricken, this time with a malarial fever. Despite the 90-degree heat, he wrapped himself in a blanket and began to sweat. In his fevered state, he thought about the question that had first sent him trekking into the Amazon, on the origin of new species. What had caused the emergence of so many unique and extravagantly different Bird of Paradise species, thirty-nine in all? Were they purely the result of external conditions, like flood and drought? What caused one species to outnumber another? He recalled the "positive checks" to the growth of human populations—war, disease, infertility, and famine—described in 1798 by Thomas Malthus in "An Essay on the Principle of Population," and he considered how they might apply to animals. Since they typically bred much more quickly than humans, animals would have overcrowded the planet were it not for similar Malthusian checks. "Vaguely thinking over the enormous and constant destruction which this implied," Wallace continued, "it occurred to me to ask the question, Why did some die and some live? And the answer was clearly, that on the whole the best fitted live. From the effects of disease the most healthy escaped; from enemies, the strongest, the swiftest, or most cunning; from famine, the best hunters."

Two hours into his malarial episode, Wallace was racing toward a complete theory of natural selection, until "it suddenly flashed upon me that this self-acting process would necessarily *improve the race*, because in every generation the inferior would inevitably be killed off and the superior would remain—that is, *the fittest would survive*." He thought of the specimens he'd gathered from forests and jungles that had been changed constantly by rising and falling sea levels, climate change and drought, and realized that he had "found the long-sought-for law of nature."

Wallace waited anxiously for the fever to break so he could start capturing his thoughts on paper. Over the next two nights, he sketched out his theory, which he excitedly addressed to the man he most revered: Charles Darwin. "I wrote a letter," he later recalled, "in which I said I hoped the idea would be as new to him as it was to me, and that it would supply the missing factor to explain the origin of species."

On June 18, 1858, Charles Darwin wrote in his journal: "interrupted by letter from AR Wallace." As he read Wallace's paper, he realized with mounting dread that the self-taught naturalist, thirteen years his junior, had independently arrived at the same theory he'd been quietly nurturing for decades. "I never saw a more striking coincidence," he wrote in a letter to his friend, the geologist Sir Charles Lyell. "Even his terms now stand as heads of my chapters," referring to the book on natural selection he'd been drafting.

"So all my originality, whatever it may amount to, will be smashed," Darwin wrote, confessing that while he hadn't been planning on publishing his own theory yet, he felt compelled to by the appearance of Wallace's paper. Then again, he did not want to be accused of intellectual theft. "It seems hard on me that I should be thus compelled to lose my priority of many years' standing," he wrote, but "I would far rather burn my whole book, than that he or any other man should think that I had behaved in a paltry spirit."

Wallace was searching for more Birds of Paradise in New Guinea when Darwin's allies in the scientific establishment settled upon a plan to resolve the question of who rightfully deserved to be credited as the originator of the theory at a meeting of the Linnean Society, the world's oldest consortium of biologists.

On July 1, 1858, a letter from Lyell was read before the society: "These gentlemen, having, independently and unknown to one another, conceived the same very ingenious theory to account for the appearance and perpetuation of varieties and of specific forms on our planet, may both fairly claim the merit of being original thinkers in this important line of inquiry." Lyell then shone the spotlight on his friend: an abstract of an essay Darwin had written in 1844 was read first, followed by a summary of a letter Darwin had sent to the American botanist Asa Gray in 1857. Wallace's paper was read last, almost as an afterthought.

When Wallace returned to his home base in Ternate, he found a pile of letters waiting for him. "I have received letters from Mr. Darwin and Dr. Hooker, two of the most eminent naturalists in England, which has highly gratified me," he eagerly informed his mother, mentioning that the paper he'd written had been read at the Linnean Society. "This assures me the acquaintance and assistance of these eminent men on my return home," he beamed. He proudly asked his specimen agent to buy a dozen copies of the Linnean Society's journal, then set off on another collecting expedition.

———

Wallace would spend several more years in the Malay Archipelago before completing his itinerary. Over an eight-year period, he had boxed up 310 mammals, 100 reptiles, 7,500 shells, 13,100 moths and butterflies, 83,200 beetles, and 13,400 other insects. But what he prized most were the 8,050 birds he captured, skinned, and shielded from hungry ants, maggots, and rangy dogs before shipping them ten thousand miles to his specimen agent in London, who set aside several thousand for research and sold the rest to the British Museum. By his own estimate, Wallace traveled 14,100 miles within the Malay Archipelago over the course of sixty or seventy separate collecting expeditions. Of the eight years, a full two had been spent in transit.

Wallace dreamed of returning to London with a living Bird of Paradise, but his attempts at caring for them always ended badly.

Whenever a hunter brought one to him, flapping in a sack or teth-ered to a stick, he would deposit the worried bird in a large bamboo cage he'd built, with troughs for fruit and water. Despite treating it to grasshoppers and boiled rice, the result was always the same: on the first day, it fluttered frantically against its confinement. On the second day, it barely moved. On the third, he found it dead on the cage floor. Sometimes the bird convulsed violently before tumbling lifeless from its perch. Of ten living birds, not one survived in Wal-lace's care into the fourth day.

So when he heard a rumor that a European merchant in Singa-pore had successfully caged two young male Birds of Paradise, he curtailed his plans to spend several more months collecting in Su-matra and paid £100 for the pair. If they survived the journey back, they would be the first live Birds of Paradise ever to reach Europe.

During the seven-week return voyage, he had "endless trouble & great anxiety" sustaining them. By the time the steamer approached Suez, his supply of bananas and cockroaches, gathered by the fistful in Bombay, had dwindled, forcing him to slip into the storeroom to sweep roaches into an empty biscuit tin. He nervously shielded the birds from sea spray and cold drafts, riding with them in the train's chilly baggage car across the desert from the Red Sea to Alexan-dria. In Malta, he obtained a fresh crop of roaches and melons to tide the birds over until the next resupply in Paris. When at last he arrived at the British port of Folkestone on March 31, 1862, eight years after departing for the Malay Archipelago, he telegrammed the Zoological Society: "I have great pleasure in announcing to you the prosperous termination of my journey and the safe arrival in England (I suppose for the first time) of the Birds of Paradise."

By the time of Wallace's return, Darwin was already famous the world over for "his" theory of natural selection; his *Origin of Spe-cies* in its third printing. If Wallace was bitter about Darwin's elevation, he never revealed it. The scientific establishment now fully embraced him: he was elected an honorary member of the British Ornithological Union and named a fellow of the Zoological Society. The biologist Thomas Huxley declared, "Once in a generation, a Wallace may be found physically, mentally, and morally qualified to wander unscathed through the tropical wilds . . . to form magnificent collections as he wanders; and withal to think out sagaciously the conclusions suggested by his collections." John Gould, England's most renowned ornithologist, declared Wallace's specimens "perfect"—a boon for future research.

He settled into a house in Regent's Park not far from his Birds of Paradise, which drew large crowds at the Zoological Gardens. He bought the most comfortable easy chair he could find for his study and summoned a carpenter to construct a long table, where he began the process of sorting through the teetering boxes of specimens and making notes for a memoir about his travels.

Six years later he completed *The Malay Archipelago: The Land of the Orang-utan, and the Bird of Paradise,* one of the greatest-selling travel narratives of all time. He dedicated the book to Darwin, "as a token of personal esteem and friendship, but also to express my deep admiration for his genius and his works." In a letter to Henry Bates, who first traveled to the Amazon with Wallace, Darwin wrote that "what strikes me most about Mr. Wallace is the absence of jealousy towards me: he must have a really good honest & noble disposition. A far higher merit than mere intellect."

Wallace's extraordinary achievement in deducing the role of evolution through natural selection has been largely forgotten. But his relentless attention to the geographic distribution of species—enabled by meticulous details on specimen tags—eventually shored up his legacy as the founder of a new field of scientific inquiry: biogeography. The deepwater strait between Bali and Lombok, which he realized formed a dividing line between species found upon the Australian and Asian continental shelves, now appears on maps as "the Wallace Line." Unfurling eastward across the Malay Archipelago is a 130,000-square-mile biogeographical zone now known as Wallacea.

In all his travels, Wallace captured only five of the thirty-nine known species of Birds of Paradise, one of which, *Semioptera wallacii*, now bears his name. In an 1863 paper, he explained why he went to such lengths to gather specimens, describing each species as "the individual letters which go to make up one of the volumes of our earth's history; and, as a few lost letters make a sentence unintelligible, so the extinction of the numerous forms of life which the progress of cultivation invariably entails will necessarily render obscure this invaluable record of the past."

To prevent the loss of the earth's deep history, Wallace implored the British government to stockpile within its museum as many specimens as possible, "where they may be available for study and interpretation." The bird skins surely held answers to questions that scientists didn't yet know to ask, and they must be protected at all costs.

"If this is not done," he warned, "future ages will certainly look back upon us as a people so immersed in the pursuit of wealth as to be blind to higher considerations. They will charge us with having culpably allowed the destruction of some of those records of Creation which we had it in our power to preserve." He challenged the antievolution religionists, "professing to regard every living thing as the direct handiwork and best evidence of a Creator, yet, with a strange inconsistency, seeing many of them perish irrecoverably from the face of the earth, uncared for and unknown."

Upon Wallace's death in 1913, the British Museum added to its large collection of his specimens by buying those that had been sold to various private collectors. Deep within the stone and terra-cotta womb of the museum, the curatorial staff unpacked and arranged Wallace's birds neatly in storage cabinets, alongside Darwin's finches. Here was a male King Bird of Paradise from the Aru Islands, captured outside the village of Wanumbai in February 1857, just north of the River Watelai at 5°S, 134°E, at 138 feet above sea level. Just as there would never be another Wallace, there could never be another specimen bearing such biological data. The curators protecting these specimens would train apprentices before retiring, just as their replacements would mentor the next generation.

But the threats to their preservation intruded at once. At the outbreak of the First World War, two years after Wallace's death, German Zeppelins drifting silently eleven thousand feet overhead dumped 186,830 pounds of bombs over London and the coast. At the start of the Second World War's Blitz, the German Luftwaffe unloaded a hail of bombs over the city for fifty-seven consecutive nights. The British Museum was hit some twenty-eight times; the botany department was nearly destroyed, and the geology department saw hundreds of skylights and windows blown out. The museum's staff resiliently worked throughout the night to sweep away the damage, but it was clear that their specimens were imperiled.

To protect them from Hitler's bombers, the curators secreted Wallace's and Darwin's bird skins in unmarked lorries to manors and mansions throughout the English countryside. Among the safe houses was a private museum in the tiny town of Tring, built by one of the richest men in history as a twenty-first-birthday present for his son. Lionel Walter Rothschild would grow up to earn many distinctions: the Right Honorable Lord, Baron de Rothschild, member of Parliament, adulterer, blackmail victim, and one of the most tragically obsessive bird collectors ever to roam the earth.

2

LORD ROTHSCHILD'S MUSEUM

In 1868, as Wallace was finishing up *The Malay Archipelago*, Walter Rothschild was born into what one historian described as the richest family in human history. His great-grandfather is credited with founding modern banking. His grandfather helped finance the British government's stake in the company that built the Suez Canal. His father was friends with princes and routinely consulted by heads of state. Walter, by contrast, consorted with dead animals.

When he was four, the Rothschilds moved into Tring Park, a 600-acre expanse anchored by a mansion of red brick and stone. Three years later, while on an afternoon stroll with his German governess, young Walter came across the workshop of Alfred Minall, a construction worker who dabbled in taxidermy. For an hour, the boy watched him skin a mouse, transfixed by the menagerie of taxidermy creatures and birds cluttering the cottage. At afternoon tea, the seven-year-old stood to make a sudden pronouncement to his parents: "Mama, Papa. I am going to make a Museum and Mr. Minall is going to help me look after it."

Terrified of infectious diseases, drafts, and sunstrokes, his mother kept him confined to the family estate at Tring Park. Walter, chubby and afflicted with a speech impediment, did not play with boys his age. Instead, he darted around with an oversize butterfly net, pinning his quarry to bits of cork. By fourteen, he had a large staff at his disposal to aid in his obsessive collecting of insects, blowing eggs, and ordering rare birds. He arrived at the University of Cambridge with a large flock of kiwis, logging an underwhelming pair of years before returning to the security of his burgeoning natural history collection at Tring. His father had long hoped his firstborn's obsession with the natural world might fade, allowing him to assume his role in the financial realm as a Rothschild, but it only seemed to intensify. By twenty, he'd accumulated some forty-six thousand specimens. For a twenty-first-birthday present, his father built him the only thing he seemed to want: his own museum, erected in a corner of Tring Park.

Walter was compelled by his father to try his hand at banking at the N. M. Rothschild and Sons New Court headquarters in London, but he was miserably out of place. Six foot three, three hundred pounds, with a stutter, he was nervous around others, but as soon as he returned to the museum after a day's work, he relaxed and bubbled with enthusiasm over the latest acquisitions. In 1892, when he was twenty-four, the Walter Rothschild Zoological Museum on Akeman Street in Tring was opened to the public. The museum soon attracted thirty thousand visitors each year, a staggering figure for a small-town museum in those days but a sign of the voracious public appetite for the strange and exotic. Floor-to-ceiling glass cases were filled with stuffed polar bears, rhinoceroses, penguins, elephants, crocodiles, and Birds of Paradise. Taxidermy sharks hung from chains overhead. Outside, a zoo of living animals wandered the grounds of Tring Park: fallow deer, kangaroos, cassowaries, emus, tortoises, and a horse-zebra cross called the zebroid. Lucky visitors caught glimpses of Rothschild astride Rotumah, the 150-year-old Galápagos tortoise he'd sprung loose from an insane asylum in Australia.

Rothschild sported a jaunty Vandyke and bowled around the

building "like a grand piano on castors." He paid no attention to the museum's budget, buying up specimens like an addict, unwrapping package after package of skins, eggs, beetles, butterflies, and moths sent by an army of nearly four hundred collectors throughout the world. And while he had an exceptional eye for the minutest details of a rare bird skin, he was a disaster when it came to the daily tasks of running a museum and such a large network of collectors. For years, he carelessly threw bills and other correspondence into a large wicker basket. Once it was full, he padlocked it shut and found another one.

Rothschild never escaped the overweening attention of his mother, and he never moved out of Tring Park. He never won the respect of his father, from whom he went to great lengths to conceal his enormous spending. After two live bear cubs were deposited on the front steps of N. M. Rothschild and Sons, his incensed father tried to put a stop to Walter's collecting, but not before his son managed to arrange for another delivery of cassowaries from New Guinea. When his father cut him out of the will and removed his portrait from the walls of the bank, Walter admitted to his sister-in-law, "My father was absolutely right—I can't be trusted with money."

Little did she know that among the many expenses Walter had concealed from his family was a blackmail attempt, made by a British peeress with whom he'd once had an affair. Cut off from the family coffers and desperate to keep the potential scandal hidden from his mother, he raised the funds the only way he could: by offering up the bulk of his bird collection for sale. In 1931 his collection of 280,000 skins was sold to the American Museum of Natural History for $250,000, in the largest accession of specimens in the New York museum's history. In the final stage of negotiations, Rothschild extracted a promise that a signed photograph of him would hang in perpetuity near his collection. "He was as jubilant over it as a schoolboy on the 'honor roll,'" wrote a bird curator at the museum: "Although he always carries the front of a Lord, he is also an extraordinarily simple man."

According to his niece, Miriam Rothschild, "Walter seemed to shrink visibly in the period following the sale. . . . He felt tired and distrait, and spent only about two hours before lunch in the Museum. It was winter—the birds had flown." When he died in 1937, what remained of his beloved collection was bequeathed to the British Natural History Museum. Upon prying open his padlocked wicker baskets, his niece discovered the blackmail demand and the identity of his blackmailer, but she never disclosed it. On his tombstone was inscribed a verse from the Book of Job: "Ask of the beasts and they will tell thee and the birds of the air shall declare unto thee."

Before it all came to ruin, Walter Rothschild's obsession had brought him the greatest private collection of bird skins and natural history specimens ever amassed by a single person. The collectors he employed risked life and limb in the pursuit of new species: one had his arm bitten off by a leopard, another died of malaria in New Guinea, three from yellow fever in the Galápagos, and still others succumbed to dysentery and typhoid fever. According to a visiting cartographer, a map depicting the locations of the Tring's collectors resembled "the world with a severe attack of measles." Alfred Newton, one of his professors at Cambridge and a champion of Wallace and Darwin's theory of evolution, chided his former pupil: "I can't agree with you in thinking that Zoology is best advanced by collectors of the kind you employ . . . No doubt they answer admirably the purpose of stocking a Museum; but they unstock the world— and that is a terrible consideration."

But if Rothschild's collectors were measles on a map, another class of hunter was the gangrene: no matter how many specimens were scooped up for the Tring, nothing compared to the widespread slaughter of birds that had begun to unfold in the world's jungles, forests, swamps, and bayous. In 1869, when Alfred Russel Wallace first expressed his fears of the destructive potential of "civilized man," he couldn't have imagined how swiftly they would materialize, in what historians have described as the Age of Extermination: the greatest direct slaughter of wildlife by humans in the history of the planet.

In the last three decades of the nineteenth century, hundreds of millions of birds were killed, not for museums but for another purpose altogether: women's fashion.

3

THE FEATHER FEVER

Before the Hermès bag or Louboutin heel, the ultimate status indicator was a dead bird. The more exotic, the more expensive, and the more expensive, the more status conferred upon its owner. In one of the stranger intersections of animal and man, the feathers of brightly colored male birds, which had evolved to attract the attention of drab females, were poached so that women could attract men and demonstrate their perch in society. After millions of years, the birds had grown too beautiful to exist solely for their own species.

If there was a patient zero for the feather fever, it was Marie-Antoinette. In 1775 she took a diamond-encrusted Egret plume, a gift from Louis XVI, and wedged it into her elaborately piled hair. Although Marie-Antoinette wasn't the first to don feathers, she was an indisputable fashion icon, at a time when new rotary printing presses enabled the proliferation of magazines, which promoted the latest styles to subscribers around the globe.

Within a century of Marie-Antoinette's death, hundreds of thousands of women subscribed to feather-filled fashion magazines like

Harper's Bazaar, Ladies' Home Journal, and *Vogue.* On its December 1892 inaugural cover, *Vogue* depicted a debutante surrounded by a gauzy cloud of birds and butterflies and ran advertisements for Madame Rallings's "elegant assortment of Paris Millinery" on Fifth Avenue in New York, and for Knox's Hats: "Riding Hats—Walking Hats—Driving Hats—Hats for the Theatre—Receptions—Weddings—Hats for every social function." The January 1898 issue of *The Delineator,* another popular American fashion magazine, announced the latest millinery trends: "Stiff wings are in high vogue for the ordinary walking hat. . . . Spangled wings, aigrettes and feather pompons from which a Paradise aigrette emerges are admired for either bonnets or hats."

The ideal Victorian woman, enshrined in these magazines, had milk-white skin to make clear that she didn't work outside the home under the sun, and she dressed in bell-shaped crinolined cages made of steel hoops that hung from waists pinched by suffocating, tight-laced corsets. She wore stiffened, heavy petticoats and chemises, and strips of whalebone were tethered to her back and sides for structure. "A large fraction of our time was spent in changing our clothes," one such woman wrote: "You came down to breakfast ready in your 'best dress' . . . after church you went into tweeds. You always changed again before tea. . . . However small your dress allowance, a different dinner dress for each night was necessary." If one wanted to go for a walk, a special outfit was required. Shopping required still another.

And thanks to the ever-changing laws of fashion, there were unique hats for every occasion, each demanding different species of bird for decoration. Women in America and Europe clamored for the latest plumes: entire bird skins were mounted on hats so ostentatiously large that women were forced to kneel in their carriages or ride with their heads out the window.

In 1886 a prominent ornithologist conducted an informal survey of the extent of the feather fever during an afternoon stroll through an uptown New York shopping district. He counted seven hundred ladies wearing hats, three quarters of them sporting whole skins. They weren't poaching birds out of Central Park; ordinary backyard birds carried little status in the hierarchy of feather fashion. The species in vogue were Birds of Paradise, Parrots, Toucans, Quetzals, Hummingbirds, the Cock of the Rock, Snowy Egrets, and Ospreys. And while hats were the main graveyard for these birds, other articles of clothing were frequently festooned with them as well—one merchant peddled a shawl made from eight thousand Hummingbird skins.

In the early years of the trade, according to the historian Robin Doughty, "plume merchants purchased stock by the individual plume; however, as millinery interests, particularly in Paris, changed over to buying by weight, bulk purchasing became everywhere the rule." Considering the weight of a feather, this meant astonishing tallies: commercial hunters had to kill between eight hundred and one thousand Snowy Egrets to yield a kilo of feathers. Only two hundred to three hundred larger bird skins were required to yield a kilo.

As the industry matured, the numbers only grew: in 1798, around the time Marie-Antoinette displayed her diamond plume, there were twenty-five *plumassiers* in France. By 1862 there were 120, and by 1870 the number had skyrocketed to 280. So many people were working in the feather-plucking and bird-stuffing business that trade groups sprang up to protect its workers, such as the Union of Raw Feather Merchants, the Union of Feather Dyers, and even a Society for Assistance to Children Employed in the Feather Industries. In the final decades of the nineteenth century, nearly one hundred million pounds of feathers were imported into France. In the auction houses of London's Mincing Lane, 155,000 Birds of Paradise were sold in a four-year stretch, part of a $2.8 billion industry (in today's dollars) that imported forty million pounds of plumage over the same period. One British dealer reported selling

two million bird skins in a single year. The American feather industry was no different—by 1900 eighty-three thousand New Yorkers
were employed in the millinery trade, for which some two hundred
million North American birds were killed each year.

As the number of birds in the wild dwindled, the value of a
feather doubled, tripled, then quadrupled. By 1900 a single ounce
of the Snowy Egret's finest plumes, which emerge only during the
courtship displays of mating season, fetched $32. An ounce of gold
was worth only $20. A kilo of Egret feathers, in today's dollars, was
worth over $12,000, driving plume hunters into Florida rookeries
to wipe out generations of birds in an afternoon.

With demand for birds like Herons and Ostriches far outpacing
supply, entrepreneurs around the world set up feather farms. Since
Herons weren't predisposed to life in a cage, farmers blinded the
birds to make them more docile, running a fine filament of cotton
thread through the bird's lower eyelid and tugging it over its upper
eyelid. There were riches to be harvested from their backs—indeed,
when the *Titanic* went down in 1912, the most valuable and highly
insured merchandise in its hold was forty crates of feathers, second
only to diamonds in the commodities market.

Darwin and Wallace had scoured the mountains and jungles for
clues to explain the emergence and disappearance of species, but
many in the West derided the very concept of extinction as folly, in
part due to the assurances of religion, and in part due to the bounty
of the "New World." The fate of the vanished species revealed
within the fossil record could be explained away as the work of the
great flood: those that survived must have made it onto Noah's ark.
In the early days of the American colonies, salmon ran in such great
numbers that they could be speared from the riverbanks with a
pitchfork. So common were they that they were ground up and used
as crop fertilizer. The skies were darkened with great clouds of mi-
grating birds—in 1813 John James Audubon once traveled for three
straight days under a single eclipsing horde of Passenger Pigeons.

The plains rumbled with bison herds so vast that it took one soldier six full days to pass through them on horseback.

As Americans looked westward toward their "manifest destiny," they took God's commands to "fill the earth and subdue it" and to "rule over the fish in the sea and the birds in the sky and over every living creature that moves on the ground" quite literally, a divine sanction for the industrializing society. In this fantasy, all the copper, iron, and gold blasted out of stone would never run out, the fish and fowl were limitless, the oak in the forests infinite. Never mind the fact that the resource-hungry human race, which numbered only one hundred million at the time Genesis was written, was hurtling exponentially toward 1.6 billion in 1900: all that was needed were machines to extract and harvest the raw materials of nature more efficiently.

Armed with repeating revolvers and a blessing from God, they razed a path to the Pacific. After Alexis de Tocqueville toured the United States in 1831, he concluded that its citizens were "insensible to the wonders of inanimate nature . . . their eyes are fixed upon another sight: the American people views its own march across these wilds, drying swamps, turning the course of rivers, peopling solitudes, and subduing nature." By the end of the century, the sixty million American bison were hunted down to three hundred, fired upon by tourists from train windows for sport. By 1901 billions of Passenger Pigeons had been hunted to the point of extinction. In the Everglades, steamboat pilots loaded their decks with shotgun-toting sportsmen who fired at alligators and Egrets in "an orgy of noise, gunpowder fumes, and death." In forests across the continent, trees older than Shakespeare were chopped down and sent to the mill. Meanwhile the feather fever spread.

As the twentieth century arrived, America's manifest destiny had been fulfilled. The 1890 census found so many settlements as to declare the extinction of the frontier. Having reached the Pacific, our forebears looked back and saw a denuded landscape: mountains

demolished and rivers fouled by the Gold Rush, and species vanishing as cities grew larger and their smokestacks taller. Between 1883
and 1898, bird populations in twenty-six states dropped by nearly
half. In 1914, Martha, the last Passenger Pigeon on earth, died in the
Cincinnati Zoo. Four years later her cage hosted the death of Incas,
the last of the Carolina Parakeets.

4
BIRTH OF A MOVEMENT

In 1875 Mary Thatcher wrote a piece for *Harper's* entitled "The Slaughter of the Innocents," suggesting that tenderhearted women "would shrink from inflicting needless pain on any creature had not the love of 'style' blinded their eyes." She assailed "the widespread belief that birds and animals were created only for the use and amusement of man" as "unworthy of Christendom."

Five years later the great suffragist Elizabeth Cady Stanton condemned the social consequences of placing women in corseted, crinoline cages to pine after the latest fashions instead of developing their bodies and minds. "Our fashions as you all know are sent us by the French courtesans, whose life work it is to study how to fascinate man and hold him for their selfish purposes," she said in a famous lecture. "God has given you minds, dear girls. . . . Your life work is not simply to attract man or please anybody, but to mould yourselves into a grand and glorious womanhood." Stanton lamented the sedentary, unstimulated life of the Victorian woman and urged her audiences to "remember that beauty works from within, it cannot be put on and off like a garment."

Simultaneously, British women were rising up against the feather trade. In 1889 Emily Williamson, a thirty-six-year-old woman from Manchester, founded a group called the Plumage League, dedicated to curbing the slaughter of birds. Two years later she joined forces with Eliza Phillips's Fur and Feather meetings in Croydon in what was soon rechristened the Royal Society for the Protection of Birds. The society, composed entirely of women, had two simple rules for its members: to stop wearing feathers, and to discourage others from doing so. It swiftly became one of the largest membership organizations in the country.

In 1896 a Bostonian Brahmin named Harriet Lawrence Hemenway, outraged by an article on the brutality of the feather trade, enlisted the help of her cousin, Minna Hall, to convene a series of tea parties to discourage their friends from wearing plumes. After nine hundred women joined, the two formed the Massachusetts chapter of the Audubon Society. Within years newly formed Audubon Society chapters had tens of thousands of members throughout the country.

In the United States and Britain, these women fought to educate others and to stigmatize the use of feathers in fashion. In London's West End, they passed out pamphlets and marched with signs illustrating the slaughter of Egrets and calling feathered hats "The Badge of Cruelty!" In America the Audubon Society held public lectures, maintained "white lists" of milliners who did not use birds, and pressured Congress to act. In one such call to arms, at an 1897 Audubon lecture held at the American Museum of Natural History in New York, the ornithologist Frank Chapman spoke of the Birds of Paradise piled up in milliners' workshops: "This beautiful bird is now almost extinct. The species fashion selects is doomed. It lies in the power of women to remedy a great evil."

The press joined the fight. In 1892 *Punch*, a British weekly best known for coining the word *cartoon*, published one of a woman with dead birds on her hat. Her arms are stretched out menacingly, large plumes extend from her back, and she has talons instead of feet. Ospreys and Egrets are winging away from her in terror. The caption reads: A BIRD OF PREY. In another cartoon, entitled THE EXTINCTION OF SPECIES, a woman sporting a dead Egret on her head is branded as the "fashion-plate lady without mercy." In the United States, the editors of *Harper's Bazaar* declared in 1896 that "it really seems as though it were time a crusade were organized against this lavish use of feathers, for some of the rarest and most valuable species . . . will soon be exterminated if the present craze continues." *Ladies' Home Journal* followed suit, offering up fashion alternatives to wearing real birds and publishing photos of bird slaughter with a warning: "The next time you buy a . . . feather for your hat think of these pictures."

In 1900 one of the first major victories for conservationists in the United States arrived with the passage of the Lacey Act, which prohibited interstate trafficking of birds (though it did nothing to halt the imports of foreign birds). In 1903, when it became clear that the Snowy Egrets of the Everglades had been hunted to the brink of extinction, President Theodore Roosevelt signed an executive order to create the first federal bird refuge at Pelican Island in Florida— one of fifty-five reserves set aside during his presidency.

Queen Alexandra of Britain soon entered the fray, declaring, via an aide's 1906 letter to the president of the Royal Society for the Protection of Birds, that she would never wear Osprey or other rare bird feathers, "and will certainly do all in her power to discourage the cruelty practiced on these beautiful birds." The queen's letter was printed in numerous journals and fashion magazines.

Now fighting for its existence, the feather industry ran sophisticated campaigns to denigrate groups like the Plumage League and the Audubon Society, calling them "faddists and sickly sentimental." The *Millinery Trade Review*, sizing up the growing stigma, issued a call to arms: "there is no alternative but for the importer and manufacturer to take up the gauntlet and meet these people in a battle royal." Lobbyists representing groups like the New York Millinery Merchants Protective Association, the Textile Section of the London Chamber of Commerce, and the Association of Feather Merchants warned lawmakers that any laws curbing the feather trade would eliminate jobs in a moment of economic insecurity. "The feather men are fighting for their iniquitous traffic with the same animosity as has so long animated the slave traders," remarked a prominent naturalist in the *New York Times*.

In the end, the conservationists won out. A procession of new bills tightened the net around the global feather trade. In the United States, the Underwood Tariff Act, passed in 1913, banned the importation of all feathers, and the 1918 Migratory Bird Treaty Act outlawed the hunting of any migratory bird in North America. In 1921 the UK passed the Importation of Plumage Prohibition Act. In 1922, an amendment was passed to ban the import of Birds of Paradise into the United States.

Other forces helped bring an end to feather fever, in particular the outbreak of World War I, which ushered in a period of austerity. Fashion trends shifted from ostentatious to more practical designs as women went to work in munitions factories and other positions vacated by men who'd gone off to fight. The arrival of the automobile meant that women could no longer wear large hats brimming with feathers in the cab of the car. Meanwhile the growing popularity of cinema rendered it unfashionable, even impolite, to wear large hats that obscured the screen. In an era when women were expected to remain at home and had yet to be granted the right to vote or own property, the abolition of the feather trade was ultimately their work.

The desire to possess something beautiful, however, could never be fully eradicated. Despite the gains of the conservation movement, some from the older generation of women found it difficult to give up the "time-honored" custom of wearing feathers now shunned by their daughters and granddaughters. At the dawn of the twentieth century, a new profession emerged to meet their demand: the wildlife trafficker. In the wake of each legislative victory came a band of scofflaws to test the limits of enforcement. In 1905 poachers murdered the first two game wardens dispatched to protect the endangered Snowy Egret in Florida. That same year authorities in the Hawaiian island of Laysan arrested a group of Japanese hunters with three hundred thousand dead Black-Footed Albatrosses in their possession. In 1921 a passenger debarking from a cruise ship in New York was found to have five Bird of Paradise feathers and eight bunches of Egret plumes hidden in the false walls of his suitcase, along with sixty-eight bottles of morphine, cocaine, and a pouch of heroin hidden within a bag of nuts. The following year the *New York Times* reported that customs inspectors were trained to observe the neck and waist of disembarking sailors: if the neck was small but the torso large, an arrest would be made: "On one occasion a suspiciously well-timbered and pompous ship captain was searched and a mere core or kernel of human being was found running through a huge structure of feathers."

The smugglers grew ever more creative in their attempts to evade the authorities. An Italian cook working on the *Kroonland* was found with 150 Bird of Paradise plumes hidden in his trousers and another eight hundred back in his room. Two Frenchmen were busted in London for concealing Bird of Paradise skins inside a shipment of egg cartons. An international Bird of Paradise smuggling ring was found to be operating out of a rural Pennsylvania town. Officials in Laredo, Texas, apprehended two men fording the Rio Grande with 527 skins of the New Guinean birds. There were reports of high-speed boat chases off the coast of Malta with exotic birds smuggled from the North African coast stashed in the hull, and midnight meetings in Bavarian forests to buy "parrot sausages," in which live birds had their beaks taped shut before being stuffed into women's hosiery to sneak past the authorities.

Undaunted, the conservationists scored another major victory in

London in 1933, when nine nations ratified the Convention Rela-
tive to the Preservation of Fauna and Flora in their Natural State.
Often described as the Magna Carta of wildlife conservation, the
convention listed forty-two species under its protection: most were
large African mammals like gorillas, the white rhinoceros, and elephants, but a few birds were included. Though the list of protected
species was incomplete, the convention provided a moral, legal, and
operational framework in the battle against wildlife traffickers. In
1973 the London Convention was replaced by the Convention on
International Trade in Endangered Species of Wild Fauna and Flora,
known as CITES, which has 181 signatories. Comprised of three
appendices that gauge the severity of threat to various species,
CITES protects 35,000 species of plants and animals. Among them
are nearly fifteen hundred birds, including Alfred Russel Wallace's
beloved King Bird of Paradise.

As the twenty-first century approached, U.S. Customs officers were
no longer checking the necks of seedy sailors. Women had long
since stopped wearing hats, much less ones festooned with exotic
birds, which enjoy more legal protection and defenders than ever
before. The membership of the Royal Society for the Protection of
Birds now numbers more than a million, maintaining more than
two hundred nature reserves throughout the UK. The Audubon Society, for its part, counts over a half million members.

But as the eyes of the law were trained on rhino horns and elephant tusks, the birth of the Internet was bringing together a small
community of obsessive men addicted to rare and illegal feathers:
practitioners of the Victorian art of salmon fly-tying.

5

THE VICTORIAN BROTHERHOOD
OF FLY-TIERS

In late 1915 a ragtag group of soldiers of the British Expedition-
ary Force was entrenched just south of the Macedonian border,
alongside an ancient Greek cemetery in Amphipolis, when an er-
rant shell blew apart the entry to a nearby tomb. Inside, Dr. Eric
Gardner, an army medic, discovered a skeleton from 200 B.C.,
clutching a handful of bronzed fishing hooks. Gardner distributed
them to the troops, who, desperately hungry as their resupply ship
had just been torpedoed, cast the two-thousand-year-old hooks
into the nearby Sturma River. After they reeled in thousands of wild
carp, the largest of which weighed fourteen pounds, Gardner reported back to command a "welcome change in the diet of the
troops" and mailed the hooks to be kept for posterity in the Imperial War Museum in Hyde Park, not far from the Natural History
Museum.

   That ancient hooks would still function so well is a testament to
the simplicity of the contract between man and fish: bait a crooked
piece of metal, tie it to a line, and cast it out. Worms work well for

bottom-feeders like the carp, but if the fish preys on winged insects skating the surface, like the trout, it helps to tie a couple of feathers to the hook.

The earliest recorded use of feathers for fishing occurs in the third-century-A.D. writings of a Roman named Claudius Aelianus, who described Macedonian trout fishermen who tied "crimson red wool around a hook, and fix onto the wool two feathers which grow under a cock's wattles." And while the practice assuredly continued over the coming millennia, no texts on fly-fishing survive from the Dark Ages. Fly-tying didn't reappear until 1496, when Wynken de Worde, a Dutch émigré running a newfangled printing press in Fleet Street in London, published *A Treatyse of Fysshynge wyth an Angle*, which included crude "recipes" for a dozen trout flies, one for each month, known by fly-fishing fanatics as the "Jury of Twelve." March's Dun Fly called for a black wool "body," with "wings" fashioned from the "blackest drake" mallard. The Yellow Fly of May recommended a body of yellow wool, with wings made from dyed yellow duck plumes. Although the *Treatyse* focused on trout, it referred to the salmon as "the most stately fish that any man can angle for in fresh water."

If there's a gap between what a fisherman casts to a carp versus a trout, there's a chasm between trout and salmon. The freshwater trout demands exquisitely realistic flies, meant to mimic the color, size, life cycles, and behavior of a wide range of aquatic insects. To "match the hatch," trout fishermen must know when to cast a nymph, which replicates the phase of the insect's life when it clings to underwater rocks, and when to deploy a dun fly, when the insects rise to the surface to split the "shucks" that cover their wings. Trout are picky, fickle, and flighty: anglers who don't pay close attention to the river's ecosystem won't have much luck hooking them. Trout flies require materials that are drab, common, and cheap: elk hair, rabbit fur, wool, and chicken feathers.

A salmon fly, by vivid contrast, is made not to resemble anything in nature but to provoke. The fish being stalked are returning from the ocean to their natal rivers to spawn eggs in gravel beds, known as redds, before dying. After they die, their carcasses release loads of nutrients that attract small larvae and other insects that will eventually become the first meals for their newly hatched offspring. During these annual journeys, known as salmon runs, the fish stop feeding, but they protect their redds from intruders by biting with canine teeth and hooked lower jaws. Salmon don't lunge at an angler's fly because it resembles an insect: they attack it because it's a foreign object in the place where they've just buried their eggs.

Catching trout requires paying close attention to nature. Salmon can be caught with dog fur tied to a hook and a bit of luck. But aristocratic anglers weren't about to let that get in the way of the romance of casting a beautiful fly to the "king of fish" in the idyllic countryside.

"Rivers and the inhabitants of the watery element were made for wise men to contemplate, and fools to pass by without consideration," wrote Izaak Walton in 1653 in *The Compleat Angler*. Beckoning to the next generation of "Brothers of the Angle," Walton described a world coursing with magical waters. There was a river that extinguished lit torches but kindled unlit ones; another that turned rods to stone. There were rivers that danced when music was played, and others that brought madness to anyone that sipped from their waters. There was a river in Arabia visited by sheep whose wool turned vermilion red upon drinking, and a river in Judea that flowed for six days of the week before resting on the Sabbath.

Of course, there were also mythic rivers closer to home, like the Dee, the Tweed, the Tyne, and the Spey, but they were far from London and inaccessible to anyone but locals or those with the means to travel across rutted terrain, ancient Roman roads and narrow bridle paths. It wasn't until the Victorian era, nearly two centuries later, that the railways opened up the legendary rivers to the lower classes. Suddenly, it wasn't just lords and kings joining the Brotherhood of the Angle, but laborers hopping a train for a break from industrialized city life.

In order to limit the intrusions of these interlopers, British lords fenced off lands and made waters private, in a series of laws known as the Enclosure Acts. Working-class anglers were suddenly barred from rivers they'd spent a lifetime fishing: landowners sitting on a good stretch of salmon water started charging a premium for the right to cast a fly.

By the end of the nineteenth century, there was "very little water left in Britain which wasn't firmly controlled either by landlords or clubs," according to the fly-fishing historian Andrew Herd, as nearly seven million acres were fenced off to the general public and protected by trespass laws. The old order was restored; only the wealthy could afford "game fishing" for the noble salmon, while the common man was limited to "coarse fishing" for lowly bottom-feeders like the carp.

With most waters now private, the sport of salmon fishing "rapidly accumulated a burden of tradition and convention." Private fishing clubs and individual aristocrats began to develop their own fly patterns, designated for each river. The flies soon took on a flashy appearance, using the pricey plumes of exotic birds. Even though there was no genuine advantage conferred by such flies, they were adopted with "near hysteria" by anglers who were, according to Herd, "egged on by local tackle dealers who had much to gain from parting the new breed of . . . salmon fisherman from their money."

After all, the ports of London were bursting with shipments of exotic bird skins intended to feed the feather fashion trade. While women competed for the rarest of plumes for their hats, their husbands showed off by tying them into their hooks. By the time the first book to consecrate the art form emerged, William Blacker's 1842 *Art of Fly Making*, the recipes had shifted from using Chicken feathers to those of South American Cock of the Rock, the Indian blue Kingfisher, the crest of the Himalayan Monal Pheasant, and Amazonian Macaws.

The Art of Fly Making was the first book to provide detailed step-by-step instructions for tying various salmon flies, and it identified the rivers on which they supposedly worked best. "They will be found most killing in the rivers of Scotland and Ireland," he promised his customers, but only if they used the correct color: fiery brown, cinnamon brown, claret, sooty olive, wine purple, stone blue, or Prussian blue. Blacker was an expert merchandizer, selling his book, the flies, the feathers, the tinsel, silk, and hooks. To achieve perfection, he recommended owning the plumes of thirty-seven different birds—among them the Resplendent Quetzal, the Blue Chatterer, and the Birds of Paradise.

For those who couldn't afford exotic birds, he provided instructions on dyeing ordinary feathers: for Parrot-yellow, a tablespoon of turmeric should be mixed with ground alum and crystal of tartar. The liquor of walnut rinds helped with subtle browns. Indigo powder dissolved in oil of vitriol yielded a deep blue. But to most, a dyed feather was never as good as the "real thing."

As the Victorian era progressed, salmon flies became ever more elaborate, and the authors of fly-tying books began to preach a pseudoscience to justify the need for such expensive and exotic materials. The greatest evangelizer of them all was the aristocratic playboy George Mortimer Kelson. Born in 1835, he dedicated most of his youth to cricket, long-distance swimming, and the steeplechase, but the passion that would eventually eclipse all others was fly-fishing and the stratified world of Victorian fly-tying.

His 1895 work, *The Salmon Fly*, is the art form's apotheosis: brashly confident, dismissive of amateurs, and obsessed with hard-to-get feathers. He opened with an entire chapter extolling the scientific rigor of his work, though his methods were questionable at best. To penetrate the mind of the salmon, Kelson dove into rivers with flies of various colors, prying his eyelids open to see what they looked like underwater. His first attempt was with a fly called the Butcher, but whenever he tried to make out the Blue Macaw or yellow-dyed Swan feathers, he stirred up the mud on the bed of the river and lost sight of them. When he took the Butcher over to a gin-clear ice-cold river, he spent so much time studying it underwater that he became slightly deaf.

"Exactitude is needed in applying our principles," he wrote, outlining the various factors that might cause a salmon to rise for an artificial fly, such as "predisposition for certain shades of color" and variations in the clarity of the water or the weather. So exact was his craft, at least in his own view, that he recommended one pattern, the Elsie, for salmon hiding between a large, upright rock and a nearby boulder.

Kelson smirked at the "uninitiated," the "novice," and those "so low down in the scale of ignorance" that they couldn't tell a Jock Scott fly from a Durham Ranger. Of course, neither could a salmon, but in order to justify paying for such costly feathers, some needed to believe that the fish could distinguish between the twenty shades of green described in the masterworks on fly-tying.

Kelson admitted in his book that the "classification" for selecting which salmon flies to cast was "artificial," but he couldn't seem to accept the full implications, indignantly recounting the time when a salmon ignored his flies for a simple fly tied by an amateur angler: "At times salmon will take anything, at times nothing. . . . In a fever of excitement the King of Fish will exercise his royal jaw upon a thing it were an outrage to call a Salmon fly . . . a one-sided, wobbling, hydrocephalic bunch of incongruous feathers." But before long he was back to preaching about the principles of symmetry and the harmony of "balanced" colors in a fly.

For Kelson, fly-tying had a kinship with the fine arts—he claimed the practice would instill a "mental and moral discipline" in his disciples. "We have here a well-bred hobby noteworthy of the attention of the greatest amongst us who are fishers, whether Divines or Statesmen, Doctors or Lawyers, Poets, Painters, or Philosophers." For such great men, Kelson's bible included eight stunning hand-colored plates depicting fifty-two finished flies, with lofty names like the Champion, the Infallible, Thunder and Lightning, the Bronze Pirate, and Traherne's Wonder.

The Salmon Fly included detailed recipes for some three hundred flies, laying out which materials were required for each part. The eye of the fly was to be fashioned out of a loop of silkworm gut. The head, horns, cheeks, sides, throat, underwing, and overwing all required special plumes. His analytical diagram of the fly reveals nineteen different components, to say nothing of the various styles and curvatures of hook.

To tie like Kelson, his readers would need a silver monkey, a gray squirrel, pig's wool, silk from the Orient, fur from the Arctic, a hare's face, and a goat's beard. There were single-tapered shanks and double-tapered shanks. Single-eyed and double-eyed hooks. Flat tinsel, oval tinsel, embossed tinsel, and tinseled chenilles. Seal's fur, in bright orange, lemon, fiery brown, scarlet, claret, purple, green, golden olive, dark and light blue, and black. Cobbler's wax. The list of materials needed in order to tie Victorian salmon flies was long, even before any mention of feathers.

Kelson rattled through his current inventory of bird skins: the Banded Chatterer (now endangered), the Great American Cock, the Nankeen Night Heron, the South American Bittern, and the Ecuadorian Cock of the Rock. But there was one skin that Kelson prized above all: "The greatest find that has fallen to my lot is the Golden Bird of Paradise. May this luck be your luck, brother Fishermen, as it has been mine! It will only cost you £10!"

He acknowledged that the dyed feathers of common birds could be used when exotic ones were out of reach, but stressed that "however well hackles may be dyed . . . they never look so well, even when fresh, or are so effective in the water as natural ones. Take, for instance, the hackles of a Golden Bird of Paradise . . . the best dyed orange hackle in creation would simply be nowhere in competition with it."

Kelson and his book were so influential that even before he died in 1920, he'd become a brand name. Burberry's offered a waterproof Kelson jacket, featuring large pockets for fly boxes and special flies. C. Farlow & Co. created a custom Kelson rod, and the Kelson Patent Silent Aluminum Salmon Winch. Morris Carswell & Co. sold Kelson enameled salmon fishing line.

Kelson knew he had his detractors—fishermen who were skeptical of the need for such prismatic creations—but he brushed them off as "narrow-minded enthusiasts—piteously hoodwinked on an exceptional day by getting a fish or two with the wrong fly presented the wrong way." Galileo had been similarly doubted in his time, he noted.

Over the course of the twentieth century, scattered pockets of fly-tiers followed the recipes of Kelson and his peers, but fly-tying didn't truly reemerge until the final decades, thanks in part to the influence of Paul Schmookler. In 1990 a *Sports Illustrated* profile of his salmon flies—which were being snatched up by collectors for two thousand dollars apiece—began with this: "If Donald Trump continues having trouble making interest payments on the Taj Mahal, maybe he should call up Paul Schmookler, one of his old schoolmates from New York Military Academy, for some money-making tips.

"To dress one fly," marveled the author, "Schmookler will use up to 150 different materials, ranging from polar bear and mink fur to the feathers of wild turkeys, golden and Reeves pheasants, the African speckled bustard and the Brazilian blue chatterer."

"The materials I use are not from animals on the endangered species list, or were collected before the Endangered Species Act was passed," said Schmookler. "When you tie artistic or classic-style Atlantic salmon flies, you not only have to know materials but you have to know the law."

Throughout the 1990s, Schmookler published a number of coffee table books with titles like *Rare and Unusual Fly Tying Materials: A Natural History* and *Forgotten Flies*, which sold for hundreds of dollars, with special edition leather-bound books with limited print runs going for over $1,500. His books appeared at the dawn of the Internet age: before long, eBay and Victorian fly-tying forums would usher in a new wave of feather addicts, hoping to tie just like Schmookler, Kelson, and Blacker.

Unlike their forebears, most of the new generation of tiers didn't even know how to fish: salmon flies were instead treated as pieces of art. But as far as materials were concerned, the new tiers were marooned in the wrong century. There were no more stevedores in London and New York unloading shipments of Bird of Paradise skins. The tackle shops advertised in Kelson's books were long gone. Feather-filled hats had been out of fashion for more than a hundred years. Many of the birds required in Kelson's recipes were endangered, threatened, or protected by the CITES convention against trafficking. The new tiers were dedicated to an art form that could no longer be legally practiced without great difficulty.

The arrival of the Internet triggered a brief flood of rare birds, as enterprising eBay users rummaged through their grandmothers' attics and uncovered Victorian hats to sell. There were online auctions of nineteenth-century cabinets, filled with curios of the natural world, including the occasional exotic bird. Offline some wealthy tiers had luck at estate sales in the British countryside. One resourceful fly-tier made off with a number of stuffed birds that he rented from a company specializing in movie props.

But there were only so many attics to explore, only so many

feathers that could be plucked from 150-year-old hats. The price of a pair of feathers from the Blue Chatterer, Indian Crow, Resplendent Quetzal, or Bird of Paradise—some of which were protected species—climbed as the practice grew in popularity. The lucky few who happened to have rare bird skins were on top, idolized by the pining mass of featherless newcomers below: by virtue of owning such exotic materials, they alone could tie the most beautiful flies.

The only way most fly-tiers could see such birds was to ogle at them behind the display cases at natural history museums like the one at Tring.

6
THE FUTURE OF FLY-TYING

I n 1705, just outside the Hudson Valley burg of Claverack, 120 miles north of New York City, a five-pound mastodon tooth, disinterred by the spring floods, rolled down a steep hill and landed at the foot of a Dutch tenant farmer working the fields. The farmer brought the fist-size tooth into town and traded it to a local politician for a glass of rum. The first remnant of an extinct animal discovered in America, nicknamed Incognitum, set off a frenzy of theological concerns: how could something vanish from God's earth? Had Noah forgotten to load Incognitum onto the ark?

By 1998, when the Rist family decamped from the Upper West Side of Manhattan to Claverack, another hundred species—seventy of them birds—had disappeared, hunted into extinction.

Many other things had vanished from the small town over the years. The town's grist- and sawmills, powered for a century by the 150-foot waterfall of the Claverack Creek, had shuttered. Gone too were the cotton and wool factories. A few thousand brown trout, stocked into the creek each year by the Columbia County fishery, fan in its pools and riffles, eyeing flies and dodging anglers.

Ten years old when the family moved north, Edwin was no field and stream child: the mere sight of red ants sent him bolting for higher ground. He spent most of his time indoors, doing his homework, practicing the flute, and playing with his younger brother, Anton.

The boys were homeschooled by their parents, Lynn and Curtis, who were both Ivy League graduates and freelance writers. Lynn taught them history, while Curtis covered mathematics. By day, Curtis wrote pieces for *Discover* magazine on an eclectic range of topics—from the physics of the basketball foul shot, to the molecular chemistry of fine art conservation and the planetary movement of Neptune. By night, he read his sons *The Iliad*. The television was rarely on.

Instilled with a love of learning, Edwin leapfrogged through his lessons, devouring new subjects. On Mondays his mom would deposit him at the nearby adult-education Spanish class, where he practiced conjugations with forty-year-olds. When Edwin developed a fascination with snakes, his parents enlisted David Dickey, a herpetologist at the American Museum of Natural History, as a biology tutor. During a family vacation to Santa Barbara, they visited the Sea Center, where a naturalist introduced the boys to camouflaged decorator crabs and a bright-orange sea slug known as the Spanish dancer. "Now *that* is what I want to be for Halloween," marveled Edwin.

His parents nurtured whatever new interests he formed. So when Edwin's first-grade music instructor told them that their son demonstrated an innate talent on the recorder, they signed him up for private lessons. He swiftly graduated to the flute, practicing with such devotion that Anton soon followed suit, taking up the clarinet. The brothers, lovingly competitive, spurred each other to new heights of achievement. Edwin took first place in the Uel Wade Music Scholarship competition and enrolled in the international master class of Jeanne Baxtresser, the principal flautist for the New York Philharmonic.

Even at a young age, perhaps as a result of the unstructured nature of homeschooling, Edwin understood that his potential in the flute would be limited only by his ability to focus. Anyone could learn scales or arpeggios: true mastery would require conquering techniques like multiphonics and flutter-tonguing.

But one day, late in the summer of 1999, Edwin wandered into the living room and became transfixed by what he saw on the television screen: his obsession began as a hobby but quickly grew so feverish that the eleven-year-old would soon be able to focus on little else.

———

As research for a piece on the physics of fly-fishing, Curtis had picked up a video called *The Orvis Fly-Fishing School*. In a segment on the rudiments of tying a trout fly, the Orvis host demonstrated each step on a thumbnail-size hook clamped between the jaws of a tabletop vise. Halfway into the process, he held up an ordinary hackle feather, harvested from the neck of a rooster. Like all feathers, hackles have tiny barbs that branch out from the feather's shaft, which is known as a rachis. But when he wound the feather around the body of the fly in a helix-like wrap, a technique known as palmering, the barbs splayed out in every direction like hundreds of tiny antennae. A palmered rooster feather helps the fly float atop the river's surface: to the hungry fish below, the barbs resemble wriggling insect legs.

Edwin was so captivated that he grabbed the remote and rewound the VHS, watching the sequence over and over, spellbound by the transfiguration of the simple feather. To tie a basic trout fly, the instructor employed a number of implements that looked as though they had spilled out of a Victorian surgeon's bag. There were spools of fine thread, clamped between the two prongs of a stethoscope-looking tool called a bobbin. To make precise midcourse adjustments to the fibers of a feather, there was a needle-shaped device known as a bodkin. To grab hold of the narrow shaft of a feather, he used a tiny pair of hackle pliers. In the final stage of the tutorial, the instructor twisted the thread into a tight knot with a quick flourish using a whip finisher, an elegant device that resembled a deconstructed paper clip.

Edwin had a habit of diving into things, so he raced down to the basement in search of materials. After uncovering a few hooks, he rummaged through drawers for thread, but the closest thing he found was a fistful of pipe cleaners. Not surprisingly, there wasn't any rooster hackle lying around, so he pulled a couple of feathers from his mom's down pillows and hurried back to his room to tie his first fly.

Over the coming weeks, he tied flies with Mardi Gras beads and aluminum foil, winding whatever was at hand before untying them and starting over. But nothing came close to resembling what he saw in the video. Knowing his son was chafing for proper materials, Curtis drove him to Don's Tackle Service, a fly-fishing shop a half hour away in Red Hook.

Don Travers, a gruff septuagenarian, wasn't thrilled to see an eleven-year-old in his store, which was lined with trays filled with carefully organized flies, but the well-behaved boy quickly won him over, returning to the register with all the tools he'd need to get started: bags of hackle feathers, hooks, thread, bobbins, and a fly-tying vise.

Like most households at that time, the Rists didn't have Internet at home, so Edwin relied on the Orvis video and a subscription to *Fly Tyer* magazine to learn the basic techniques. His brother Anton became interested, and the two were soon begging for proper instruction. In 2000 the boys began taking regular fly-tying classes at Don's, where they met other tiers and discovered new feathers and techniques. The materials required for trout flies weren't particularly costly: a pinch of elk hair, a couple of inches of thread and tinsel, and an ordinary hackle feather tied to a basic hook amounted to about twenty cents.

Their first instructor was a seventy-five-year-old Princeton-educated evolutionary biology professor named George Hooper, an expert on insect life and an avid fly-fisherman. He approached tying like a biologist, using head-mounted dissection magnifiers and microscopes, referring to fish by their Latin binomial names, and selecting from among what seemed to Edwin like ten thousand colors of wool to fill out the bodies of his flies.

Under Hooper's tutelage, Edwin tied piles of flies that he had no idea how to cast: he didn't even own a fly rod. He just liked the challenge of replicating what he saw in the Orvis video and in his magazines.

Impressed with their budding talent, Hooper urged Edwin and Anton to enter fly-tying competitions, which took place at conventions throughout the country as well as Europe, where hook makers, specialized booksellers, feather peddlers, pelt hawkers, and the stars of the show, tiers, met to sell their wares and show off their talents. The competitions had a straightforward format: entrants must tie a particular fly pattern three times in a row in front of a panel of judges, who graded for quality and consistency.

Always willing to encourage their sons' passions, Curtis and Lynn loaded the eager boys and their gear into the car, driving to shows like the Arts of the Angler convention in Danbury, Connecticut, where Edwin tied an astonishing sixty-eight trout flies in an hour to take the title. At the Northeast Fly-tying Championship in Wilmington, Massachusetts, Anton was assigned the Hellgrammite Fly, which mimicked the look of an underwater centipede-like insect known in the Ozarks as a Devil Scratcher. He tried his best to replicate the hideous fly but was frustrated with each attempt. The boys were perfectionists at the vise and fixated on the slightest inconsistency or inaccuracy.

It was at that moment, awaiting the judges' verdict, when Edwin saw the glimmering thing that would take a hobby and distort it into an obsession. As the brothers wandered the aisles of fly-tiers and feather dealers, Edwin's eyes came to rest on a huge display of sixty Victorian salmon flies, all painstakingly tied according to the nineteenth-century recipes found in George Kelson's *The Salmon Fly*.

Edwin had never seen anything like these spectral bursts of iridescent turquoise, emerald, crimson, and gold: compared to the ugly brown and black Devil Scratcher fly, they seemed to belong to some other planet. Many trout flies were the half the size of a penny; salmon flies were huge, tied on jet-black hooks up to four inches long. Edwin could tie a trout fly in under a minute; a single salmon fly demanded ten hours or more behind the vise.

The man who'd created them was standing nearby, watching as the boys examined each fly with reverence. He tried not to eavesdrop on their hushed conversation, but he grinned when he heard them murmur about the structural complexity of the flies. These weren't normal kids. They were tiers.

And so it was that the brothers met Edward "Muzzy" Muzeroll. Muzzy, a marine designer who worked on Aegis-class destroyers at the Bath Iron Works shipyard in Maine, spent most of his spare time hooking trout and salmon in the Kennebec River. When it was too cold to fish, he tied flies and was considered a master of the Victorian salmon fly— his work had even graced the glossy cover of *Fly Tyer*. (The accompanying article was entitled: "Tying with Exotic Materials: Avoiding the Long Arm of the Law.")

The judges announced that the boys had won first place in their respective categories, but Edwin was so entranced by Muzzy's creations that the world of drab trout flies was rapidly losing its hold on his attention.

Edwin pleaded with his dad to arrange lessons with Muzzy. By a happy coincidence, Muzzy's hometown of Sidney, Maine, happened to be the site of the New England Music Camp for gifted young musicians. The boys were accepted, and Edwin began counting down the days until he could learn to tie his first salmon fly.

———

On the day Curtis and his boys headed over to Muzzy's for their first lesson in salmon flies, Edwin wore a bright red novelty T-shirt depicting a "Note from the desk of Toto," the terrier from *The Wizard of Oz*: "Dear Dorothy: Hate Oz, took the shoes, find your own way home!" He was only thirteen, with oval-framed glasses and a spiked crop of hair, but as Muzzy escorted him through the fly shop toward the small table set up for tying Victorian salmon flies, he had the brooding quiet of a reverent pilgrim.

Next to the vise, George Kelson's *The Salmon Fly* was opened to a recipe.

THE DURHAM RANGER

Tag: Silver twist and yellow floss
Tail: One topping with indian crow over
Butt: Two turns of black ostrich herl
Body: Two turns of orange floss. Two turns of orange seal's fur followed by black seal's fur
Ribs: Silver lace and silver tinsel
Hackle: Over the wool only a red-coch-y-bondhu hackle
Throat: Light blue hackle
Wings: A pair of long jungle cock feathers with double tippets on both sides. Outer tippets reaching to the first dark band of the inner tippets with a topping over all
Cheeks: Chatterer
Horns: Blue Macaw
Head: Black Berlin Wool

The Durham Ranger, introduced in the 1840s by a Mr. William Henderson of Durham, England, demanded the crest feathers of the

Golden Pheasant from the mountain forests of China, black and fiery orange breast feathers from the Red-ruffed Fruitcrow (known to fly-tiers as Indian Crow) of South America, ribbon-like filaments of Ostrich herl feathers from South Africa, and tiny turquoise plumes from the Blue Chatterer of the lowlands of Central America. The fly was like a snapshot of the British Empire at midcentury: employing plumes shipped up by Ostrich farmers in the Cape Colony, Blue Chatterer and Indian Crow extracted from British Guiana, and Golden Pheasant crated in the port of Hong Kong.

But Edwin would not tie with rare feathers that morning. Muzzy laid out a series of substitute feathers, or "subs," from game and breeder birds. Instead of hard-to-get Indian Crow or Blue Chatterer, there was Ring-Necked Pheasant, dyed Turkey, and feathers from the more common Kingfisher.

Over the next eight hours, Muzzy introduced the brothers to the arcane tricks of tying Victorian flies, regaling them with stories about the godfathers of the art form like Blacker, Traherne, and Kelson, who tried to one-up each other with increasingly extravagant flies.

He spoke of the magic of tying with "real" feathers instead of substitutes like Turkey feathers, which have a round quill that is vexingly difficult to lash to a hook without it slipping. As Edwin tried flattening them with needle-nose pliers, Muzzy rhapsodized about how much easier it was to tie with Indian Crow.

At one step in the process, Edwin slipped on a pair of white silk gloves to prevent the oils in his hands from tarnishing the fly. The lost era of the art form seemed so close: he was communing with it, using the same types of tools, following the rules of century-old books. The only thing that had changed was the law, which placed the feathers in Kelson's book frustratingly out of reach.

As the boys tied, Muzzy tried to make small talk, but he could see how engrossed they were by their partially completed Durham Rangers. They would check in on each other's work, offering compliments and critiques before firing off another technical question at Muzzy. When he asked what they did for fun back home, he wasn't surprised by their response: they tied flies.

On the second day, they tied the Baron, a fly praised by Kelson for use in the rivers of Norway. The original recipe required feathers from twelve different species of birds across the globe, plucked from Ostriches and Peacocks, Indian Crows and Blue Chatterers, Swans and Summer Ducks, Jays and Macaws, Golden Pheasants and Jungle Cocks.

In *How to Dress Salmon Flies*, one of the Victorian compendiums of fly-tying published in 1914, T. E. Pryce-Tannatt encouraged aspiring tiers to get Duck and Partridge skins from friends who hunted local game birds, but when it came to finding Brazilian Blue Chatterer skins, the Brit had no practical advice: "I only wish I possessed such a friend!"

Of course, the Migratory Bird Treaty Act of 1918 had made it illegal to buy feathers of birds as common as the Blue Jay—even if one dropped lifeless from the sky and landed at Edwin's feet, he could be fined for picking it up.

After sixteen hours of instruction, Edwin had tied his first two flies. Before they piled into the car for the drive home, Muzzy approached Edwin with a small envelope. "*This* is what it's all about," he murmured to the boy, who opened it to find $250 worth of Indian Crow and Blue Chatterer feathers in tiny Ziploc bags, enough for about two flies. The feathers were legal but rare and prohibitively expensive to a thirteen-year-old.

"Don't tie with them yet—not till you're ready," he told the wide-eyed boy. "You gotta work up to these things."

Back in Claverack, Edwin and his brother commandeered the garage and converted it into a laboratory for Victorian salmon flies, where they built upon the foundation Muzzy had laid. They called themselves the Fly Boys.

Working with substitutes, they boiled, steamed, oiled, glued, bent, twisted, crimped, stripped, trimmed, and massaged the fibers into shape. When they hit a wall, they'd call their teacher or experiment by trial and error until they figured it out. When Edwin ran out of wax, he went into the yard with a power drill and bored a hole into a pine tree, collecting the sap that bled out.

He learned how to use a cauterizer to burn away any unwanted feather fluff. When the cauterizer broke, he turned a blowtorch on his awl-like bodkin until it was red hot and ready to burn off extraneous fibers.

The learning curve was steep. Sometimes, after hours hunched over the vise, Edwin's fingers would slip up, and the fly would unravel. There were disasters, like when their dad flipped on the overhead fan in the garage and inadvertently stirred up a tornado of formerly organized feathers.

Edwin relentlessly pursued his hobby, trying to replicate what he saw in *Fly Tyer* and in Kelson's and Blacker's books. Once he was skilled enough, he emulated the masters by inventing his own flies, with names like the Weirdo Fly and Edwin's Fancy. "They would spend all day out there if we let them," Edwin's mom told a local journalist who had come to profile the Fly Boys. "But occasionally, my husband and I force them to come in and eat."

That fall Edwin was accepted as an early admit to nearby Columbia-Greene Community College. The thirteen-year-old planned to study fine arts.

But Edwin's artistic pursuits behind the fly-tying vise were hampered by the fact that he didn't have the "real" feathers. Through brute repetition, he had developed the technical skills needed to tie Victorian flies, but he was constantly frustrated. To an untrained eye, his creations looked exactly like Kelson's, but to him, they were adulterated, compromised by the use of substitutes like Turkey and Pheasant.

It was only when he finally got online that he realized he wasn't alone in his obsession.

———

After a member of ClassicFlyTying.com, the largest online forum for Victorian fly-tiers, wrote in a post, "There is something . . . to a fly tied with the old materials," Bud Guidry, the site's administrator, responded swiftly. "I've met this 'Something.' I'm haunted by it constantly now," wrote Guidry, a shrimp-boating Cajun from the tiny bayou town of Galliano, south of New Orleans. It's "like a drug, nothing else matters, nothing else compares. . . . When it touches my fingers I feel the history. I'm taken back to a time when fish were as big as logs, fresh from the sea . . . reds, yellows and shades of blues. Their texture and color have that power to push you to do your best, there is nothing else that compares to that power."

But the opportunity to experience that "something" was available only to the wealthiest tiers, those who could afford feathers from the birds cited in the original recipes, now even more expensive and elusive than they were in Kelson's day. Aware that their flies were a kind of status symbol, they presented them in decadently staged photographs: one hooked a Jock Scott, with fifteen different species of birds—Toucan, Bustard, Macaw, Indian Crow, and more—into the cork of a bottle of twenty-year single malt, a cut-crystal scotch glass nearby. The backgrounds of such pictures were often littered with piles of priceless feathers, whole skins of rare birds, or patches of polar bear and monkey fur, an homage to Victorian excess.

Edwin was desperate to gain access to this level of tying. On Muzzy's recommendation, he reached out to one of the kingpins of the exotic feather trade, a grizzled, chain-smoking retired detective from Detroit named John McLain, who ran a website called FeathersMc.com. "If you're going to tie good flies you have to have good materials," proclaimed McLain's site, which offered nearly every kind of feather.

For Edwin, a fourteen-year-old student, the prices were astronomical. The Argus Pheasant, a near-threatened bird that roams the lowland hill forests of the Malay Peninsula, is prized by fly-tiers for its thirty-inch quills that are marked with olive-colored eye spots known as ocelli. Linnaeus named the species after Argus Panoptes, the hundred-eyed giant from Greek mythology that never slept. McLain sold its feathers for $6.95 an inch, making a single quill worth more than $200.

Ten Blue Chatterer feathers went for $59.99. Ten Indian Crow feathers, each no larger than a fingernail, sold for $99.95, with a limit of one packet per customer "to ensure everybody that wants some of the real thing will be able to get them."

With dreams of Argus, Edwin went to work, wading into the waist-high ferns behind his home to gather firewood for his neighbors, who paid him a few bucks an hour to run pine through their wood splitter. When McLain got a call from a teenager wanting to buy a few hundred dollars' worth of Argus and other feathers, the former detective was suspicious. "Do your parents know you're calling me?" he asked. Edwin put his mom on the line.

When the feathers finally arrived, Edwin handled them gingerly. He had worked so hard for them that he was reluctant to cut into them: it was like learning how to sculpt on a priceless slab of marble.

As McLain got to know Edwin, he quickly realized that the boy's appetite for feathers far outstripped what he could afford, so he began to impart some of his strategies for finding feathers. Edwin found a retired ornithology professor willing to sell full bird skins on the cheap. He called up the Bronx Zoo, which sent him feathers from the autumn molt of Macaw, Spoonbill, Tragopan, and other species in their collection. He wrangled some Kori Bustard and Toucan feathers from species preservation societies.

He began to scour eBay for exotic birds—in the early days of the auction site, sellers occasionally posted antique bird cases with little knowledge of the rarity of each species—but was usually outbid by grown men with deeper pockets. Sometimes when a rarity like the Blue Chatterer was listed, tiers would join forces to outbid others, splitting the spoils among themselves. Others bid on antique salmon flies, solely to razor them apart for their feathers. Everyone searched for Victorian hats, but they rarely appeared on the auction site. When a well-known fly-tier died, community members would publicly express their condolences and privately move on the feathers he left behind.

Supply never kept up with demand. McLain sold a lot of valuable feathers, but when it came to the most sought-after—Blue Chatterer, Indian Crow, Resplendent Quetzal, and Birds of Paradise— there was a veritable drought. Most of the posts on ClassicFlyTying .com were made by tiers obsessively searching for plumes: some threads read like confessionals, where the authors admitted the birds they coveted most in wistful tones. Indian Crow, Blue Chatterer, and Resplendent Quetzal topped the list.

It was a seller's market; anyone who found a new source of the rare birds stood to make a lot of money, fast.

———

As Edwin's prominence in the community grew, master tiers would occasionally send him a few feathers to help him complete a particular fly. One of them was Luc Couturier, a French-Canadian renowned for his extravagant flies. In 2001 he earned the distinction of tying all twenty-eight Traherne flies, named after a nineteenth-century British soldier whose flies were seen by many as the pinnacle of the art form. Kelson himself had declared him "the master of infinite elaboration . . . there are no salmon flies in creation requiring so much patient work to dress well as Major Traherne's." A single fly, known as the Chatterer, called for an astonishing 150 to

200 Blue Chatterer feathers—which, if anyone could locate such a quantity, would cost nearly $2,000.

Couturier was an evangelist for taking salmon flies to new aesthetic heights, breaking free of a slavish adherence to nineteenth-century recipes. He pioneered what he called "thematical flies," inspired by a close study of a particular species of bird: chiefly, the Indian Crow, Blue Chatterer, and Birds of Paradise.

When Edwin first saw Couturier's orenocensis fly, named after the *orenocensis* subspecies of the Indian Crow, he thought it was a painting. The fly, which Edwin once described as a "satanic moth," was loaded with priceless feathers, including those from the Condor's tail. After Edwin came across Couturier's Paradisaea Minor Fly, celebrating the Lesser Bird of Paradise, he nervously reached out to the Québécois master, asking him for guidance.

When Couturier replied, Edwin felt as though he had a message from Michelangelo or da Vinci in his inbox. They struck up a correspondence, trading several e-mails a day as Edwin absorbed his secrets. Couturier sent him rare feathers and special hooks and even designed a fly dedicated to Edwin and his brother.

In a 2007 article written for the website of Ronn Lucas, a legendary hook maker, Edwin wrote, "Fly-tying is not merely a hobby, it is an obsession we seem to devote a substantial part of our time to . . . examining feather structure, designing flies, and coming up with new techniques for getting exactly what we want out of a fly."

He scrimped and saved to pull together enough materials for one such creation, nicknamed the Blacker Celebration Fly in honor of the art form's patriarch, William Blacker. The fly included feathers from the Indian Crow, Golden-headed Quetzal, Flame Bowerbird, Superb Bird of Paradise, and Cotinga. When he posted a picture of it on the forum, the community was gobsmacked. "Good grief, Edwin!" replied one tier: "The only materials on that fly that aren't on the CITES list are the flosses, the tinsels and the GP crests!" referring to the Golden Pheasant. "Do you and Anton live in an aviary, perchance? That at least would explain how you get your young hands on so many rare and exotic feathers!"

———

Even as his hobby became an obsession, Edwin had other things in his life. He was traveling to New York City each week for flute lessons and performances, having earned a spot in the New York Youth Symphony's orchestra, chamber music, and composition programs, as well as in the Interschool Orchestra of New York.

At sixteen, Edwin became a regular at the American Museum of Natural History, when David Dickey, his former biology tutor, secured him an internship in the herpetology department. He was given a key card to the back offices and was taught about the procedures for handling the museum's collection of reptile and amphibian skeletons, which were stored in a locked room monitored by security cameras.

Around that time, his parents were debating how to make use of their spare land in Claverack. Lynn had wanted to grow an herb garden, while Curtis thought it'd be fun to raise American bison, which had come back from the brink of extinction, thanks to Congress's 1884 decision to authorize the army to protect the final few hundred from poachers. They settled on breeding hypoallergenic Australian Labradoodles—a cross between a Labrador and a poodle—that would fetch up to several thousand dollars a puppy. Edwin pitched in as webmaster for the newly named Hudson Doodles business.

But whenever there was free time, he was back in the garage tying flies. He was now teaching others in the community, sharing twenty-page step-by-step instructions with close-up photos and running commentary on ClassicFlyTying.com. He wrote with the chatty confidence of a host on a cooking show, noting that the "fly looks a little droopy" in one picture, but that when preening a fly, it is "ridiculously easy to over rub or break a crest" feather. He took questions from grateful tiers, happily sharing his tricks.

Within a few years of first laying eyes on Muzzy's salmon flies, Edwin and his brother had joined the small fraternity of masters. In early 2005 Dave Klausmeyer, editor of *Fly Tyer*, formalized their ascension by proclaiming: "They are two of the finest young gentlemen you'd hope to meet, and they prove that the future of fly tying is in good hands."

But Edwin never saw mastery as having an end. As an artist, believing he had perfected any technique was anathema to him: fly-tying was an endless search for perfection. Some days he tied better than others. Some days he made mistakes he thought he'd long since moved past. He approached the art form with a humble, monkish devotion. As Muzzy put it, in a profile on Edwin and Anton that ran on McLain's website: "All they need to remember is they are entering a school you never graduate from."

Like Couturier, he was trying to achieve something transcendental. Fly-tying had become a search for something more profound than tying turkey feathers to a hook. "I'm toying with the idea of tying a series with each species of Cotinga and Crow," he told John McLain, referring to the five different subspecies of Indian Crow and seven species of Cotinga—the Blue Chatterer—one of which was on the endangered species list, "but that may not be practical right now."

And while the demands of the flute took priority, visions of all the Victorian patterns he had yet to tie floated through his mind like apparitions, always beckoning. He regarded the "future of fly tying" moniker as an obligation to strive even harder, but the higher he climbed, the more difficult it was to distinguish himself. Couturier had tied all twenty-eight Traherne flies. It took years for Marvin Nolte, another master, to tie 342 flies for a private collector in Wyoming. There were dozens of recipes in Blacker's *Art of Angling* and close to three hundred in Kelson's *The Salmon Fly*. At his current rate, Edwin would be chasing feathers for a hundred years before he had enough to tie them all.

———

In 2006, at sixteen, Edwin earned an associate's degree in fine arts from Columbia-Greene Community College, with a spot on the president's list.

Having decided to become a professional musician, he applied to the Juilliard School in New York City and the Royal Academy of Music in London, two of the most competitive music institutions in the world, which admitted only a handful of flautists each year. He dreamed of becoming the principal flute chair in the Berlin Philharmonic: it was perhaps the most coveted spot there was, but he knew it was pointless to pursue anything but the best.

Following his older brother's lead, Anton enrolled at Columbia-Greene as a thirteen-year-old, with aspirations of performing as a concert clarinetist.

In the spring of 2007, Edwin was accepted by the Royal Academy of Music in London. He would live on the southern edge of Regent's Park, home to the London Zoo, which had housed the first live Birds of Paradise that Wallace had brought back from the Malay Archipelago.

Suddenly the Berlin Philharmonic didn't seem like such an outlandish goal. That summer, as he packed his things, he decided to leave behind his fly-tying materials and feather collection. He was worried customs officers in the UK might seize them, but more important, he was going to London to study the flute, not to tie flies. He needed to stay focused.

On the eve of his departure, he got an e-mail from Luc Couturier, telling him about a magical place in England he had to visit. Attached were photos of the bird-filled drawers of the Natural History Museum in Tring.

II.

THE TRING HEIST

7

FEATHERLESS IN LONDON

I n the fall of 2007 Edwin Rist began his studies at the Royal Academy of Music. It had taken over a decade of devotion to the flute—a relentless schedule of private lessons, rehearsals, and practice—to earn a coveted spot at the school, whose alumni are launched into the finest orchestras or, like Elton John, pop superstardom.

Edwin's schedule was demanding—in between classes and practice, there was an endless offering of guest lectures and performances by distinguished musicians. He didn't struggle with the transition from the solitude of homeschooling to college life in a big city. He was no stranger to the world of overachieving musicians, and he had little difficulty making friends, knowing instinctively how important it was to get along with everyone since they all performed together.

But it only took four weeks after arriving to London for his other passion, the one he'd intended to set aside during his studies, to reassert its hold on him.

On October 10, 2007, he logged onto ClassicFlyTying.com to see if anyone would be willing to split the cost of a hotel room at the upcoming British Fly Fair International (BFFI), a couple of hundred miles north of London at the upmarket estate of Trentham Gardens. Like the shows that he'd frequented in the United States, the BFFI would host dozens of fly-tying demonstrations, alongside some eighty vendor booths brimming with feathers, silks, vises, and hooks.

"Unfortunately I'm not tying at the show (Customs wouldn't like my birdie bag . . .)," Edwin wrote, referring to the feathers he'd painstakingly collected over the years, "but I'd still like to see some old faces." A forum member reminded him that the fair was only an hour away from the fishing cabin of Izaak Walton, author of *The Compleat Angler*, built in 1671 on the banks of the River Dove.

He'd been tying flies for nearly as long as he'd been playing the flute, and here he was, in the land that spawned his beloved art form, without any feathers or materials. As if to add insult to injury, when he set out for Trentham Gardens, an eight-hour train delay kept him from attending the BFFI.

Two months into term, he visited the Natural History Museum in South Kensington, snapping photos of specimens and curios on display: cases full of stuffed Birds of Paradise, sapphires and diamonds. In the Mammals Hall next to a massive whale skeleton was an American mastodon—not Incognitum, from his hometown, but Missourium, exhumed in the 1840s from a spring in Missouri. Back at his dorm, he posted pictures of his visit to Facebook, including images of the Flame Bowerbird and the velvety-black Bird of Paradise known as Lawes's parotia. But the magnificent collection he'd heard about from Luc Couturier, the vast repository with hundreds of thousands of birds, was somewhere out of sight, walled off from the public.

In January 2008 Edwin received an invitation to demonstrate his mastery at the Bristol Fly Dressers' Guild. He leaped at the opportunity. His host, a prominent British tier named "Terry," asked what fly he hoped to tie. Edwin shared some recipes from Kelson's *The Salmon Fly* but stressed that he was completely without materials.

A month before the presentation, Terry took down the required materials for the Stevenson fly like a grocery list. Edwin had very specific requests: twisted silkworm gut, ultrafine white thread, a six-aught-size hook, Lagartun silk. When Terry, who had agreed to put him up in his Bristol flat for several days, asked what kind of food he liked, Edwin replied, "I will eat absolutely anything (as long as it's not disgusting, a la McDonald's), and in large quantities. . . . I am after all still a student, and a fairly starved one at that."

"I'm trying to sort out how I can bring over materials from home for next semester," Edwin added. "Life without tying is fairly harsh, but having a fortune in feathers confiscated by customs would be worse."

To tie in England, he'd need to rebuild a collection of materials from scratch. He had poked around London's antique shops in a vain search for Victorian-era hats and bird-filled natural history cabinets, and on the few occasions when he found a bird skin auction of a recently deceased aristocrat, the items were far beyond the reach of his student budget.

The screen name he used to upload videos from his time at the academy to YouTube, edwinresplendant, might have reflected his longing. The emerald Resplendent Quetzal feathers were prized by anyone hoping to tie rarities like the Ghost Fly or Wheatley's Fly no. 8 of 1849, which also calls for King Bird of Paradise plumes. But King Bird of Paradise feathers rarely appeared on the marketplace. The Resplendent Quetzal was endangered, listed in Appendix I of CITES, making it all but impossible to possess.

His early efforts to source feathers thwarted, he found his thoughts returning again and again to the e-mail Luc Couturier had sent him, and he decided he needed to see the greatest collection in the world.

According to the Natural History Museum's website, its ornithological collection included 700,000 skins, 15,000 skeletons, 17,000 specimens in spirit—full birds, pickled in large jars—4,000 nests, and 400,000 sets of eggs. Over two kilometers of shelves were needed to hold the birds in spirit alone. The specimens safeguarded there represented about 95 percent of the world's known species. Many of them had been gathered before the British Museum was founded in 1753.

Edwin clicked through to the "Access to the Collections" page and saw that researchers and artists could visit by prior appointment. He doubted the museum would grant him access if he said he was a fly-tier keen on seeing exotic birds. He considered his options. He had always wanted to write a book in the tradition of Kelson, to share his expertise with the next generation of tiers: perhaps he could request access in order to take photographs of beautiful specimens to include in it. But the museum was unlikely to admit someone without a background in writing, much less someone without a publisher.

Finally, he struck upon a solution: he would write in the name of research. On February 9, 2008, four days before he was scheduled to tie at the Bristol Fly Dressers' Guild, Edwin e-mailed the museum under his own name, saying that a friend at Oxford who was working on a dissertation on Birds of Paradise had asked him to take high-resolution photographs on his behalf.

As part of its security protocol, the museum asked Edwin for the e-mail address of the Oxford student in order to verify his request. Edwin created a fake e-mail account under his friend's name. When the museum sent the verification e-mail, they were in fact writing to Edwin. Access was granted, and a date was set in March for him to come photograph Alfred Russel Wallace's Birds of Paradise.

The day before the demonstration in Bristol, Edwin and Terry stopped at Veals Fishing Tackle, a short walk from the Broadmead shopping mall in the center of town. Edwin bought a pair of Jay wings, which were easy to purchase in the UK but prohibited in the United States. Across town Little Egrets, once sold by the millions for the millinery trade, flapped through the open-air section of the Bristol Zoo known as the Alfred Russel Wallace Aviary.

That night they did a practice fly-tying session at Terry's home, so that Edwin wouldn't feel rusty. But there was no need for concern: the following evening he dazzled several dozen of Terry's friends in the Fly Dressers' Guild, tying the Stevenson. The fly's body was a bright shock of orange-dyed seal fur, with silver tinsel threaded throughout. Wings of black-tipped orange Golden Pheasant feathers enveloped a pair of black-and-orange cream-colored Jungle Cock feathers. The pattern was remarkably similar to the first salmon fly he'd ever tied, with Muzzy: the Durham Ranger. Like Muzzy, Terry supplied Edwin with substitute feathers from ordinary birds for his demonstration.

Terry had seen Edwin's flies on the forum, but when he witnessed the eighteen-year-old's talents in action, he was overcome. "He is the BEST salmon tyer I have EVER seen. He is probably in the top five in the world," Terry raved in a note to the national president of the Fly Dressers' Guild, urging him to book Edwin at as many of its chapters—which number several dozen throughout England—as possible. "Everyone who attended . . . was amazed."

When Edwin got back to his dorm room at the Royal Academy, he dashed off a thank-you note to Terry. "I look forward to coming back," he added. "Hopefully by then I'll have my own equipment and materials here and will be able to put on a real show."

On the day of his appointment to photograph the Birds of Paradise, Edwin returned to the South Kensington campus of the Natural History Museum in London. The curators in charge of the bird skin collection had told him to cut through the parking lot and ring the buzzer on a door to the Ornithology Building, located behind the public museum. He could scarcely contain his excitement as he wandered around the lot, high-end digital SLR camera in hand, searching for the entrance.

A security guard noticed him and offered his help. When Edwin mentioned his appointment to visit the ornithological collection, the guard smiled and told him he was at the wrong branch of the museum, in the wrong city. The skins hadn't been in London for decades.

Embarrassed, Edwin returned to his dorm room and began re-searching how to get to the tiny town of Tring.

The public portion of the Tring museum is a striking example of Victorian architecture, with steep-pitched roofs, red brick walls, high-peaked gables, chimneys, and dormers. Kids play in the adja-cent park while parents refuel at the Zebra Café next to the mu-seum entrance. By stark contrast, the building housing the largest ornithological collection in the world is a four-story brutalist for-tress of concrete, looming in a corner of the museum complex.

On November 5, 2008, Edwin strode through the main entrance of the Ornithology Building. A security guard standing behind a counter welcomed him and asked for his ID. He signed his name in the visitors' logbook while the guard phoned the staff's office to an-nounce his arrival.

A staffer escorted him into the bird vault, where the museum's hundreds of thousands of bird skins are carefully stored in fifteen hundred white steel cabinets, occupying tens of thousands of square feet spread over several floors. The air was thick with the smell of mothballs, used to protect specimens against insect damage. To shield the birds from damage from ultraviolet rays, there were nar-row windows that only let in a faint amount of sunlight.

The staffer deposited the visitor in front of the cabinets marked PARADISAEIDAE, the Birds of Paradise. Before wandering off, he mentioned the locations of a number of other species he thought the photographer might like to see, gestured to a colleague in the corner of the room, and instructed Edwin to "let him know when you're done."

Edwin opened the cabinet doors. Inside were rows of drawers, some two dozen in each cabinet. He slowly pulled one out to reveal a dozen adult male Magnificent Riflebirds lying on their backs. He removed his trembling hand from the drawer pull. He'd never seen a full skin before, much less a dozen of them. The birds, about a foot in length, had a robe of deep black feathers, accented by a breastplate of metallic bluish-green feathers that turned purple in the right light. Their eyes had been stuffed with cotton, and biodata labels hung from their legs, recording the altitude, latitude, longitude, date of capture, and name of the collector. Several bore the faded handwriting of Alfred Russel Wallace.

The drawer below held another dozen, and the drawer below that, a dozen more, all in perfect condition. Riflebird feathers were rarely listed for sale on ClassicFlyTying.com, and when they were, their scarcity made them more valuable. In 2008 ten Riflebird breast feathers had sold for fifty dollars on the forum; with more than five hundred feathers per breast, a single skin might fetch $2,500. Tens of thousands of dollars were resting in the drawers of the first cabinet he opened alone, like lightweight, iridescent bricks of gold. And rows of cabinets stretched down the hallways for what seemed like miles.

Standing inside the Tring museum was like being in the vault of Fort Knox, the repository of centuries of mining, where the United States' gold bullion is stored. At some point, the value becomes incomprehensible.

Once he pulled himself together, Edwin carefully removed one of the birds from the drawer, brought it over to a research table, and took a picture. After he returned it, he surreptitiously snapped a photograph of the cabinet.

He moved to the cabinet that held the King Bird of Paradise. As Wallace described the specimens he'd gathered in the forests of Aru, ten of which were now within Edwin's reach: "the head, throat, and entire upper surface are of the richest glossy crimson red, shading to orange-crimson on the forehead . . . shining in certain lights with a metallic or glassy lustre."

Edwin took a photograph of his favorite specimen, snapped another of the corridor of cabinets that housed hundreds of skins from all thirty-nine species of the Birds of Paradise, then moved on to the museum's collection of Central and South American Cotingidae family of birds, which included the coveted Indian Crow and Blue Chatterer.

He selected a specimen to photograph—the small Blue Chatterer's turquoise body practically glowed in his hands. Most Blue Chatterer skins for sale were half destroyed, their feathers picked and plucked at by generations of tiers. A set of ten feathers could fetch fifty dollars. Here were dozens of flawless, untouched specimens, each of which could be sold for at least two thousand.

Each time he photographed a new species, he snapped a picture of its location. His camera's memory chip slowly filled up with a visual map of the vault.

Edwin's mind raced beyond the sheer monetary value of the Tring's birds to the creative potential they represented. Ever since he tied his first Victorian fly, five years earlier, his pursuit of perfection behind the vise had been defined by struggle; he'd made do with unconvincing substitute feathers, while watching wealthy tiers outbid him at auctions of exotic birds. Despite his fame in the community, there were so many flies that he still hadn't tied—not least of which were the exorbitantly plumaged "thematical flies" of his mentor, Luc Couturier.

To now wade through a seemingly endless supply of birds unstoppered a river of creative possibilities in Edwin's imagination. There was nothing he couldn't tie. It was as if he'd stepped back 150 years to the era of Kelson and Blacker, when ships still sagged with crates full of exotic birds.

He'd had two unsupervised hours to take as many photographs as he wanted. He knew Couturier had seen this room, and maybe only a few other salmon fly-tiers in the world. It had been an achievement to bluff his way in.

But as soon as he walked out into the bright light of day, he knew he had to find a way back inside.

8

PLAN FOR MUSEUM INVASION.DOC

E dwin wandered back toward the train station in an altered state, charged by a magnetic reaction to the birds he had just seen. He had to find a way to see them again.

It won't be easy, he thought as the train sped back to London. He'd gained access under false pretenses, and the museum was unlikely to fall for the same ruse twice. Since he had signed in using his real name, he couldn't return under a different identity—too many staffers had seen him.

For months, he thought about how to get back inside the Tring. At first it was a game, something to occupy his mind while he was sitting through lectures and practicing for ensemble performances. But as he descended deeper into his thought experiment, he realized that it wasn't simply about seeing the birds again. It was about taking them.

If he owned these birds, he would have an unrivaled stash of feathers for the rest of his life. In a community defined by its longing for the unobtainable, he would be king, and his extravagantly plumed flies would be unmatched. Even better, he could feature them in the book on fly-tying that he hoped to write, cementing his place in history alongside Kelson.

But his desire to possess the birds was driven as much by pragmatism as by obsession. The global financial meltdown of 2008 had dealt a blow to Hudson Doodles, the Rist family's dog-breeding business, nearly wiping out its customer base. In the face of a recession, five-thousand-dollar dogs were unnecessary luxuries. Edwin occasionally sent a little money home from student loan checks, but he knew it wasn't helping much.

At the same time, auditions with orchestras were only a year or so off, and just as tiers longed to work with expensive feathers, flautists yearned to perform with flutes forged from the rarest metals. While a nickel-silver flute could be bought for fifty dollars, the prices skyrocket as the metal becomes scarcer, from pure silver to 12-karat gold, 24-karat gold, all the way to $70,000 for a platinum flute. Despite multiple studies demonstrating that experts couldn't hear a difference—and that he'd be auditioning behind a screen— Edwin had his eyes on a $20,000 golden flute, roughly the equivalent of what four Indian Crows would fetch on the forums.

At twenty, the idea of stealing the Tring's birds glowed with potential—to advance his ambitions as a flautist, to give him the life and status he coveted, and to provide for his family. Even better, the birds would be an inoculation against future hardship: their value would only increase in time.

And why, he asked himself, did the museum need so many birds, after all? What earthly good was it serving to lock up dozens of skins from the same species? With such a vast collection, would they even notice if a few went missing?

Maybe, he thought, if he could persuade the curators to let him back into the building, he could put a couple of birds in his pocket without anyone noticing. It'd be easy to do this with species like the Cotinga, which were only six inches long and a tenth of a pound— the weight of a golf ball. But Indian Crows were a foot and a half long; Resplendent Quetzals were three and a half feet in length. How could he pocket a King Bird of Paradise without destroying its delicate tail feathers? Even if he found a way to conceal birds during a visit, how many trips would it take to build a respectable collection? How many times could he realistically do it before arousing suspicion?

It would be better to steal them all at once.

As he ducked in and out of class and rehearsal rooms, he thought through the details of the plan. How would he get inside? What route would ensure he remained inside the museum for the minimum amount of time? Should he start with the Birds of Paradise, the Blue Chatterers, or the Indian Crows? How often did the guards make rounds? How many guards were there? Where were the security cameras? If he entered through a window, how would he climb back out with a suitcase full of birds? Would one suitcase suffice?

He created a Word document titled "PLAN FOR MUSEUM INVASION" and started compiling a list of tools he'd need: grappling hooks, a laser glass cutter, and latex gloves to conceal his fingerprints.

Sometimes during rehearsal an inner voice would emerge and say *This is ridiculous!*, but it was faint, always drowned out by the other voice pushing him forward. *If you're going to do it*, that voice told him, *you need to start taking concrete steps to pull it off.*

The moment when Edwin's plans emerged from the realm of fantasy into that of reality transpired during a routine checkup at a doctor's office. While he was waiting in the examination room for the physician to arrive, his eyes fell on a box of latex gloves. *I'm gonna need a pair of those*, he thought, pocketing them.

And so Edwin's preparations began in earnest. On June 11, 2009, seven months after his first visit to the Tring, he ordered an 8mm diamond-blade glass cutter through his eBay account:

Fluteplayer1988. To protect the spoils from insects, he ordered a box of fifty mothballs.

He transferred the photographs from his camera to his computer and studied the proximity of one cabinet to another, assessing how long it might take to cover each of his coveted species.

He pored over a map of the museum. He went online and studied maps of the town of Tring, its main streets, side streets, and alleyways. The train station was east of the town center, over a good two miles of dimly lit country road. It would be easy enough to slip into Tring, but once he arrived at the intersection with Akeman Street for the final quarter-mile south to the museum, he'd be face to face with the Tring police station.

But he had already discovered a less conspicuous approach. He had noticed a narrow alleyway running parallel to Akeman, weaving behind the houses and restaurants. The path—Public Footpath 37—would deposit him directly behind the Ornithology Building.

There was a wall, but he could easily scale it. There was barbed wire, but he could easily snip it. There was a museum window on the second floor, just a few feet from the wall, but he could reach it.

All that remained in his planning was to select the optimal date. If he was to do it before the Royal Academy of Music's term ended on July 1, when he would return home to New York, he was running out of time.

The morning of June 23, Edwin woke up ready, confident. He performed at the academy's "London Soundscapes," a daylong tribute to composers who had left their mark on the city over the past few centuries, among them Purcell, Pepys, Handel, Hayden, and Mendelssohn. In his concert hall locker, he stashed an empty suitcase, a miniature flashlight, a wire cutter, the gloves, and the glass cutter. After the performance, he swapped his flute for the suitcase, made his way to Euston Station, and boarded an evening train to Tring.

The Midland train is painted parrot green and toucan yellow, its

ride quieted by a coffee-colored carpet. Just before the Kings Lang-
ley stop, halfway to Tring, the Grand Union Canal appears and
runs between the tracks and the A41 highway the rest of the way. A
woman's voice murmured the name of each stop, "*Wembley Central, Harrow & Wealdstone, Bushey, Watford Junction . . .*"

Edwin had nine stops and thirty-five minutes to change his mind.

––––––––

His well-rehearsed plan had quickly gone off script—after he lost
the glass cutter, it had taken several nerve-wracking minutes to
bash enough of the window away to make room for his suitcase, but
he was too charged with adrenaline to worry about cuts as he wriggled past the window frame's jagged edges into the museum.

Fifteen hundred unlocked steel cabinets lined the route he'd
plotted, containing hundreds of thousands of birds. Only a small
placard bearing Latin scientific names indicated their contents. His
flashlight cast a faint dome of light as he hurried down the hallway,
scanning for COTINGIDAE, which included the Indian Crow.
He'd originally planned to take only a handful of each species, but
when the moment came, he couldn't resist emptying out entire trays.
The only Indian Crows he left behind were the smaller females and
juvenile males, which hadn't yet grown their orange breastplates.

Forty-seven Indian Crows, weighing about a half-pound each, fit
neatly in his suitcase. Before proceeding to the cabinets containing
the seven species of Blue Chatterers, he carefully shut the cabinets,
to avoid arousing the suspicion of the museum staff.

After relieving the Tring's drawers of ninety-eight tiny Blue
Chatterers, he made his way to the birds of the Malay Archipelago.

He pulled out a tray labeled SERICULUS AUREUS, containing the
nine-inch-long Flame Bowerbird of New Guinea, famous for a hyp-
notic courtship dance in which it raises its wing like a matador
while dilating and contracting its pupils. He wedged seventeen tan-
gerine and golden skins into his suitcase.

At last he made his way to the Birds of Paradise. He maneuvered twenty-four Magnificent Riflebirds into his luggage, which was now brimming with several continents' and centuries' worth of specimens. Still, he managed to find room for twelve Superb Birds of Paradise, a species renowned for its bouncing courtship dance in which it shows off a stunning breastplate of iridescent aquamarine feathers.

Upon arriving at the cabinet containing Alfred Russel Wallace's beloved King Birds of Paradise, he gingerly laid thirty-seven of the birds, five of which bore Wallace's handwritten tags, into his suitcase.

Edwin realized he had lost himself in the plunder: he had no idea how many birds he'd taken or how long he'd been inside, but he knew the guard's next round must be coming up soon. Whether he managed to get back out the window and into the anonymity of the street before their paths collided would depend on how efficiently he moved. He walked briskly through the corridors, wheeling his full suitcase behind him. By the time the guard finally got up from the soccer match, Edwin was gone, having climbed out the way he came in.

As he made his way up the footpath, a tremendous wave of fatigue overcame him as his adrenaline subsided. He reverted to a kind of limbic motor movement, instinctively shuffling one foot in front of the other, breathing heavily as he emerged from the alleyway onto High Street. As he headed east, the storefronts yielded to houses, the houses to farms, and soon he was alone in the blackness of the ancient trees that formed a canopy over the narrow road, quietly counting off the forty minutes until the faint lights of Tring Station rose in the distance.

His original plan was to catch the 10:28, or failing that the 11:38, direct back to London. The last train left at 12:16 a.m., but he was certain he'd be finished well before then. When he finally arrived at the station and checked the time, he realized he'd missed them all.

By his estimation, he had been inside the Tring for nearly three hours. The next train home wasn't until 3:54 in the morning. As he sat on the platform, with maybe a million dollars' worth of birds in his suitcase, he began to worry—for the first time in months of planning—about getting caught.

What if the guard noticed the broken glass on his next round? Had he remembered to close each of the cabinets? Had he left any fingerprints on the glass cutter? Was that a cut on his hand? Had any drops of blood fallen inside the Tring? Could they identify him by his blood? Had he walked in front of any security cameras? Where *was* that glass cutter?

What if they were already doing a dragnet at that very moment, fanning their way steadily outward from the scene of the crime with flashlights and bloodhounds, primed with the scent of dead birds, working their way toward the station?

He was exhausted, but he couldn't risk sleeping. Whenever someone walked over the nearby bridge spanning the tracks, adrenaline shuddered through him, snapping his weary mind awake with dread.

The Midland train slipped into Tring at 3:54 a.m., its headlights scattering the shadows on the platform. He clutched his suitcase and waited impatiently for the doors to open, desperate to get far away from the museum and back to the city, where he could blend into the crowd of Londoners and luggage-toting tourists.

He boarded, but the doors lingered open. A high-pitched beeping sounded from a box above the door. Had the conductor received some kind of alert?

At last the pneumatic doors shut with a solid, reassuring thump. A comforting prerecorded voice bade him *"Welcome aboard this*

London Midland service to . . . Euston Station." Most of his fellow passengers were fast asleep. Rather than using the overhead rack, he kept the suitcase and its precious contents between his legs, resisting the urge to peek inside.

As the train approached the next station, he peered nervously out the window, searching for flashing police lights or constables with K9 dogs on the platform. But no such thing appeared. With each stop, the museum slipped farther away, and he began to relax.

Forty minutes later the automated voice announced, *"We are now approaching London Euston, our final destination."* Commuters gathered by the doors, snapping purses shut, zipping up jackets. *"Please remember to take all of your personal belongings with you when you leave the train."*

He was almost there. Dawn broke as he hurried down the street toward his flat, suitcase wheels clacking noisily over the seams of the sidewalk.

Hoping not to wake his housemates, he tiptoed through the apartment. Back in his room, the sunlight was already starting to filter in through the windows. Safe at last, he unzipped the suitcase and peered in at a flash of turquoise and crimson, indigo and emerald, hundreds of lifeless cotton eyes. As he spread them out on his bed with mounting excitement, he felt it was the greatest day in his life. It wasn't a dream. They were all his.

He cleared a space on his bed and fell into a deep sleep.

9

THE CASE OF THE BROKEN WINDOW

On June 24, 2009, the Natural History Museum's on-duty security guard was halfway through his round when he noticed shards of glass near the base of the building. Perhaps a drunk had tossed an empty bottle over the wall of the nearby public footpath? He scanned the area until his eyes settled on the smashed-out window overhead.

He hurried inside to inform the Tring's curators that there seemed to have been a break-in.

The police arrived and began searching for evidence, examining the bird skin cabinets in the immediate vicinity of the broken window and scanning the ground outside. Mark Adams, the senior curator responsible for the Tring's bird skin collection, raced to the stacks containing the museum's most precious specimens.

On the museum's staff since 1990, Adams had recently coauthored a journal article, "Extinct and Endangered Bird Collections: Managing the Risk," noting that "damage and theft" were increasing concerns.

To protect these rare specimens, the Tring's staff had moved them to "a high-visibility area adjacent to the curators' offices where any activity in the collection may be easily monitored." Adams acknowledged the risks inherent in consolidating everything into one area—a fire could consume the entire collection in one swoop, for example—but he stressed that their approach meant that "only a few key areas need additional protective measures to maintain security."

Now, with an active crime scene, he feared the worst as he nervously unlocked the cabinets containing the Tring's treasures: the Galápagos finches collected by Darwin during the voyage of the *Beagle*, skins and skeletons of extinct birds like the Dodo and the Great Auk, a collection of John James Audubon's birds, and an original bound edition of his *Birds of America,* the most valuable book in the world.

Mercifully, nothing seemed to be missing.

Asked by police for an estimate on when the window had been broken out, the security guard could suggest only a twelve-hour period.

All were puzzled about what the intruder had been after. The police mentioned that there had recently been a rash of smash-and-grabs around town by petty thieves looking for laptops and other electronics, but after a search of the staff offices, nothing of value appeared to be missing.

A relieved consensus was forming. It appeared as though their culprit had poked his head in, looked around, and finding nothing of obvious value, left empty-handed. He'd have become a rich man if he'd known how much Darwin's finches might fetch on the black market, or that *Birds of America* had recently sold for $11.5 million at auction.

And so no systematic audit of the Tring's collection was ordered. Even if it had been, with over fifteen hundred cabinets housing 750,000 specimens and a small staff, a complete audit—which hadn't been conducted for at least a decade—could take weeks.

Dr. Robert Prys-Jones, the museum's collections manager, was relieved that nothing appeared to be missing. A brief police report was written up, and the case of the broken window was considered closed.

The glow of Edwin's successful heist was fleeting. He couldn't brag about it to his friends, his girlfriend, or his brother. He couldn't leave the birds out in the open in his apartment. He now had one of the greatest private collections of birds in the world, but he had to keep it a secret—or, eventually, come up with lies about where he had found the specimens.

In the days that followed, he was consumed with paranoia and guilt. When the buzzer on his front door rang unexpectedly, a bolt of fear shot through him. He started sensing that people were following him when he walked through his neighborhood. Were the police already on his trail? What had they found that linked him to the crime? Even the ring of his telephone startled him.

He considered taking them back. If he deposited them in front of the Tring and slipped off into the night, it would be as if the theft had never happened. Or instead of returning to the scene of the crime, he thought about leaving them on a random street corner and calling the police with an anonymous tip. But both scenarios sparked new fears of getting caught: walking away from a suitcase in a major city is pretty suspicious behavior, and there was no telling if cops were staked out by the museum.

And why go to such lengths to take the birds, just to return them a few days later?

After all, nothing had changed. He wasn't giving up his hobby: the mere sight of his haul made him ache to start tying again, but the rest of his equipment—the vise and bobbins and tinsel and threads— was back in New York. And while he was set to return home in a matter of days, it would be folly to risk bringing the birds through customs. He would have to wait until the fall to start tying, when he could bring his tools back to London.

He still needed a new flute. His parents were still struggling. And the demand for a new supply of feathers within the fly-tying community, which had recently named Edwin "Fly Tier of the Year" in the forum, was as intense as ever.

Before long, the fear and guilt receded, taking with them any notion of returning the birds. Why should anyone care about some old birds taken from a musty museum, especially when it had so many to spare?

He returned to the plan, beginning with an inventory. He carefully placed each specimen on his desk, unfurling the two-foot-long tails of the Resplendent Quetzals and gingerly cradling the King Birds of Paradise as their iridescent jade disc-plumes wobbled back and forth. He opened up a blank file on his computer and made a tally. He was astounded by the numbers. Had he really grabbed *forty-seven* Indian Crow skins? *Thirty-seven* King Birds of Paradise? *Thirty-nine* Resplendent Quetzals?

By the time he finished, he had logged 299 skins from sixteen different species and subspecies. All the obstacles he had faced over the past decade of tying flies—the drudgery of splitting wood for hours just to be able to afford a few of John McLain's feathers, trudging to estate sales and antique shops in vain hopes of finding a bargain, calling zoos in search of molted feathers, tying flies with cheap substitutes while prized birds on eBay were snapped up by wealthy men—vanished beneath the pile of birds around him. Over a century earlier George Kelson had bemoaned the difficulty of finding good Bird of Paradise feathers, but Edwin now had more than old Kelson could've imagined.

Edwin had an unrivaled supply of product in a marketplace not dissimilar from the drug trade—crowded with self-professed feather addicts, white- and blue-collar, young and old, near and far. There were two obvious ways to push the feathers: he could approach wealthier tiers—doctors, dentists, and lawyers with capital—and offer to part with an entire skin. Under this model—essentially wholesale—he'd pull in a lot of cash up front, but the total revenue would be considerably less than if he harvested the feathers and sold them in individual packages. Such an approach—more similar to retail—would require dealing with a much higher volume of customers and smaller increments of cash, but he'd earn more in the long term. The easiest thing to do, of course, would be to sell the entire haul to a rich collector, but that would have negated one of the main goals of the heist, which was to obtain materials to last him a lifetime of tying.

The retail model carried significantly more risk. If he sold to fewer people, he was much less likely to get caught. He probably wouldn't need to post anything online, thereby avoiding leaving a trail of incriminating evidence. If anyone asked where the skins came from, he could just say that he found them in a London antique shop or some unpublicized Victorian estate sale.

Retailing would also require considerably more work, both in terms of the feathers themselves—harvesting them and searching for matching pairs from each side of the cape, wing, throat or breastplate—and on the business side, drafting copy and photographing each feather for every posting. He'd need packaging, probably thousands of Ziploc bags. He'd need to handle distribution, figuring out how to send his product to buyers without attracting attention. He'd need to manage the finances, setting up accounts for online payments, not to mention customer service. When he wasn't at rehearsals, there would be the time-sucking distraction of constantly running down to the post office to mail feathers to impatient customers.

He decided to try more than one approach. He would sell some individual feathers on the forum and eBay, and at the same time reach out privately to a few people who he knew might be able to afford a full skin.

Laying out each skin on a dark gray piece of fabric, he trained his camera on the portions that would be most prized by his fellow tiers, concealing the labels tethered around the birds' legs, the words MUS. BRIT. stamped in the corner.

Using tweezers, he began the first harvest, plucking the rich, orange feathers from the breastplate of an Indian Crow. When he was younger, his dad had shelled out $2,500 for a full Indian Crow skin from a collector on his deathbed in New Jersey—beating the line of eager fly-tiers waiting at the door—but Edwin had never been able to bring himself to pluck all the feathers. Now, with forty-seven of them on the desk before him, he had no qualms tweezing the plumed bounty from the bird. The rest of the bird's black plumage was worthless to fly-tiers, so once he'd removed the breast feathers and matched them into pairs, he tossed the skin into a large cardboard box by his closet. He started on the next one, and before long he had a small pile of bagged feathers. With only six feathers not much larger than a pinkie fingernail, a single baggie might fetch a hundred dollars.

With his departure for summer break imminent, Edwin packed the birds and packets of feathers into a large cardboard box, carefully scattered mothballs inside to protect his collection from any interested insects, and stowed it in his closet, which he secured with an additional lock. Everything he wanted to sell was ready for distribution when he returned. So long as he snipped the tags from the skins before sending them off, no one would ever connect them to the Tring.

As he boarded his flight home, weeks after the heist, nobody was looking for him. No one at the Tring even realized anything was missing.

10

"A VERY UNUSUAL CRIME"

O ver a month after the theft, on the morning of July 28, 2009, when Mark Adams showed up for work at the Tring, he had no idea how bad his day was going to get. While guiding a visiting researcher down the fluorescent-lit hallways into the bird collection, Adams pointed out the locations of various avian families and genera along the way. *Pyroderus scutatus is here,* he said, as he opened a cabinet, just as he'd done countless times before with other researchers. But when he pulled out a tray of Red-Ruffed Fruitcrows, known to fly-tiers as Indian Crow, all the adult male skins were gone.

Heart racing, he yanked out another tray. Empty. Another tray. Empty. With the exception of one adult male skin wedged out of sight in the back corner, all that remained of the species were juvenile males, which hadn't yet grown their cherry-orange breast feathers.

An all-hands-on-deck call was sent out, and the Tring's staff scrambled to see if anything else had been stolen. They checked other brightly colored members of the Cotinga family in nearby cabinets and discovered more empty drawers. Scores of Blue Chatterers were gone. They flung open the cabinet doors to the Trogon family, which includes the Resplendent Quetzal, and found them empty. They expanded their search to include the Birds of Paradise and realized that dozens, including five of Wallace's, had vanished. Only the dull-colored females were left behind.

They rang the Hertfordshire police to inform them that the case of the broken window needed to be reopened.

Over the next couple of weeks, fifteen hundred cabinets were opened and thousands of trays pulled, as the devastated curators took stock of the loss: 299 birds from sixteen different species. While it was too early to know for sure, they were beginning to sense that it hadn't been a scientific theft, since an obsessive collector trying to complete a collection of species would have taken the females and immature specimens as well. As their sweep continued, it became clear that whoever did this was after exotic birds with iridescent plumage.

Who would steal a bunch of dead birds?

At first the question seemed almost comical to Detective Sergeant Adele Hopkin as she headed over to the museum. A single mother with shoulder-length brown hair and a warm yet no-bullshit demeanor, she had been on the force for nearly twenty years, making detective just a few years prior to the break-in. She worked plainclothes units. Did undercover work. Did her time on the drug squad and also worked the safe neighborhoods programs, protecting vulnerable residents from fraud and harassment. As detective sergeant, she was now running a team in the Hertfordshire county constabulary investigating robberies, burglaries, and violent assaults.

She didn't live far from the museum but hadn't visited often. Before getting the call that day, she'd never heard of Alfred Russel Wallace and had little sense of the importance of the Tring's collection. She did, however, understand that the investigation was already hampered by the length of time it had taken for the museum to realize it had been burgled. Whoever did this had quite the head start: had it not been for the request from the visiting researcher to examine the Indian Crow skins, it's unclear how much more time might have elapsed before anyone noticed something was missing.

CCTV surveillance footage was held for twenty-eight days. It had been thirty-four days since the break-in. As discouraging as this was, Adele doubted that the footage would've solved the crime for them. Tring wasn't a heavily monitored town, and she knew there weren't any cameras on the stretch of road between the town and the train station: "It's about four miles of nothing," she said.

The thief's motive wasn't clear, nor were his methods. Had the birds been taken all in a single night or over several months or even years? After all, it had been a decade since the last full inventory of the collection. Was it a single perpetrator or more than one? Did they arrive by car or on foot? Could it have been the work of a crime syndicate? For years, a network known variously as the Irish Travellers, the Rathkeale Rovers, or the Dead Zoo Gang had been involved in a series of thefts of rhino horn and Chinese jade from museums across the globe, including in the UK.

Initially, Adele wondered if it was an inside job, someone sticking the precious specimens down their trousers, a couple of skins at a time, but she quickly ruled out the possibility. Interviews with the museum's staff revealed how crushed they were by the theft.

She asked the museum to point out the window that had been broken. The beat policeman had inspected it back when it was first reported, but she wanted to take another look.

It was about six feet off the ground. A tall enough person could hoist himself in, but it wouldn't be easy. Her eyes swept the area beneath the window and settled upon a gutter meant to catch bits of cladding and debris that might fall from the roof. Crouching down, amid the broken glass, she found a bit of a latex glove and a glass cutter. On one of the shards, she found a drop of blood. She bagged up the evidence her colleagues had missed and sent it off to the national forensics laboratory.

As Adele poked around the crime scene, the museum was beginning to come to terms with the scope of the theft and the specter of a public relations crisis. The loss of so many irreplaceable skins, which would create a significant gap in the scientific record, was a deeply embarrassing blow. That it had apparently been so easily accomplished only made things worse.

As the tally of missing skins mounted, so did the scale of the Tring staff's sense of failure as custodians of natural history. Mark Adams was hit hard by the burglary; he saw himself and the others as just one link in the centuries-long chain of curators entrusted with looking after the specimens, and they had failed.

But it wasn't the first time the Tring had been burgled.

In 1975 a man in a wheelchair appeared at the museum's entrance, asking to speak with a curator about the egg collection. Mervyn Shorthouse explained that he'd been severely injured in an electrical accident at work and was now on disability, and that eggs were now his only joy in life.

"The museum took pity on him," recalled Michael Walters, then head of the Tring's egg collection, and granted access on compassionate grounds. Over the next five years, Shorthouse paid over eighty-five visits to the Tring's eggs—until a suspicious curator spotted him slipping some of them into his pocket. When police searched him outside the museum, they found 540 eggs in his baggy overcoat and in his car. Back home were another ten thousand. It was soon discovered that the "electrical accident" that had disfigured Shorthouse had in fact occurred in the midst of another theft, when he had attempted to steal cable by hacksawing through a live high-voltage line.

At the trial, the prosecutor lamented the "incalculable damage to part of the national heritage" and established that Shorthouse had been selling eggs to other private collectors, often removing any identifying markings to cover his tracks. Shorthouse was sentenced to two years for his crimes, while Walters spent the next twenty-five years and the rest of his career trying to sort through the damage to the integrity of the collection.

In another infamous case, Colonel Richard Meinertzhagen was banned from the British Museum's Bird Room for unauthorized removal of specimens. But Meinertzhagen, a distinguished officer in the Levant during the First World War and a prolific birder and ornithologist, had Lord Walter Rothschild lobby the London museum to revoke the ban. After only eighteen months, the colonel was allowed back in, but for the next thirty years, the curators remained suspicious that he was stealing birds. Upon his death in 1967, his private collection of twenty thousand specimens was donated to the museum, but it was decades before the scientific community realized what Meinertzhagen had been up to: in an attempt to burnish his legacy as a world-famous collector, he had replaced the labels on birds collected by others and fraudulently claimed them as his own discoveries. In doing so, he cast into doubt the veracity of the invaluable biodata on the labels of many of the affected species, none of which were part of the newest theft.

Dr. Prys-Jones, the bird collections manager at the museum, had spent a depressing amount of time over the past two decades evaluating the extent of Meinertzhagen's fraud. He knew that there had been a series of bird skin thefts in previous years at other museums, whose curators hadn't rushed to publicize what happened. Between 1998 and 2003 a pest controller at the Australian Museum named Hendrikus van Leeuwen had stolen more than two thousand skulls and skeletons during his unregulated nighttime access to the collection. More recently the Naturkunde Museum of Stuttgart had suffered a loss of bird skins—mostly from the Cotinga family—but the thief was never caught, and as so often happened, the burglary was not made public.

Prys-Jones was particularly invested in tackling the challenges faced by natural history museums throughout the world. In

November 1999 he convened a conference in Aston Clinton called "Why Museums Matter: Avian Archives in an Age of Extinction." One hundred thirty curators from twenty-five countries participated, representing natural history museums in Europe that housed nearly four million bird skins among them. The Tring was the most prestigious, with four times as many skins as the second-largest collection, in the Naturalis Biodiversity Center in the Netherlands, and dwarfing the few thousand skins held by museums in Luxembourg, Norway, and Italy. All faced similar pressures: public funding was on the wane, while the threats posed by theft were constant.

Following the conference, the electronic Bulletin Board for European Avian Curators, eBEAC, was established to bring together the extensive community of curators and to help time-strapped staffers stay abreast of the countless obsessions driving black markets for particular specimens. If a museum suffered a theft by an organized network, other curators throughout the world would be on heightened alert. The Tring volunteered to host the computer running eBEAC.

In this case, the system hadn't worked: the Tring's staff had had no idea that these particular species had become valuable enough to steal.

Making the theft public would mean risking their reputation, but the museum's directors reasoned that it was worth risking embarrassment to try to recover the skins. Plus, Adele needed leads. It would take a while to get forensics results from the national fingerprint database, and if there wasn't a positive match to a known criminal, she wouldn't have anything to go on. Their best hope was that a member of the public might come forward with information.

Beyond finding the culprit, she had another urgent mission: after the Meinertzhagen and Shorthouse affairs, in which labels were either removed or changed, it was vital that she recover the birds with their biodata labels intact. Finding them without their tags would create an impassable void for researchers, as few meaningful inferences could be drawn from a skin without knowing the date and geographic details of its collection. An educated guess could be made based on the types of materials and cotton used to stuff a specimen, but it would be a painstakingly slow and less-than-conclusive process.

With Adele's assistance, the museum drafted a press release announcing the theft.

"It is very distressing that we should have been deliberately targeted in this manner," Richard Lane, the Natural History Museum's director of science, lamented in the release. "Our utmost priority is working with the police to recover these specimens to the national collections so that they can be used by future generations of scientists."

"This is a very unusual crime," Adele's supervisor, Detective Inspector Fraser Wylie, was quoted as saying. "We are appealing for anyone who may have seen any suspicious activity around the museum in the time around when the break-in was, before it or subsequently." The police included their contact information along with a Crime Stoppers hotline number where anonymous tips could be shared.

A handful of media outlets in the UK, including the BBC and the *Telegraph*, ran brief articles, and a few sites like Nature.com and the Association of Academic Museums and Galleries posted about it, but the release found its widest distribution in the various online fly-tying forums: FlyFisherman.com, FlyTyingForum.com, and Edwin's favorite online haunt, ClassicFlyTying.com.

11

HOT BIRDS ON A COLD TRAIL

"**S** omebody stole birds from a museum!" Anton exclaimed on the other end of the line. "It's on the forum!"

Edwin had just returned to London from summer break. He hurried over to his computer and found the press release. A statement from Detective Inspector Fraser Wylie caught his eye: "We would ask any collectors of such specimens to keep a watchful eye out in case they are offered anything resembling them."

The police were still groping in the dark: Wylie suggested the birds might have been stolen by a "gang of thieves" on behalf of a collector, and that 299 birds would fill up to six garbage bags. When asked by journalists why these particular birds might have been targeted, he shared his working theories—that a dressmaker or jeweler might have commissioned the theft in pursuit of iridescent feathers for their craft. "We keep an open mind," he added, mentioning one other theory: "There may also be a need within the fishing market."

At that point, with a formal investigation under way and a public call for leads, Edwin knew that it was too late to return the birds to the Tring with a simple apology. He considered stowing the birds away for years, maybe decades, selling them only after the police stopped searching. Or he could go ahead with his plan, making sure that he supplied a good enough cover story for each sale he made. How bright were these people anyhow, he reasoned, if it took them a full month to realize they'd been robbed? Surely they'd forget about them soon enough.

In October, shortly after starting his third year at the Royal Academy, Edwin purchased eleven hundred small Ziploc bags, 2.25 by 3 inches, ideal for storing individual feathers. He also ordered five hundred medium-size bags, 4 by 5.5 inches, perfect for storing patches of feathers sliced from the skin. On November 12, he logged on to ClassicFlyTying.com, navigated to the "Trading Floor" section of the forum, and created a new post: "Indian Crow Feathers for sale, Buying new flute!"

"The time has come for me to upgrade my instrument," he wrote, "and I am selling some crow feathers to help this along." In describing his wares, he used *P.S.* for the Latin binomial *Pyroderus scutatus*: "There are two subspecies, P.S. Scutatus, and P.S. Granadensis. All are super A quality. I have limited numbers of Granadensis so first come, first serve! There is no limit on the number of feathers you can buy at a time. Prices are: Scutatus large—10 feathers/$95; 10 medium/$85; 10 small/$80. Granadensis 10 large/$120; 10 medium/$95; 10 small/$90." The post included high-resolution photographs of the black-and-orange-tipped feathers.

The response was ravenous. The following day he ordered more Ziploc bags, these ones large enough to ship full bird skins. Two days later he logged back in to announce that only a limited number of Indian Crow feathers remained, "so if you still want some, now is the chance!"

On November 28, Edwin uploaded a photo of the small turquoise Blue Chatterer to eBay.co.uk, using an account he'd registered a couple of months prior to his first visit to the Tring: Fluteplayer 1988. When news of the auction hit the forum, there was a surprised reaction.

> **Angler Andrew:** From Britain as well, I've never seen one on Ebay from Britain. Anyway there's about 10 mins left and still no bids. Man if I won the lottery!
>
> **Monquarter:** Hmm the seller is "Fluteplayer 1988." Edwin Rist sold some Indian Crow to pay for a new flute recently. Coincidence? Maybe however I suspect the seller is Mr. Rist so it should be good quality and from an honest seller.
>
> **mitch:** anyway I wish him well and hopefully gets his flute before Christmas. Cheers.

Meanwhile Adele was still waiting on the forensics results from the bit of latex glove, the drop of blood, and the diamond-blade glass cutter. She was skeptical that a match would come back. A more experienced burglar, the kind with prints already on file, would have been more careful about removing potentially incriminating evidence. In the meantime, she contacted the National Wildlife Crime Unit, charged with enforcing anti-trafficking laws. Formed only three years earlier, the police unit specialized in gathering intelligence on wildlife crime, working closely with various branches of law enforcement, including the UK Border Force, which maintained a dedicated CITES team trained in identifying protected species at Heathrow Airport. Adele asked them to be on the lookout: if an agent discovered someone with a bunch of exotic birds, she wanted to be the first to know.

Around this time, "Mortimer," a dentist and avid fly-tier from the Pacific Northwest, landed in London for an eight-hour layover on his return from a fishing expedition in Africa. He took a cab to the Jurys Inn, where he found Edwin waiting in the hotel restaurant.

Edwin didn't seem particularly concerned about displaying his wares. He ordered a beer and laid out a handful of species that his customer had expressed an interest in over e-mail. As Mortimer inspected the skins, Edwin told him he was helping a pair of aristo-cratic collectors sell off their collection as a way of funding his stud-ies. Mortimer, unsure of their legality, was wary of returning to the airport with the birds, so he put a hold on three of the choicest skins: a Flame Bowerbird, an Indian Crow, and a Blue Chatterer. He sent Edwin a check for seven thousand dollars. When the pack-age arrived at Mortimer's dental practice, he found a U.S. Fish and Wildlife Service inspection sheet inside, which meant either that Edwin had forged documents or that the federal agency had opened it mid-shipment, examined the birds, and waved them along.

At eighty-seven, Phil Castleman is arguably the community's longest-running feather supplier. Proprietor of Castle Arms of Springfield, Massachusetts, he has been selling feathers for sixty-four years to a mailing list of customers that approaches fifteen hundred names. His showroom, which includes pelts of fur, taxi-dermy birds, and a collection of more than one hundred framed salmon flies by the world's best tiers, is open by appointment only. Castleman kept a close eye on movements in the marketplace, and he would generally hear if a competitor was about to off-load a lot of skins or an obsessive collector was looking to buy. Shortly after Edwin started selling, Castleman's phone began ringing, as fly-tiers tipped him off to the auctions of rare birds in England, wondering whether they could be legally shipped to the United States. He did a lot of business in Europe but didn't know anyone in England with a collection like that for sale.

But while Castleman fielded calls from cautious fly-tiers, Edwin found that his buyers, many of whom he had known since his earli-est days tying, weren't asking questions. He knew that their addic-tion to these birds meant they wouldn't ask questions to which they'd rather not know the answers. For those whose conscience demanded it, though, he offered a menu of fabricated stories regarding each skin's provenance. Some had been discovered in overlooked corners of antique shops, others scooped up at a provincial estate sale. His Birds of Paradise had come from a friend in Papua New Guinea as part of a trade.

As 2010 approached, the search for the thief—or gang of thieves—was short on leads. The curators had reviewed their e-mail correspondence with people who had expressed an interest in the species targeted in the theft. Two initial suspects emerged: a Canadian named Luc Couturier and an American named Ed Muzeroll. Just a couple of years prior, both had inquired about the possibility of buying some of the museum's skins but had been turned away. Adele ruled them out as culprits but remained unaware of how close she had come to the thief, who had learned to tie his first salmon fly with Muzeroll, and had first heard about the Tring's collection from Couturier.

Although the museum's curators had publicly expressed a strong desire to recover the skins, they had privately come to the conclusion that the stolen specimens had likely already been broken up and separated from their tags and were no longer of scientific value. Whether this pessimistic assumption colored the police investigation is unclear: what is clear is that the thief was right under their noses. One of the working theories was that a fly-tier was behind the theft, and any Web search for the species in question would have yielded a number of hits at ClassicFlyTying.com, including discussions of Edwin's bird skin sales on eBay. His forum posts had used the Latin names for each species, the very names now affixed to empty cabinets at the Tring.

The two previous major thefts at the Tring—Shorthouse's eggs and Meinertzhagen's skins—had been perpetrated by known visitors to the specimen stacks. Had the latest thief also come to the museum prior to robbing it? No more than a couple of hundred visitors were likely to have entered the vault during the previous calendar year: if their culprit had staked out the museum under false pretenses, surely his or her name would be in the logbook.

The name Edwin Rist was, of course, there, on a page dated November 5, 2008. If they had run an online search for "Edwin Rist," they would have found a number of websites connecting him to the world of salmon flies and his eBay listings. But six months after the robbery, they were still in the dark.

Adele's day-to-day work—tackling domestic abuse cases, breaking and entering, and other robberies—continued apace. If the Tring's curators ever turned up a good lead, she'd investigate, but for the time being, the case moved into the unsolved bracket.

At the dawn of the new year, everything was coming up aces for Edwin. Whenever he needed an infusion of cash, he'd post some feathers on eBay or the forum, which would sell in less than a day. A quick trip to the post office, and the money would pour in; repeat as necessary.

On March 6, he packed a number of skins he was open to selling if the price was right and headed up to the Spring Fly Fishing Show in Newark, a few hours north of London. Dave Carne, who had recently sent Edwin $3,500 that he'd borrowed from his elderly mother for a cape of feathers from a prized subspecies of Indian Crow, was excited to finally meet him in person. Carne had been tying salmon flies since he was thirteen, when he often spent his pocket change on Florican Bustard and Jungle Cock feathers from the fishing tackle shop where he worked.

At the show, Carne saw Edwin sell a full Blue Chatterer skin to Jens Pilgaard, a Danish blacksmith renowned for his collection of hand-forged blades of mottled Damascus steel, medieval weapons, and Viking jewelry. Pilgaard also sold fly-tying materials as the proprietor of Fugl & Fjer Fluebinding—Danish for Bird & Feather

Fly-tying. As the Dane tied a fly in front of a small audience of admirers, Edwin approached him with his skins. "Why are you selling
this?!" he asked, as he and his audience marveled at the quality of
the feathers. When Edwin replied that he needed money to buy a
new flute, the Dane bought a breast patch of Indian Crow, a Flame
Bowerbird cut into a few pieces, and a Blue Chatterer skin. The bill
came to about $6,000, along with a commitment to send a Ma-
layan Peacock Pheasant skin—worth another $4,500—from his
collection back home in Århus, which Edwin could sell to his growing customer base.

In April 2010 Edwin hopped on a flight to Japan: he had recently
started taking Japanese at King's College London, even taking part
in the International Japanese Speech Competition. He bought a
travel pass, visited Tokyo and Kyoto, and rode the bullet train. He
packed some materials so that he could tie a Popham Fly in the park
under the *sakura* cherry blossoms, wrapping fine silk around Indian
Crow and Blue Chatterer feathers.

When he got back to England, he sent a follow-up note to Jens,
letting him know he'd spoken to his Bird of Paradise contact and
that he would be able to get several King Birds of Paradise. Pilgaard
had seen only a couple of skins of that species over decades in the
feather business: how had a twenty-one-year-old American student
in London managed to find a supplier?

Even as the online residue of his transactions spread and spread,
Detective Hopkin and the Tring curators were still without a suspect. The National Wildlife Crime Unit hadn't turned up any bird
skins at the airports. The forensics on the drop of blood, the latex
glove, and the glass cutter hadn't yielded anything useful. The
search for the missing skins had officially gone cold.

Safe as he felt, Edwin had no way of knowing that in one month's
time, hundreds of miles away in a small Dutch town, one of his
customers would make an offhand comment that would bring it all
crashing down.

12

FLUTEPLAYER 1988

If there was one specific moment when Edwin's plans began to unravel, it was in late May 2010, at the Dutch Fly Fair outside the small city of Zwolle, an hour and a half east of Amsterdam.

The festival, convened every two years, was held in crisp white pagoda tents beneath the Swedish, Dutch, and Icelandic flags that flapped over the shores of the Drontermeer Lake west of town. Massive salmon steaks were roasted on cedar planks over medieval coal baskets, and a pair of bagpipers announced the entrance of the king, who strutted about comically with a velvet robe and a scepter-shaped fishing rod.

In the main tent, where dozens of tiers from around the world convened to demonstrate their skills on an elevated stage, a Dutch construction engineer named Andy Boekholt was at work on a salmon fly, using hard-to-get feathers. Nearby was Chuck Furimsky, manager of the International Fly Tying Symposium in Somerset, New Jersey, known for his trademark handlebar moustache. Vintage reels and fly rods gleamed from nearby glass cases.

Also present was a man from Northern Ireland. "Irish" was two decades into a career in law enforcement. He had operated undercover during the worst years of the Troubles, narrowly surviving multiple bombings and shootings. To keep sane in those dark times, he had taught himself to tie, starting with simple shrimp flies used to catch sea trout. He had recently begun to dabble in classic salmon flies and had come to Zwolle to see the masters in action— but he didn't share the community's obsession with rare birds.

Irish wandered through the tent until he arrived at Boekholt's booth. Next to the bespectacled Dutchman's vise was a Victorian cabinet containing twenty slender trays, originally designed to store antique microscope slides. Boekholt pulled them out one by one, revealing hundreds of flies with many thousands of dollars' worth of rare feathers tied into them.

When Irish and Boekholt started talking about hard-to-get feathers, the Dutchman couldn't resist showing off one of his latest purchases, a flawless full Blue Chatterer skin. To Irish, it didn't look like the birds that occasionally popped up on eBay after being pried out of a Victorian hat with outstretched wings and legs: its eye-sockets were stuffed with ancient-looking cotton, and the wings and feet were tied closely to the body.

"Where'd you get this?" he asked casually. Nearly a year earlier, he had seen reports about the Tring heist, so when he saw the Dutchman's museum-grade skin, something fired in his mind, and his suspicions flared.

"Some kid in England named Edwin Rist."

When he got home, Irish logged onto ClassicFlyTying.com and began clicking through the items being sold on the Trading Floor. The night before the Dutch Fly Fair, a listing had gone up: "Flame Bowerbird male full skin for sale." The post had already amassed 1,118 views. He discovered several other links on the forum to eBay listings of Birds of Paradise, in which forum members mentioned that the skins were located in England. Irish found that most of the auctions were posted by the same seller.

He rang the Hertfordshire Constabulary and told them to look into the eBay username "Fluteplayer 1988."

———————

The message made its way to Adele, who petitioned eBay for the legal name and address of the person holding the account "Fluteplayer 1988."

When the name Edwin Rist came back, she ran him through their system and discovered that he was a student at the Royal Academy of Music. When she shared this information with Mark Adams and Robert Prys-Jones at the Tring, they confirmed that someone by that name had visited the museum six months prior to the theft.

Adele wasn't easily excitable, but this was the best lead she'd had since the case was assigned to her. She quickly dialed the school administrators to locate Edwin but discovered that she had just missed him: he had boarded a plane back to the States for summer break only two weeks earlier, and had moved out of the apartment eBay had on record.

Thirteen months had passed since the burglary. And now they were fourteen days too late?

Her department didn't have much in the way of a travel budget—she had a hard enough time getting approval for a train ticket to London—so a flight to New York to interrogate Edwin was off the table. But she was concerned about the fate of the skins—the more time passed, the more likely they were to be separated from their tags, rendering them worthless to the Tring. Had he taken them with him to the United States? If he had left them in England, where were they?

The United States was unlikely to grant any favors by extraditing Edwin back to England. She would have to wait until he returned on his own and hope that he hadn't traveled with the skins.

When the Royal Academy of Music's fall term commenced on September 13—the start of Edwin's fourth and final year of study—Adele was still trying to determine his exact whereabouts. She couldn't get a search warrant authorized without a valid address, and she was still waiting on the school to notify her once Edwin registered his new off-campus address.

Meanwhile Edwin was back and moving product. In an e-mail to his network of customers, he announced his September 2010 offerings, including a Blue Chatterer with "full plumage" for one thousand dollars, excluding shipping. A few weeks later he was sending messages to Jens Pilgaard, hoping to sell the Dane some Birds of Paradise.

Perhaps in anticipation of a new wave of sales, he logged into eBay and updated his account with his new address.

Shortly thereafter eBay responded to Adele's request for an updated address for her suspect: a flat in Willesden Green, an eighteen-minute ride on the underground line from the Royal Academy.

The last online listing of Edwin's feathers on ClassicFlyTying.com went up on November 11, 2010. "A Mix pack for sale" was posted, along with an image showing nine pairs of feathers neatly arranged on a dark canvas backdrop. Beneath each pair, the subspecies and available quantities were typed in a white bold font.

That night Edwin and his girlfriend went to bed on the earlier side—he had a rehearsal the following morning and wanted to be at his best. His dream of playing for the Berlin Philharmonic wasn't far from reach: he would soon graduate with a degree from one of the world's best conservatories, positioning him for auditions with the finest orchestras. He already had an invitation to audition with the Boston Symphony Orchestra. He had just turned twenty-two.

Early in the morning of November 12, 2010, Adele and two of her colleagues drove down from the Hemel Hempstead police station to London, their GPS set for the address of Fluteplayer 1988. If she had had only his name, she would have been skeptical that

Edwin, an American music student without any prior record, was her man. But she had his eBay records, which included listings of exotic birds and purchases of mothballs, Ziploc bags, and a diamond-blade glass cutter. She knew he'd visited the Tring. She was pretty certain.

A little bit before eight in the morning, Edwin's doorbell rang. He was awake, trying not to disturb his sleeping girlfriend as he got ready for his rehearsal. At first he ignored it. He wasn't expecting any packages and was a bit pressed for time. But now someone was banging on the door

"Who is it?" he asked through the door.

"It's the police," Adele said. "Open the door."

Five hundred and seven days after he broke into the museum, Edwin opened the door, glanced at Adele, and asked, "Is something wrong?"

13

BEHIND BARS

When Adele told him they were there to investigate the Tring robbery and had a warrant to search his apartment, Edwin confessed immediately. He knew they would find the birds; there was no point in trying to hide what he'd done.

He led them to his room, where his girlfriend was just waking up, confused by the commotion. He gestured at the large cardboard boxes containing what remained of the skins.

"I was having some psychological problems," he said. "I was depressed. I regretted it. . . . I was going to put the stuff back the next day, and I'm sorry." He pointed out a flatscreen TV in the corner, telling them he had stolen it from the Royal Academy's International Student House—though no one had asked.

Adele's colleagues snapped pictures of all the birds as he had stored them in his apartment, which was now a crime scene. They bagged up all the skins, patches of birds, and packs of feathers, including some that hadn't come from the museum, such as the Malayan Peacock Pheasant he'd received from Jens Pilgaard. They unplugged his laptop and seized his camera and passport.

In that moment, Edwin finally succumbed to the shock of what was happening, suddenly feeling hollowed out. Despite all his planning, he had never imagined this moment.

Adele placed him under arrest and led him down to the squad car below. With a guilty suspect in the backseat and a trunk full of dead birds, Adele drove to the police station halfway between London and Tring, in Watford, which was equipped with sixteen "custody suites"—or jail cells. They took a mug shot and a DNA swab, which would be run against the drop of blood found at the crime scene, and deposited Edwin in a cell by himself to wait.

As the bars locked shut, he became extremely agitated. He had no idea how long he'd be there. Nobody even knew where he was. Apart from the first few days after the heist, during which he'd been hounded by anxiety that he'd be found out, he had been certain he wouldn't get caught. But now that he was behind bars, all he saw was uncertainty. Would he go to prison? What would happen to his family? What would happen to his audition with the Boston Symphony? His future as a musician?

Adele called up the Tring to tell the curators the good news. Knowing that the skins would require special handling, she summoned them to the station. It was a high moment in her career. She had come to know the museum's staff well, particularly Dr. Prys-Jones, who had introduced her to the world of Alfred Russel Wallace and the scientific importance of the bird skins. Her newfound appreciation of the specimens' value—which went beyond the monetary—had motivated her to solve the case, and she had done it. The thief was behind bars. All that remained for her to do was the interrogation, and then the Crown Prosecution Service would take over. Since Edwin had admitted his guilt, his case wouldn't go to trial: it would proceed straight to sentencing.

Mark Adams arrived in Watford and began the work of identifying each skin. Of the 299 skins that Edwin had taken, 174 intact specimens had been recovered in his apartment. Unfortunately, only 102 skins still retained their labels.

A massive blow had been dealt. Only a third of the birds were recovered in a scientifically uncompromised condition. For some of the individual species, the numbers were even more dispiriting. Of the seventeen missing Flame Bowerbirds, nine had been recovered, but all of them were missing their tags. Of the forty-seven Indian Crow skins, nine were recovered but only four with tags. Three of Wallace's Birds of Paradise were recovered, all without tags. (The only detached labels discovered in Edwin's apartment were two written in Wallace's handwriting.) Of the King Birds of Paradise, only three out of thirty-seven skins were recovered with labels.

And those were only the full skins. There was also a heap of Ziploc bags filled with individual feathers or hacked-off segments of breasts, capes, crests, and necks. Identifying the species and subspecies would be challenging, and more devastatingly, it was ultimately pointless: the bird fragments were scientifically useless.

After several hours, Adele had Edwin brought into the interrogation room. She asked if he wanted an attorney. Thinking that if he cooperated, it might all blow over, Edwin waived his right to counsel and confessed. He rattled off the names of those who had bought skins—Jens Pilgaard, Andy Boekholt, Dave Carne, Mortimer, and others—and how much they had paid for them. He didn't feel particularly bad naming names—it was their mistake to have trusted him.

By that point, Adele's colleagues had already combed through the e-mails, Skype chat records, and other files on his laptop. They wanted to know who else might have been involved in the burglary.

Had someone put him up to this? she asked Edwin. She went through the various fly-tiers with whom he had exchanged e-mails prior to the break-in, but he insisted, again and again, that he had acted alone.

In the middle of the interrogation, a fly tumbled out of a ceiling duct onto Adele's notebook.

"Oh my god! Is that a *fly?!*" she shouted, flicking it from her page. It catapulted across the table and landed next to Edwin, who swiftly trapped it beneath a glass of water.

After about an hour, Adele had what she needed. She gave him a slip of paper informing him of the terms of his arrest and the date of his court hearing and released him from custody. Edwin didn't even know where he was.

He was equal parts indignant about and confused by his treatment at the hands of the police. An excruciating day in that cell, and all he had was a slip of paper about a court appointment.

As he wandered around Watford trying to get his bearings, he wondered why they hadn't strapped one of those anklets on to track his movements, and an idea flashed through his mind: *I could just leave!*

14
ROT IN HELL

A s he made his way back to his apartment in Willesden Green, Edwin knew he couldn't just flee. He wouldn't make it past security at Heathrow; Detective Sergeant Hopkin had confiscated his passport. He braced himself for the phone call he knew he had to make.

His mother answered. Confessing to her was worse than his time in the cell, as he began to sense how the crime would affect his family. When Anton, who was headed off to Juilliard that fall, learned that it was his own brother who had stolen the Tring's birds, he burst into tears. Edwin could hear him crying in the background. There was no one else to blame. Telling everyone he was sorry wouldn't change a thing.

After the initial shock, the conversation pivoted toward the more practical question of how to keep Edwin out of prison. They would need to find a lawyer and figure out how to cover legal fees. His father also wanted to locate, buy, and return as many of the stolen skins as he could, with the hope that this might reflect favorably on his son's character. His mother would fly to London in time for his first court appearance two weeks later.

Following such a monumental event, one expects the world to stop, or to at least reconfigure itself in response to the news. But in those first few days, with the exception of Edwin's family, nobody around him knew what had happened. The morning after his arrest, he reported to rehearsal and played an orchestral piece along with his classmates. But as he practiced, his mind was consumed by the prospect of being deported, which would mean he couldn't graduate.

Graduation was only six months away. If he left England without a degree, all his hard work would be for nothing. The coveted spots in the most prestigious orchestras would slip from his reach. There were, of course, more immediate fears: after all, it wasn't some petty theft to which he'd pleaded guilty—the birds were worth about a million dollars, and he'd broken all sorts of international conventions protecting endangered species by trafficking skins and feathers throughout the world.

To survive this, he would need an incredible defense attorney.

At his first court appearance, on November 26, 2010, at the Hemel Hempstead Magistrate's Courthouse, Edwin shuffled into a large glass box for defendants in the middle of the courtroom and pleaded guilty to burglary and money laundering, while his mother and a few friends looked on from the gallery.

All criminal cases in the UK begin at the level of the magistrate's court, which typically deals with minor offenses like speeding or drunk and disorderly conduct. But Edwin's prosecutors, armed with a guilty plea and the pile of evidence that Adele had unearthed in his apartment, felt that the sentencing powers of a magistrate judge were insufficient to address the severity of the crime.

In the hopes of obtaining leniency, Edwin's lawyer, Andy Harman, characterized his client's actions as a youthful flight of fancy—a mistake made in the spur of the moment—and Edwin himself as an earnest naïf who, propelled by an obsession with fly-tying and fascination with James Bond, had begun to have "extremely childish fantasies" about breaking into the museum. He said his client had taken only a couple of weeks to plan the theft, pointed out that he used the train as his getaway vehicle, and noted that he hadn't used "exotic tools" to break in. "He didn't even take a torch"—a flashlight—"and has been described going around trying to get light off his phone," he added incorrectly. "It was a very amateur burglary."

The judge was unmoved and accepted the prosecution's petition to transfer the case to the Crown Court, comparable to a superior court in the United States.

The British press covered the now-sensational news story much more widely than it had the Tring's original call for help recovering the skins. "Flute player admits theft of 299 rare bird skins," the BBC announced. "Exotic bird pelts 'worth millions' stolen from Natural History Museum by musician acting out 'James Bond' fantasy" ran the *Daily Mail*'s account. (For all the 007 references, though, the British press neglected to mention that Ian Fleming had found his spy's name after stumbling across a copy of *Birds of the West Indies*, written by the American ornithologist James Bond.)

It was only a matter of hours before the news hit the forums. On FlyTyingForum.com, someone posted an article about the arrest under the headline "RARE FEATHER THIEF BUSTED . . . and he's one of us. Shocking." On FlyFishing.co.uk, a user wrote: "I hope Rist, if found guilty, is jailed and then deported, his feathers and fly collection should be confiscated, for incineration." Another replied, suggesting that Edwin might be innocent: "Although it would be nice to think that the police only ever arrest the guilty, that is far from the case. The allegations against this man have yet to be proved, and to convict him on this forum is to usurp the function of the courts."

There was, however, one poster on FlyFishing.co.uk who knew Edwin well. Terry, who had hosted Edwin at his fly-tying guild in Bristol a couple of years earlier, wrote that he was "devastated to hear" how Edwin had "train-crashed his whole life not only as an extremely talented & world class fly tyer but as a highly gifted musician."

In the heart of the feather underground, at ClassicFlyTying.com, a user posted a link to one of the articles about the arrest. Before it was deleted by Bud Guidry, the site's administrator, the thread had generated eighty-five comments and 4,596 views, one of the largest in the site's history.

The same tiers who were overjoyed by the flood of rare materials Edwin had introduced were now outraged to learn how the college student had obtained them. Anton soon appeared in the comments, defending his brother from what he described as "irresponsible accusations." But the more Anton insisted the articles weren't conveying the whole story, the more attacks came. Finally he asked Guidry to remove the thread. On November 29, 2010, three days after Edwin's initial court appearance, Guidry made an announcement:

> for reasons i won't disclose, all posts concerning this topic of stolen birds have been deleted. i would appreciate a compliance by all members at this time to restrain from making any other post on this subject.
>   thanks
>   the administrative team

John McLain, the retired Detroit detective who had sold Edwin his first feathers, appended an update to his website, where he had once written: "You may not have heard of the Rist brothers before, but you certainly will in the future."

"There is no way to condone Edwin's apparent actions and no real way for me to really understand them," wrote McLain. "The

Salmon Fly tiers in general do not deserve a 'Black Eye' over this now, they as a group had absolutely nothing to do with it. There may be an individual or two that knowingly helped after the fact and I sincerely hope that will be handled by the proper authorities, 99.99% of the fly tiers that covet these feathers are as shocked by this as I am."

McLain surely recognized that he was one of the more public figures in the community and that any journalist Googling "Edwin Rist" would find his site. He, like Bud Guidry, wanted to do whatever he could to ensure the Tring heist was not a stain on the collective reputation of salmon fly-tiers and that the responsibility was borne by Edwin alone.

Guidry, perhaps anticipating increased scrutiny from the authorities, also deleted many of the illegal sales posted on the forum's Trading Floor, which meant they would no longer appear in a Google search. Unless someone had the specific URL for each post, they were irretrievable.

Still an active member of the forum, Edwin saw vicious comments made by people he had known for nearly a decade. Some of his former friends, mentors, and customers were saying he should rot in hell for what he'd done.

Edwin's sentencing began on January 14, 2011, at the St. Albans Crown Courthouse, an hour north of London.

The Honorable Judge Stephen Gullick asked Edwin to identify himself, before asking one of his lawyers, Peter Dahlsen, a series of rapid-fire questions.

Referring to documents submitted by the defense, the judge asked, "Are you going to invite the sentencing Court to go down some form of mental health route?"

"I'd certainly invite the Court to consider a sentence which would not involve immediate custody," Dahlsen replied.

"That's not my question," Judge Gullick snapped.

"I know it's not your question."

"It's a deliberately phrased question," the judge stated. "Are you seeking some form of disposal which involves, albeit in the community maybe, some form of mental health requirement?"

"Yes," Dahlsen answered.

If Edwin's sentencing was to revolve around a mental health defense, the court would need a professional assessment. Dahlsen said he had someone in mind, but it might take several weeks to schedule an analysis. Their exchange concluded, the judge turned to Edwin.

"Edwin Rist, just stand a moment. You must come back on the 11th February, on which day I hope that sentence can be passed in your case."

"I'm adjourning your case for the purpose solely of seeing whether or not there is a mental health package which can be formulated and placed before me, but I must make it clear to you that the fact that I'm giving that opportunity to you and your lawyers does not mean that I'm necessarily going to follow it."

15

THE DIAGNOSIS

At the psychological evaluation, Edwin stared at the stack of forms before him. One of them asked him to rank between 1 (definitely agree) and 4 (definitely disagree) his reaction to a long list of statements, including:

- "I prefer to do things the same way over and over again."
- "I live life for today rather than the future."
- "I find making up stories easy."
- "I don't like to take risks."
- "When I talk on the phone, I'm not sure when it's my turn to speak."

How on earth was he supposed to respond to "I would never break a law, no matter how minor"? Three, "mildly disagree"?

The man observing him had lean features, thinning hair, and a posh London accent. He peered at Edwin through wire-framed lenses, studying his mannerisms. "Sorry, am I making you uncomfortable?" he asked.

"Ummm . . . yeah?" Edwin replied.

The man was Dr. Simon Baron-Cohen, director of the Autism Research Centre at Cambridge University, and Britain's leading authority on autism and Asperger's syndrome. He also happens to be a cousin of Sacha Baron-Cohen, the comedian behind the famed *Borat* character. Baron-Cohen is occasionally approached by legal defense teams to conduct psychiatric evaluations of their clients and draft expert reports. His diagnosis of Gary McKinnon, a Scot who hacked into the Pentagon in 2001, gave the British government a basis to decline the U.S. extradition request, on the grounds that American prisons were ill-equipped to care for him. It was the McKinnon affair that gave rise to the term *Asperger's Defense.*

Because of the way Edwin had spoken about the theft—that he didn't see taking the birds from the museum as such a big deal and that he never thought he'd get caught—his attorneys thought his actions might be explained by some form of autism. Now Baron-Cohen was charged with determining whether Edwin suffered from the disorder.

After Edwin filled out the questionnaire, he talked to Baron-Cohen about fly-tying, his childhood, his goals for the future, and all the terrible things that were being said about him in the forums. In his four-page report, which was presented to the court on University of Cambridge letterhead, Baron-Cohen spoke admiringly about Edwin's hobby, noting that he'd "taken fly-tying to the highest level of an art form, and is deeply immersed in the subject both as an artist and from a historical perspective."

The report included a photo of one of Edwin's flies, known as the Green Highlander. "He explained to me how each feather is different," Baron-Cohen wrote, "and how his deep interest is in understanding the nature of each feather." Following a century-old pattern, the fly called for feathers from the Ostrich, Summer Duck, Swan, Bustard, Peacock, Golden Pheasant, Mallard, Jungle Cock, Blue and Yellow Macaw, and above all, Indian Crow. The doctor was apparently unaware that some of these birds were protected by domestic and international conservation laws.

"He had not been motivated by money," Baron-Cohen stressed to the court. Edwin had told the professor about the glory days of Kelson and the Victorians, back when longshoremen unloaded ships full of exotic bird skins at the nearby Port of London. He said he'd taken the birds only "to help bring about the second such golden age," and that he dreamed of producing a book on fly-tying with photos of the stolen birds. According to Baron-Cohen, it wasn't greed that drove Edwin but an "'obsessional' interest in fly-tying" that made him "so over-focused on this art-form (and all of its intricate detail) that he developed a classic form of 'tunnel vision' in only being able to think about the materials and the products he aspired to make, and not about the social consequences (for himself or others)."

When viewed in this light, "breaking into the museum had seemed entirely logical," Baron-Cohen wrote. "He had felt the only bad thing he had done was breaking the window. . . . It had not dawned on him that he had done anything bad in taking the stuffed birds, and he certainly never wished to upset the specialist fly-tying community in which he was one of the most highly respected artists internationally." Baron-Cohen reported that Edwin "now understands he upset them by breaking their trust, but at the time this had not even been on his radar." To the psychopathologist, the fact that Edwin hadn't anticipated that his fellow fly-tiers might be angry with him and even publicly condemn him for implicating them in his crime was consistent with Asperger's.

After detailing the principal challenges faced by people with the syndrome—struggling to make friends or read cues in social situations—the professor wrote that Asperger's "also prevents the individual from conforming to social norms and leads the individual vulnerable to getting into trouble with the law through social naïveté or poor decision-making."

"All of these issues apply to Edwin," he informed the court, adding that the student's scores on the diagnostic forms "are very much in line with this diagnosis, and he shows all the signs of the condition: a pattern of over-focus on small details (which can also be the basis of his talents, in fly-tying, music, and photography, for example) alongside difficulties in social understanding."

In conclusion, Baron-Cohen wrote: "I am persuaded that the shock of being arrested, the shock of how his reputation as a very serious artist and a world-leader in the fly-tying community has been badly affected, and the feedback from that community and from the police and negative media coverage of the crime, have all led to him learning a sobering lesson, such that the risk of him committing a similar crime in the future is negligible." He recommended that, rather than imprisonment, Edwin be given resources and counseling.

He also felt it would be best for Edwin to continue his hobby. "Therapeutically," he wrote, "I have encouraged him not to drop out of the fly-tying world or to drop his long-standing desire to write an important and scholarly book, but instead to complete this writing project and also include an autobiographical chapter in it to explain how his undiagnosed [Asperger's] led him to commit a crime which he now regrets."

In the initial hearing, Judge Gullick had made clear that an exploration of Edwin's mental health was no guarantee of a light sentence, but now that they were armed with a diagnosis of Asperger's from such a prominent authority, Edwin's attorneys began looking for ways to tie the judge's hands.

16

THE ASPERGER'S DEFENSE

A ll rose as Judge Gullick entered the chamber. It was April 8, 2011—coincidentally, that day also marked the end of spring term at the Royal Academy of Music. Depending on how the judge ruled, Edwin could either march across the graduation stage in a few months' time or shuffle out in chains that very afternoon. The maximum sentence for his crimes would put the twenty-two-year-old behind bars until his early thirties.

David Chrimes, the prosecutor for the Crown, knew of the Asperger's diagnosis but nonetheless felt confident in his argument. To him, Edwin seemed fully aware of the consequences of his actions and should be sentenced in accordance with the law, without special consideration of Baron-Cohen's report.

Contrary to Baron-Cohen's contention, that Edwin had committed the crime for art, Chrimes stressed that the "offence was committed for financial gain" and that it was not impulsive but carefully planned. He introduced twenty-seven pieces of hard evidence, covering everything from the logistics of the burglary to what was found on Edwin's computer and in his apartment. He ticked through the facts that Adele had uncovered. On November 5, 2008, seven months before the burglary, Edwin had visited the museum under false pretenses, posing as a photographer "to help out another researcher." He had photographed far more than bird skins, "taking photographs of the area around the museum, paths, windows and fences included, showing the Defendant at that particular stage was planning his means of entry and, indeed, exit from the museum." They had found a document on his computer, dated July 4, 2008, entitled "PLAN FOR MUSEUM INVASION."

The prosecution directed the judge's attention to notes from Adele's interrogation, during which Edwin had "explained that he used the money to buy a new flute," that he "had student debt, and . . . that his parents in America also had financial problems," arguing that "even in his interview the Defendant was accepting that there was a significant financial element" to his crime. Chrimes then referred the judge to an August 30, 2008, online chat between Edwin and his roommate, in which "the Defendant talked about—and I quote—'a scheme for raising money by stealing birds from the British Museum of Natural History.'" This kind of prosecution didn't require courtroom antics: just a steady accumulation of damning information.

Chrimes must have suspected that the quirkiness of the case—a flautist stealing birds from an old museum to sell to men obsessed with an obsolete Victorian art form—might lead the court to overlook its gravity, so he read from a report submitted by Dr. Richard Lane, the museum's director of science, who described it as "a catastrophic event . . . not only a loss to the UK" but to the "knowledge and heritage" of the planet.

Dr. Lane's report spoke of the degradation of the skins that were returned, the tags that had been snipped off, and the skins that were still at large. He explained that researchers couldn't go into a jungle to gather new specimens to replace a two-hundred-year-old skin—their scientific value was derived in large part from their age. They were archival relics of a lost era. In taking them, Edwin had been "stealing knowledge from humanity."

Lane, who had worked at the Natural History Museum for over forty-two years, had sat through hours of proceedings over the previous several months, waiting for the gears of justice to turn, only to see the sentencing hearing delayed and delayed. Now that it was finally time, he was optimistic, despite the prosecution's warning that in the courtroom, "things didn't always go as you might expect them by natural justice."

Sitting in the defendant's box, Edwin tried to hold on to a shred of dignity. After all, he and his father *had* tried to recover some of the birds by messaging a number of his customers, but there was no mention of this. As Chrimes continued and the evidence against him mounted, Edwin felt his most basic sense of self under assault. The prosecution was making him out to be some kind of demon.

"There's one TIC to be put to the Defendant," said Chrimes, referring to an additional piece of information that the Crown wished to be Taken Into Consideration in the sentencing: Edwin had stolen a TV from a Royal Academy of Music common room.

Upon Edwin's admission, the judge agreed to take it into account, and the prosecution rested.

Judge Gullick, who ran an efficient courtroom, turned to Edwin's barrister. "Now, Mr. Dahlsen. I have read an abundance of paper."

Dahlsen had submitted a sheaf of documents for the judge's consideration. Since his client had already admitted his guilt, the barrister's aim was to mitigate the severity of the punishment. In addition to Baron-Cohen's diagnosis, he had pulled together character references in support of the young flautist from David Dickey, Edwin's childhood tutor at the American Museum of Natural History; Ed Muzeroll, his first instructor in Victorian salmon flies; John McLain, the proprietor of FeathersMc.com, who had first taught Edwin the ropes of sourcing rare feathers; and Luc Couturier, who had encouraged Edwin to visit the Tring Museum in the first place.

But the judge didn't seem particularly interested in these references. He wanted to talk about the precedents from British case law that the defense had flagged for his attention as a guide for deter-mining a fair sentence. And while the prosecution had introduced a damning pile of evidence—that the act was premeditated and moti-vated by financial gain—it took all of ninety seconds and one prec-edent for the defense to wrest control of the hearing. All it had to do was mention the case of *Crown v. Gibson*.

"Before we go any further," said the judge, "as far as you're aware the case of *Gibson* presumably is the only that's come up on the system with Asperger's on it?"

"It is," replied Dahlsen.

"Well, it doesn't seem to me that this case is any different from that case," the judge stated.

"It's not." Dahlsen echoed, "I can speak at some length, Your Honour—"

"I'm sure you can."

"If Your Honour wants me to. Or if Your Honour—"

"Well," the judge interrupted. "Put it this way. If I were to take a view which possibly, I don't know which newspapers are here, but if certain newspapers took the view that this young man should be locked up forever . . . I think the Court of Appeal might take a dif-ferent view."

"Yes. I absolutely agree, Your Honour," Dahlsen replied, surely beaming with the knowledge that he'd won before even stepping into the court that day.

"*Gibson*," remarked Gullick, "is in one sense even more shock-ing on its facts as to what the individual did."

———

A decade earlier, in December 2000, twenty-one-year-old Simon Gibson and two of his friends crept into Arnos Vale Cemetery in the heart of Bristol, established in the early nineteenth century just off the southern banks of the River Avon. Near its entrance looms an arched memorial, erected in 1921 for the five hundred service-men killed during World War I. "THE GLORIOUS DEAD A.D. 1914–1918" is carved deeply into its Bath stone.

Gibson and his friends crept past the monument before stopping in front of a large crypt. The door was secured with a padlock, which Gibson broke off with a hammer. Inside were thirty-four cof-fins dating from the 1800s. Before each hung a head-plate bearing the name of the deceased.

They had meant only to look around, but when they noticed a damaged tomb, they cleared away the stones, pried open the coffin, and stole a skull and some vertebrae. On their way out, they locked the crypt with a replacement padlock that Gibson had purchased for the occasion. Back at their apartment, they washed the skull in bleach, hosed it off in the garden, and fashioned a necklace out of the vertebrae.

When they went back a second time, they brought a crowbar. After opening another coffin and discovering that the body had not decomposed fully, they left it alone, but on their way out, they stole a memorial flower vase.

They made a party of their third visit, bringing booze, candles, and a camera. As they drank, they posed with the dead, snapping photos inside the crypt. In one, Gibson held up a skull like Hamlet's poor Yorick.

When they brought the film to be developed at Broadmead, a shopping mall in Bristol, they accidentally dropped a few of the pho-tos on their way out. When a security guard discovered them, the police were notified. When they descended upon Gibson's home, they found the human remains and the vase, which was resting in the middle of the dining table.

The Crown Court judge sentenced Gibson, the ringleader, to eighteen months, declaring his actions "offensive to the public and disrespectful of the deceased." His friends received lighter sen-tences.

Edwin's attorneys were drawn to the case not by what happened during the trial but by what had transpired during Gibson's appeal.

Gibson, as it turns out, had been diagnosed with Asperger's. The court of appeal judge, who described Gibson's obsession with skeletons as nearly uncontrollable—that seeing the open coffins was akin to "a chocoholic being let loose in a Cadbury's factory"—believed the Crown Court judge had erred by not taking the diagnosis into account when determining the young man's sentence.

Gibson and his friends were released two days later.

Judge Gullick adjourned to his chambers to decide on a sentence.

When he swept back into the courtroom at 4:05 p.m., Edwin shot to his feet.

"Edwin Rist, you may sit," he began.

"You're twenty-two years old. You've no criminal convictions. You are a gifted and highly intelligent musician who's currently studying at the Royal College of Music. You were in your teens a gifted and internationally known fly tyer. In November 2008, you fraudulently obtained permission to photograph items at the National History Museum in Tring. Using your knowledge of what was there, you broke in to a block at that museum on the night of 23rd to 24th June 2009 and stole 299 bird skins. They were taken, I have no doubt, for financial gain but principally to enable you to use the feathers for fly tying.

"The loss of their birds is a natural history disaster of world proportions. These were in effect priceless specimens, both in terms of their financial value but also in terms of their scientific interest. They are literally in many cases irreplaceable."

The judge then referenced Baron-Cohen's report, which stated that Edwin was "suffering at the material time from Asperger's Syndrome, and it is that condition which is behind this behaviour."

"The public may consider that such a serious offence as this would quite properly merit a lengthy prison sentence," Gullick continued. "However, I have been directed to a case called *Gibson* in the Court of Appeal almost ten years ago, which has much in it to assist me to evaluate how the diagnosis of Asperger's should be dealt with by the Courts."

The judge then read out five paragraphs from the *Gibson* ruling, verbatim. "I have read extensively from that case to assist not only you but members of the public, and . . . to assist those who may read the newspapers to understand why it is that I am taking the course of action which I do.

"Mr. Gibson's case," he went on, "in terms of his obsessional behaviour is in one sense no different from yours." As he neared his ruling, Gullick explained the bind *Gibson* had put him in: "were I to pass a substantial prison sentence upon you, which would be wholly merited by the value if not pricelessness of the items that you stole, no doubt on one view, the public would commend me, and on another view the Court of Appeal in my judgment would severely criticise me in the light of the attitude which they display in the case of *Gibson* as to the appropriate course that trial Judges should take when faced with somebody suffering from this syndrome."

He turned to Edwin. "All that can be done is to try to support you and attempt to ensure that this sort of behavior is not repeated."

Then the sentence came down: twelve months, suspended. So long as he didn't commit any new crimes during that period, Edwin would never spend a night behind bars.

17

THE MISSING SKINS

The fly-tiers' reactions to Edwin's sentencing ranged from outrage to bewilderment to conspicuous silence. "Asperger's as a defence??? fuck right off, mate . . . this was well planned," one wrote. An Australian tier was shocked by the way Edwin had skittered through the courts: "If I gain the trust of the curator, rob the museum and sell the goods afterwards I'm going to do a bit of shovel"—slang for spending time in prison. "Even if he was kept out of prison he should have suffered a serious fine and deportation." Terry chimed in with skepticism about the Asperger's diagnosis. When the young tier had given a demonstration at his Bristol Fly Dressers' Guild, he wrote, "he certainly did not display any of the symptoms one would associate with it."

By comparison, the reaction from Edwin's conservatory was muted. In the hierarchy of misbehavior that might trigger expulsion from an elite institution like the Royal Academy of Music, a felony theft of scientifically invaluable bird skins didn't rate. Not only was Edwin going to graduate, he'd be flying to Germany on June 7 to audition for an orchestra. He couldn't believe his luck.

On June 30 he received his diploma along with the rest of his class. The only thing still hanging over his head was the Proceeds of Crime Act confiscation order, the final step in the sentencing process that would determine the size of his fine. The appointed day was July 29.

The proceedings were brief. The prosecution's rough math—based on an estimate by a London auctioneer—put the value of the stolen skins at £250,300. It would only later become evident just how conservative this valuation was. To calculate Edwin's fine, they decided to halve that amount. This led to a confiscation order in the amount of £125,150, or $204,753. According to Chrimes, Edwin had £13,371 "available to pay" in his bank account at that moment but suggested a deadline of six months for payment, arguing that the Crown wouldn't want the defendant "to lose his piccolo and flute."

The judge agreed.

"Should he come into more money at a later date," Detective Sergeant Joe Quinlivan of the Hertfordshire Constabulary's Economic Crime Unit told reporters, "police will be seeking this from him up to the total outstanding figure."

"This is a very positive result for us and sends a strong message that making money through crime never pays," he added.

Though Edwin had volunteered a number of his customers' names during the interrogation, as far as the police were concerned, the case was closed. They didn't have the resources to troll through forums and eBay and PayPal records in hope of recovering more of the skins, which would likely have been separated from their tags and therefore worthless to the Tring.

But the fallout continued to reverberate through the fly-tying community. Several of Edwin's customers, including "Mortimer," the American dentist, and Dave Carne, sent birds in varying degrees of degradation back to the museum. A number who had done so were now planning to bring personal lawsuits against Edwin, seeking restitution.

Jens Pilgaard, the Danish blacksmith, returned a number of birds that he'd bought from Edwin. He had already sold the Flame

Bowerbird to another fly-tier, but when he discovered it was part of the Tring heist, he insisted on buying it back so that it could be sent to the museum. He asked Adele if the $4,500 Malayan Peacock Pheasant he'd traded Edwin might be returned to him, cc'ing Edwin's father, Curtis, on his e-mail. Curtis had reached out to a number of the angriest buyers, seeking to make right by them. "If you can give me a full accounting, in dollars, I will send this off to you," he wrote to Jens, at the same time making clear that he would not do so if Jens was planning to sue his son. "You cannot have it both ways, I am sure you understand." He now found himself warding off potential fraud claims against Edwin. Jens returned the skins but was never compensated by Curtis.

Dave Carne, who had borrowed thousands of dollars from his mother in order to purchase an Indian Crow cape, first found out about Edwin's arrest when Curtis e-mailed him "out of the blue" to see if he knew anyone who'd bought full skins from his son. Carne nearly cried at the disappointment of thinking he would lose a skin he'd been trying to get hold of for five years.

He recalls Curtis saying that if he didn't return his patch to the Tring, he might "get raided by the police"—a terrifying prospect. "Having a load of local bobbies piling into the house would of course have been disastrous since they in ignorance would have just collected every feather in my tying and then I'd have had to spend months proving they hadn't come from Edwin—and would probably STILL not have had them back now."

Carne was angry. When he returned the Indian Crow cape to the museum, he was informed by authorities that he could make a claim against Edwin for extracting money under false pretenses. Months after being persuaded by Curtis not to press suit, Carne finally received compensation.

The spring 2011 issue of *Fly Tyer* magazine, which had previously heralded Edwin as the "future of fly tying," featured a new section called "The Fly-Tying Crime Report." In a brief account of the burglary, Dick Talleur, a longtime columnist for the magazine, told the reporter about the time he'd seen two men arrested at a fly-tying show in Massachusetts: "We haven't had any problems with the legal people in some time. I'm now afraid that good people who are trying to do it properly are going to be under the gun."

But at ClassicFlyTying.com, Bud Guidry assiduously enforced his policy of "No Discussion of the Tring Incident." If a newcomer made the mistake of referencing the name Edwin Rist or the Tring heist, he promptly deleted it. Before long, the community returned to normal. Within a few months, members began to post Indian Crow and Blue Chatterer feathers again. Birds of Paradise and Resplendent Quetzal feathers made regular yet brief appearances on eBay—suggesting they were being scooped up quickly. Whether any of these feathers had been plucked from the Tring's missing skins was unclear, but the community's hunger for feathers only continued to grow.

Back in Tring, Adele had mixed feelings about how the case had turned out. She was proud that she'd arrested the burglar and recovered so many of the skins for the museum in the process but was frustrated that Edwin wasn't going to serve any time. She kept faith in the system, though, knowing it was the judge's decision to make and his alone.

Chrimes, the Crown prosecutor, believed Dr. Baron-Cohen's diagnosis of Asperger's had swung the whole case. "Had there not been such a report," he said, "it is likely that Mr. Rist would have received an immediate custodial sentence of some length."

At the Natural History Museum, Dr. Prys-Jones was still reeling from the events of the past year. "The whole thing was a complete kick in the guts," he said. "It was desperately, deeply depressing." Despite its staff members' private dismay, the museum maintained a more neutral public posture. In a press release dated April 8, the day of Edwin's sentencing, Richard Lane, the museum's head of science, was quoted as saying: "We are pleased the matter has been resolved. We would like to thank the police, media, public and fly-tying community for their help in recovering many of these priceless specimens but there has still been a terrible impact on our national collections."

There were still a lot of birds missing, though. Of the 299 stolen, only 102 intact birds had been recovered with their labels attached. Seventy-two more had been seized from Edwin's apartment without any labels, and another nineteen skins—all missing their tags—had been mailed to the museum by customers who were either named by Edwin or were compelled by conscience to return them. And while the curators at the Tring had numerous Ziploc bags with individual feathers, 106 birds were still missing.

The value of the outstanding Indian Crow, Cotinga, King Bird of Paradise, and Resplendent Quetzal skins alone easily topped $400,000, and this didn't account for the missing Crimson Fruit-crows, Flame Bowerbirds, Magnificent Riflebirds, Superb Birds of Paradise, and Blue Birds of Paradise, which hit the market so infrequently that determining their true worth was difficult.

All this presumes selling the birds in one piece, wholesale. If someone were to pluck the feathers and sell them individually, the value would climb even higher.

Had Edwin already sold the 106 skins and hidden his profits somewhere beyond the reach of British authorities?

Had he stashed the skins somewhere else?

Had he sent them to someone he trusted for safekeeping?

But at this point, no one was looking for them, and no one was asking these questions.

Except for one guy, wading up a river in New Mexico.

III.

TRUTH AND CONSEQUENCES

18
THE 21ST INTERNATIONAL
FLY TYING SYMPOSIUM

Two weeks after Spencer Seim told me about the Tring heist, and only four months after Edwin's sentencing, I dialed into a meeting with the National Security Council from a writer's retreat in Taos, New Mexico. A handful of refugee organizations, including the List Project, had been invited to speak to the president's senior advisers. The call didn't go well. I was combative and frustrated, tired of hearing the same official excuses for inaction. As soon as I hung up, I gathered up my fishing gear and sped off toward the snow-dusted Sangre de Cristo Mountains, anticipating the moment my phone lost its signal.

I parked my car on the eastern rim of the Rio Grande river valley and hiked down the Little Arsenic into the gorge. The sound of water breaking over truck-size boulders echoed against the canyon walls, drowning out my thoughts. After about an hour, I reached the river and assembled my fly rod. My waders clung tightly to my legs in the frigid water, and my breathing slowed as I started to cast.

The fly, a tuft of elk hair fashioned into the shape of a mothlike caddis fly, drifted quickly across the surface of the river. As I sloshed along in solitude, searching for trout, I wondered how I would ever put the war behind me. I had spent a year trying to rebuild a country whose citizens didn't want us there, a year recovering from a near-death experience and post-traumatic stress, and the subsequent half decade struggling against my own government on behalf of refugees that nobody wanted here. I might have been depressed, were it not for the strange story of the feather thief.

In the short time since I'd heard about the incident, I had become consumed by the crimes of Edwin Rist. It was so bizarre as to be distracting. After Spencer mentioned the ClassicFlyTying.com forum, I signed up and searched for "Edwin," finding two posts from November 2009, where he said he was selling Indian Crow feathers in order to buy a new flute. I printed them out, then copied down the names of everyone who had replied. I found Bud Guidry's post, declaring that all subsequent Tring-related discussions would be removed, and I wondered what else had been deleted. I found customer reviews for "Fluteplayer 1988" on eBay and videos of Edwin on YouTube.

I didn't have a strategy. I didn't have any experience tracking thieves. I didn't know anything about birds or salmon flies. In my free time, I clicked away, printing out the conversations of a strange subculture that had spawned this almost unbelievable crime.

I kept asking Spencer for help deciphering the jargon in the forum. Whenever we fished, I peppered him with questions about Victorian fly-tiers and the feathers they used. In an effort to understand the allure of the art form, I spent six hours at his home learning to tie the Red Rover, a yellow, orange, and red fly described in Kelson's *The Salmon Fly*. While his tawny lab, Boomer, dozed at his feet and Townes Van Zandt warbled from an unseen radio, Spencer explained the arcane techniques required to tether plumes to a hook, patiently answering my barrage of questions.

I mentioned an article in the British press that suggested the Tring was still missing more than one hundred of its birds, allegedly worth hundreds of thousands of dollars, and asked if he thought the fly-tying community still had them.

"If you *really* want to find out," he said, with a glint in his eye, "get yourself to Somerset."

Two weeks later, after discovering that I had been removed from the National Security Council's invitation list for future meetings, I found myself searching for plane tickets to attend the 21st International Fly Tying Symposium at the DoubleTree Hotel in Somerset, New Jersey. I was aware that I was running from my problems, but I had the crazy thought that if I just showed up, I might stumble upon the missing birds of Tring.

Outside the DoubleTree, semis barreled down Interstate 287 over the Raritan River. In the late November chill, I cut across the parking lot and saw John McLain—immediately recognizable from photos I'd seen on the forum—burn a cigarette down in what seemed like three drags near a hotel side door. The proprietor of FeathersMc .com had a fresh gash running across his forehead and a "don't ask" look on his face. I considered posing some questions about Edwin, but when he shot a steely glance at me, I nervously hurried past him.

Inside, hundreds of tiers milled about, their shopping bags glowing with brightly colored feathers as they wandered the grand hall. In a nearby booth, a customer held a lime-green dyed pelt of chicken neck feathers up to the light, squinting at it as if inspecting a diamond's clarity. Behind him were hundreds of skins and patches and packets of feathers, piled in bins, hanging on racks. In aisle after aisle, vendors hawked hooks, books, tinsel, and fur. Small clusters of men with handlebar moustaches and Members Only jackets gathered quietly around the booths of celebrity fly-tiers, who bowed over their vises in monastic concentration, peering through visor magnifiers as they coaxed feathers onto the hook.

What the hell was I doing there?

Poking around an online forum was one thing, but traveling to their convention was a serious escalation. I suddenly felt ridiculous and unsure of myself. I had a small pile of printouts related to the Tring theft, but what did I really know? I couldn't tell one subspecies from the next or which were protected by CITES; I barely knew anything about tying. Surrounded by these strange men and their dead birds, I felt wildly out of place.

I slinked over to a booth belonging to Roger Plourde, a man whose name I recognized from the forums. He was tying a salmon fly before a handful of spectators. During a particularly challenging step in the process, when the slightest twitch or loss of tension in the thread could cause the whole thing to unspool, a compact, bespectacled man of fifty held his breath and puffed his cheeks before blowing out a prolonged whistle of admiration that sounded like a bomb plummeting to earth. The others nodded and huddled closer.

Plourde had first caught my attention when I stumbled across a fly he had designed as a response to the attacks of 9/11. To commemorate the departed, the America fly used gold tinsel, red, white, and royal blue silk, and the feathers of seven birds, among them Kingfisher, Kenya Crested Guinea Fowl, and Blue and Gold Macaw. America went for $350 at auction, but I could tell from one look at Plourde's booth that the real money wasn't in selling flies; it was crammed into waist-high crates of bird parts—wings, tails, capes, breasts, necks—for sale in his booth. One bin was filled with Ziplocs of severed Parakeet heads, all frozen in midchirp.

"Got any Indian Crow or Chatterer?" I asked, trying to sound casual.

Plourde glanced up from his vise and sized me up with a stern look. After a moment, he produced a large binder from beneath the table and handed it to me. My heart raced as I flipped through page after page of iridescent blue and tiny black and orange feathers. Why had he hidden them under the table? Were these from the

Tring's birds? Was it even legal for him to sell these feathers? What if an agent from Fish and Wildlife saw us?

"How much for this set?" I asked, my voice quivering as I pointed to a sleeve of eight Indian Crow feathers.

"Those are ninety."

"Wow, okay."

Plourde saw in an instant that I wasn't a serious customer and turned back to his fly. Impulsively, I said I was thinking of writing something about the theft of birds from the Tring. A flash of anger appeared on his face as he took the binder, returned it to its hiding place, and resumed tying. An uncomfortable silence hung, until he finally spoke, without looking up from his fly:

"I don't think you want to write that story."

"No? Why not?"

"Because we're a tight-knit community, fly-tiers," he replied, locking eyes with me, "and you do *not* want to piss us off."

Taken aback, I looked around at the other spectators. The whistler was glaring at me.

Between Fallujah and battling the government, I was used to all manner of threats, but there was something exhilarating about receiving one from a man with a pinch of feathers in his hand. It felt as though I were onto something.

"Just so you know," muttered Plourde, "I didn't buy any of those birds."

It didn't take long for the rest of the symposium attendees to identify me as an outsider. I had come without a plan and had seemingly blown my chance, within a few minutes of arriving, to find out what happened to the rest of the Tring's birds. I spent most of the day walking around with two hundred hefty men scowling at me. If I asked for Birds of Paradise or Indian Crow, all I'd get in return was a contemptuous smile and feigned look of surprise.

Not wanting to leave empty-handed, I screwed up my resolve and marched over to the booth of the man I'd seen outside, who had sold Edwin his first feathers.

John McLain wore a baggy black thermal shirt, his trousers hoisted up by suspenders. His white hair was close-cropped, and his eyes were weary. As I watched him interact with a customer in his FeathersMc.com booth, something about the former detective seemed out of place, as though he couldn't believe where retirement had taken him. When I asked if he'd speak with me about the Tring heist, he considered it for a moment before throwing on his winter coat. "What the hell, it's time for my smoking break." I followed him out the side door into the parking lot.

"Okay, so whaddya wanna know?" he asked, lighting a cigarette.

"Well, first off, how worried should I be?" I joked, telling him about Plourde's comment.

"Yeah, Guido's gonna come after you!" McLain chuckled, shaking his head. "They gonna shut you up. . . . East River's calling!"

When I asked him about Edwin, he said he could never have imagined Edwin would do something so stupid as to break into a museum, but at the same time, he recognized the spell these birds cast over the community: "*Everybody* joneses after real Indian Crow! You look at these adult men that get weak in the knees, all over a handful of stupid little feathers! I mean, it is really bizarre when you think about it." But he wasn't too concerned about the legacy of the Edwin's theft. "There's no huge impact," he said—except that "probably no fly-tier will ever be let into the back room of a museum again.

"I go back to my life as a career police officer. What did he steal? Feathers? Well yeah, but it's still property crime." He lit another cigarette. "To me, *violent* crime needs to be locked up."

We sat for a moment in silence. Yes, Edwin hadn't physically hurt anyone in the act of stealing the Tring's birds, but it seemed more significant to me than property crime.

"But John," I said, "he took two hundred and ninety-nine birds! And a lot of them are still missing! Where are they?"

McLain seemed to have anticipated my question. "Ask Tring the last time they counted all their birds!" he said.

"What do you mean?"

"They have an inventory, and okay, now there's a shrinkage. How do they determine what was taken?" he asked. "They could have trickled out over a period of ten years! Maybe somebody borrowed one to show their show-and-tell at school, you know, somebody put it in the wrong drawer, you know, a thousand reasons!"

He paused to let his theory sink in. "All I'm saying is based on what I know . . . they *thought* two hundred and ninety-nine specimens were taken, but they didn't know for sure, because they didn't know how many they really had to begin with! 'Cuz nobody counted them!"

I was at a loss for words.

"They didn't count them!" he exclaimed, as he stood up. "They didn't count them the day before Edwin came. They didn't count them once a year. They didn't count 'em!"

With that, he stamped out his cigarette and headed back inside.

Disoriented, I walked back to my car. Had I imagined a mystery where there was none? Could someone else have taken skins prior to Edwin? Could it be that the Tring simply had its numbers wrong—that, in a collection with hundreds of thousands of specimens, they couldn't possibly have a precise sense of the numbers? What if everything had been recovered from Edwin's apartment the day of the arrest? What if there were no missing birds?

There were only a few people who could answer these questions. Shortly after returning from Somerset, I sent Edwin an e-mail, asking if he'd be willing to tell me his story. He politely declined. Given that he was still within the window of his probation, I wasn't surprised.

That left the curators at the Tring. But every time I wrote the museum, trying to arrange an interview, they sent noncommittal replies, attaching press releases I'd already seen.

Unless I could determine if the Tring had an accurate count of the missing birds, I was at an impasse. Finally I gave up waiting and bought a ticket to London, informing the museum that I was on my way with a list of questions.

19
THE LOST MEMORY OF THE OCEAN

I t was mid-January when I boarded the Midland rail to Tring, gliding through snow-dusted fields, crows shivering on the winter-stripped trees. Hopping off at the town's small station, I wondered on which bench Edwin had anxiously waited with his suitcase of stolen birds. Above one hung a large poster for the English National Ballet's production of *Swan Lake*; the lead dancer wore a tutu made of feathers.

I bounded up the station steps and briskly walked the two miles into Tring. Like Edwin, I'd studied the route so many times that I didn't need a map. There was the Grand Union Canal, with a houseboat anchored in frigid water a hundred yards downstream. Beggar's Lane. Pendley Farm. The Robin Hood pub. I turned onto Akeman Street as naturally as if I'd grown up there, passing the police station en route to the museum. I had sent a last-second interview request to Detective Sergeant Hopkin but hadn't yet heard back from her.

I had an appointment the following day with the Tring's curators, but having come this far, I couldn't wait until then to start poking around. I wandered through the galleries, snapping pictures of taxidermy birds and bears that had been on display for more than a century.

I turned a corner and stumbled upon two high schoolers making out next to the rhinoceros exhibit. After they scampered off, I couldn't help but notice a small security camera mounted on the wall. I approached a placard hanging next to the rhinos:

FAKE HORN

The horns on these rhinos are fake, because of the real threat of theft for their supposed medicinal properties. Although fake horns have no value, the market for real horns now threatens many species in the wild.

I assumed that the sign and cameras had been installed in response to the events of August 27, 2011. Only a few months after Edwin's sentencing, a forty-two-year-old Brit named Darren Bennett had punched through the front window of the museum and hammered the horns off the Indian and white rhino specimens. With only six left in existence, the northern white rhinoceros is a functionally extinct species, after centuries of being hunted for the perceived medicinal benefits of their horns. In the past few decades, the demand has been fueled by Chinese men who believe it will cure erectile dysfunction, and Vietnamese clubgoers, who take it as a party drug. Though the horns are composed of keratin, the same protein responsible for fingernails and horse hooves, the four kilos stolen by Bennett would have fetched over $350,000 on the black market.

Had they been real, that is. Months earlier, after Europol issued an alert about an organized crime network of rhino horn thieves responsible for dozens of museum burglaries, the Tring had replaced the real horns with plaster replicas.

But while Edwin skated, Darren Bennett was sentenced to ten months in prison for stealing two pounds of horn-shaped plaster.

I arrived for my meeting the next day with a simple goal: before embarking on some half-baked mission to hunt down the missing skins, I wanted to hear directly from the curators that their numbers were correct—that there were, indeed, unrecovered birds. McLain had called the museum's competence into question, and given that Bennett's break-in happened so soon after Edwin's, I wondered if McLain might have a point: just how easy was it to rob this museum?

I walked in the front door of the Ornithology Building to the sound of a security alarm, beeping frantically. The guard at the entrance smiled as if nothing were amiss and asked me for my passport. As I signed my name into the guest log, I asked about the alarm.

"I'm doing my very best to ignore it," she said with a wink, before explaining that it had been triggered during a routine cleaning of the sprinkler system's smoke heads.

I started flipping through earlier pages in the guest log in search of Edwin's name but was quickly intercepted by a young press flack, who escorted me to a fluorescent-lit conference room. As I waited for the curators, I peered out a window onto the brick wall that Edwin had climbed and wondered if it had been the one he'd smashed.

In the corner were several cream-colored plastic trays, containing many of the skins that had been recovered from Edwin's apartment. Most of the birds were still sealed in crime scene evidence bags. One tray was loaded with individual Ziploc bags, stuffed with Indian Crow feathers. Edwin had drawn smiley faces on some of the Ziplocs with a Sharpie pen.

Dr. Robert Prys-Jones and Mark Adams arrived, not appearing excited to discuss the events of June 23, 2009, especially with a refugee advocate moonlighting as an amateur bird heist investigator.

I began by relaying some of the curious opinions about the role of natural history museums I'd heard at the Somerset show. Some fly-tiers had questioned why, with hundreds of thousands of bird skins, museums needed so many "copies" of the same bird—they'd be better off selling them, wouldn't they? Hoping to provoke a response, I told the curators that several tiers had suggested that "what they do—heralding the beauty of these birds by tying them into flies—is better than locking them in some museum basement."

"The United Kingdom doesn't spend millions of pounds on the Natural History Museum so the stuff isn't used. . . . It's underwriting a resource that is of immense importance scientifically!" said Prys-Jones, peering at me through his glasses, his brow furrowed. "I'm not able to make an intelligent response to that nonsense."

The world already owed a debt to the knowledge unlocked by these specimens, he and his colleague explained. Wallace and Darwin had drawn upon them to formulate their theory of evolution through natural selection. In the middle of the twentieth century, scientists compared historic specimens in the museum's egg collection to show that shells had grown thinner—and less viable—after the introduction of the DDT pesticides, which were ultimately banned. More recently, feather samples from 150 years' worth of seabird skins were used to document the rising mercury levels in the oceans, which contributes to declines in animal populations and creates public health implications for humans who eat mercury-laden fish. The researchers described the plumes as the "memory of the ocean."

Many of these birds were already in museum storage cabinets before the word *scientist* was even coined. Over hundreds of years, each advance—the discovery of the cell nucleus, viruses, natural selection, the concept of genetic inheritance, and the DNA revolution—ushered in new ways of examining the same bird: a researcher peering at a skin through a simple microscope in the early nineteenth century couldn't have comprehended what would be revealed by mass spectrometers in the twentieth or by nuclear magnetic resonance and high-performance liquid chromatography in the twenty-first. The Natural History Museum's curators made the bird skins available to hundreds of scientists each year, hailing from increasingly specialized branches of inquiry: biochemists, embryologists, epidemiologists, osteologists, and population ecologists.

Scientists can now pluck a feather from one of the Tring's eighteenth-century specimens and, based on the concentration of carbon and nitrogen isotopes, understand the bird's diet. This in turn allows them to reconstruct entire food webs throughout history and to see how species have changed or where they migrated when food sources vanished.

Specimens in the collection are currently aiding efforts to preserve the endangered California Condor by extracting DNA from ancient bone samples. The budding field of de-extinction, also known as resurrection biology, relies in part upon extracting DNA from museum specimens in order to bring lost birds like the Passenger Pigeon back to life.

I realized that the preservation of these birds represented an optimistic vision of humanity: a multigenerational chain of curators had shielded them from insects, sunlight, German bombers, fire, and theft, joined by the belief that the collection was of vital importance to humanity's pursuit of knowledge. They understood that the birds held answers to questions that hadn't yet even been asked.

But their mission depended, in large part, on trusting that those who came to study in the collection shared this belief. Edwin had preyed upon that trust in order to plot his heist. And now, with so many skins missing or separated from their tags, there was a devastating hole in the scientific record. The only hope of closing that gap was to recover as many of the skins as possible, with their tags attached.

To underscore his point, Prys-Jones walked over to the trays of bird remnants and removed a Flame Bowerbird, sealed in a plastic bag, its tags missing. The seventeen skins Edwin stole, he explained, constituted not only the Tring's entire collection but more than half the Flame Bowerbird specimens in all of the world's museums: a serious blow to modern research.

Another tray contained what remained of the Tring's Resplendent Quetzals. Of the thirty-nine birds, which are protected by CITES, the museum had recovered twenty-nine with their tags still attached—but Edwin had sliced off the two-foot-long emerald-green tails from many of them. Next to the full skins were freezer-size Ziploc bags stuffed with hundreds of small iridescent green-tipped feathers, presumably plucked from the bodies of skins that were still at large.

Intact, the Resplendent Quetzal is nearly four feet long, from beak to tail. In early press accounts of the theft, police had speculated that the birds might have filled up to six garbage bags. But Edwin's lawyer later claimed that a single suitcase was used.

"Have you ever thought about how he managed to get all these birds out logistically?" I asked.

"I've thought a *huge* amount," exclaimed Prys-Jones, momentarily letting his emotions show before he caught himself and fell silent.

"We've got no evidence or knowledge of how he did it, other than what he told the police," Adams said. The press officer shifted in her seat.

"But do you think he had an accomplice?"

"As you will be aware," Prys-Jones volunteered, "Rist pleaded guilty. This meant there may not have been a level of investigation that might otherwise have been."

In doing so, Edwin had, in effect, halted the search for the Tring's missing skins. While the museum's curators were relieved that a third of the birds had been recovered with their tags attached, they no longer had Adele to help them search for the skins that were still missing.

Or possibly missing.

What if McLain was right—that all the detectives in the world wouldn't have found the missing skins because the Tring didn't know how many birds were stolen in the first place? As we stood next to the destroyed birds that they'd been charged with protecting, I felt like a jerk asking, but I hadn't come this far to leave without knowing the truth. I told them that some fly-tiers believed the Tring wasn't missing any skins, that everything had been recovered the morning of Edwin's arrest.

"They think any discrepancy in the numbers is due to poor record keeping . . . that you're just making guesses," I said, wincing as I added McLain's suggestion that they "should 'check in another drawer.'"

Prys-Jones glared at me as though I'd just slapped him in the face. "What knowledge does he have of Tring? Zilch!"

"Just shows that he doesn't know how a collection runs," Adams murmured.

At that, Prys-Jones handed me a spreadsheet he'd brought to the interview. It meticulously noted the exact number of skins gathered from Edwin's apartment the morning of the arrest (174), the number of those with tags (102) and without (72), and the number of skins subsequently returned by mail (19).

"What if I can help you get the missing skins back?" I blurted out, surprising myself.

Adams gestured at the pile of Ziploc bags, filled with scientifically useless feathers, and told me that the birds would need to be recovered intact, with their tags attached.

As the press officer chimed in to say that my time was up, I realized how animated I'd grown during the interview, charged by the idea of reopening the investigation that had ended the morning of Edwin's arrest. I smiled and said I would find it difficult to be as restrained as Prys-Jones and Adams were, had I been in their position.

"We're British. We're not American," Prys-Jones said.

"But how does it make you feel that he never went to jail? That he still got a degree from the Royal Academy?"

"If he'd gone to jail, how would it materially alter the situation we now find ourselves in, scientifically?" he replied.

"Emotionally, wouldn't it have been somewhat satisfying?"

"What is the wider interest in an individual's emotional response?" Prys-Jones snapped. A silence hung before he conceded, "It's a sense of complete desperation, because we are here to look after these research collections in perpetuity and to make them available. To find that a portion of them has been vandalized is depressing in the extreme.

"We will be doing work on this for decades to come," he continued, "trying to work out what information we might be able to restore to some of the specimens. Not necessarily succeeding. There are decades of wasted time in this."

He shook his head. "It's completely senseless. A crime committed by people who are delusional and obsessed."

As our meeting ended, Prys-Jones handed me a small stack of printouts, on the top of which were the museum's press releases. Having already read them many times over, I folded them up and tucked them into my back pocket.

Later that night I dropped into the Akeman pub for a pint of Tring red ale. It tasted like a slurry of flat Diet Coke and even flatter beer. Across the street, just next to the police station, the town's tourist office was filled with pamphlets touting local attractions and history, among them a card boasting that George Washington's great-grandfather John had hailed from Tring: he'd left in 1656 on a trading voyage to Virginia but remained there after a shipwreck on the Potomac.

As I forced down the ale, I tried to reconcile the many claims I'd heard from the fly-tying community with what Dr. Prys-Jones and

Adams had shown me. Fly-tiers had an obvious incentive to claim the Tring was just guessing at the number of birds Edwin stole: if there were no missing skins, there was no ongoing criminality, and the fallout from the Tring heist could be limited to one person— Edwin Rist.

The curators claimed that Edwin had been shown the list of birds during his interrogation and had admitted to its accuracy. The spreadsheet not only gave me confidence in the Tring's numbers but also put the lie to the idea that Edwin was the one bad apple in the fly-tying community. Only nineteen birds had been mailed back to the museum by Edwin's customers following news of the arrest, representing some 6 percent of the total number. How many were still floating around the community, their owners aware that they were in possession of stolen goods?

Before I went to the Tring, the only number I'd seen, in press accounts of the arrest, was that 191 skins had been recovered. According to the spreadsheet, two more skins had been returned by mail since then, bringing the number to 193. Since the total number of specimens stolen was 299, this left 106 skins for me to track down.

But what about the Ziploc bags full of loose feathers and fragments that had been recovered from Edwin's apartment? In one article, I'd seen a police evidence photo displaying five Indian Crow breastplates alongside a Flame Bowerbird cape, sliced from the back of the bird. Edwin had severed the patches containing the most desirable feathers from the original skins, which had presumably been thrown away and were now in some landfill outside London. Surely that would bring down the number of missing skins?

Fortunately the Tring's spreadsheet included a column indicating the "approx no. of specimens represented by feathers and skin fragments" for each species of bird. I pitied the curators for having to undertake such an assessment. No part of their training had prepared them to answer the questions now before them: How many feathers made up a Resplendent Quetzal? If they had two Bird of Paradise wings but no body, did that represent one specimen? After sifting through the Ziplocs, they concluded that the total number of skins still at large was sixty-four.

Having the spreadsheet was like possessing one half of a map that revealed the coast of an unknown country. The column delineating the number and species of birds still missing shimmered like the starting point of a trail that disappeared into the terra incognita of an ongoing crime.

My mind raced through all the obstacles to finding them. To identify Edwin's customers, I'd need to figure out how to dig up the evidence of his sales on the forum that had been deleted. I'd need to somehow convince him to talk to me. I'd have to determine if he had worked alone or with an accomplice. I'd have to find a way to break through the wall of silence surrounding the Tring heist in the fly-tying community and earn enough trust for people to start sharing their secrets.

I distractedly paged through the sheaf of press releases that Prys-Jones had given me, not expecting to find anything new. But at the bottom was a single sheet of paper with the heading "Information From Police from Interview with Edwin Rist."

Immediately, the official story put forward by Edwin's attorneys began to unravel. In the articles quoting their remarks to the court, they painted Edwin's actions as impulsive and amateurish, claiming that he'd spent only a "couple of weeks" plotting it out. But the notes from the interrogation included a timeline of Edwin's planning, reflecting that he'd first written to the museum under false pretenses in February 2008, fifteen full months before the theft. He admitted to having discussed his plot over Skype with a roommate three months before he first visited the museum to photograph the birds. In the month leading up to the burglary, he purchased the glass cutter and a box of mothballs. In the interrogation, he admitted to putting an extra lock on his door to protect the birds and to buying fifteen hundred Ziploc bags in order to sell feathers.

The second half of the document included a short list of individuals whom Edwin had named as customers, along with the prices he'd charged. Four buyers and nine birds were listed, for a total of $17,000 in sales. Conspicuously absent, however, were Edwin's listings of Indian Crow feathers I'd seen on the ClassicFlyTying .com forum. If he hadn't volunteered those during his interrogation, what else had he hidden? Who else had bought from him? Had the four named buyers returned the skins to Tring?

I don't know if the museum meant to pass me the document, but it was the hardest evidence I had, opening up several new leads.

As I stepped back outside into the freezing air, my phone buzzed with a call from Detective Sergeant Hopkin, agreeing to meet with me the next day. Exhilarated by my proximity to the scene of a crime I was now determined to solve, I turned up Public Footpath 37 in search of the spot where Edwin had climbed over the wall. The darkness was complete, and in the distance, the medieval bells of the St. Peter and St. Paul Church began to ring ghostlike through the cold air. The footpath's brick walls amplified every shuffled footstep, and as I quickened my pace, the echoes galloped after me. I was surprised by my thumping heart, and when at last I arrived behind the Ornithology Building, I looked around, wide-eyed. Nobody would have seen him back here. Unless someone had been passing by, nobody would've heard the sound of a window breaking. And while a tall person could have scaled the wall, I sure would have wanted someone there to help out. I got on my tiptoes to look for the window, wondering how big a suitcase Edwin might have fit through it, but I couldn't get a good view.

For a moment, I considered trying to hoist myself up but imagined how the conversation would go if the Tring's security guard happened to be passing on the other side of the wall.

———

"I looked you up, suspicious copper in me," Adele said with a smirk, as she led me down the footpath behind the museum the following morning. At the time of my visit, the exterior of the Ornithology

Building was under renovation, encased with scaffolding and blue mesh bunting to prevent pieces of cladding from falling off and injuring workers. Large PERMANEX SECURITY signs, emblazoned with the logo of a scowling American Bald Eagle, hung from the scaffolds.

She had a clipped speaking style; pronouns were dropped, and only the essential information was conveyed. "Obviously had been here before. Then came along here," she said in reference to Edwin, pointing to a portion of the wall running behind the museum. "Shimmied up. Cut the glass here." In the light of day, I could see that there were now bars on the window Edwin had bashed out, but there was still an opening in the barbed wire, which the museum believed he had snipped away. She pointed to the area where she'd discovered the latex glove fragment, the glass cutter, and the drop of his blood.

"Do you think he acted alone?" I asked, staring at the gap in the barbed wire.

"I was question-marking whether there was another person," she said, as her police radio beeped quietly on her hip. "I'm never going to be able to prove that he was on his own. I'm not going to prove he wasn't on his own. I can only go on objectively what I've got. So . . ."

"Did you ask him about the missing skins?" I asked.

She told me he gave her a few names—the same ones that appeared on the document the Tring's curators gave me—but that he "couldn't remember" exactly what he'd sold. Their search for what was missing was limited to a public appeal. Several people had responded by returning skins, but "the difficulty is they're all over the world, so it's not easy to do the follow-on inquiries."

Sensing that I was a bit underwhelmed by her reply, she echoed what Dr. Prys-Jones had told me: Edwin's admission of guilt had essentially concluded the investigation. She told me they had looked into a Canadian and a couple of Americans whose names had come up in the investigation, but that she didn't have the time or resources to track down every last skin. She was charged with solving the crime, and she had done it.

"But don't you feel like justice has been denied?" I pressed, since Edwin hadn't gone to prison.

"As the police officer you do your bit, then the next bit is down to Crown Prosecution. . . . All the negotiations between barristers and stuff, I'm not necessarily involved in. Don't necessarily agree with them either, but that's not my part of the story."

I knew from reports on the sentencing hearings that Dr. Baron-Cohen's diagnosis of Asperger's disorder had played a crucial role in keeping Edwin from being incarcerated, but whenever I asked fly-tiers who knew him whether they thought he had Asperger's, they just laughed, as if they couldn't believe my naïveté. Since she'd been the one to interrogate him, I asked Adele her opinion.

"There's your million-dollar question, isn't it! And I can't answer it for you." She paused to consider the next part of her reply: "However, if I had Asperger's, I'd be really cross that someone's saying because they've got it, they're a criminal . . . otherwise everyone with Asperger's would be committing crimes."

We were interrupted by a phone call from her son. When she finished, I asked her if she would reopen the case if I ever found out who had the Tring's missing birds.

She said she would have to run it up her chain of command and, depending on where the birds might be, check with Europol or Interpol, "but, yes—if there was evidence, it'd be brilliant. We'd try to retrieve those skins."

I left England with two conclusions. First, contrary to the fly-tying community's claims, the Tring's inventory was accurate: they were still missing at least sixty-four skins, potentially worth hundreds of thousands of dollars. I didn't know if the birds had all been plucked to smithereens and their tags removed, or whether they were stored in perfect condition in the attic of an accomplice, who was waiting for things to blow over before he started chopping them up for sale. Hell, Edwin himself might still have them, stashed in a long-term storage unit somewhere.

Second, no one else was going to hunt them down but me.

20

CHASING LEADS IN A TIME MACHINE

Initially, the story of the Tring heist—filled with quirky and obsessive individuals, strange birds, curio-filled museums, archaic fly recipes, Victorian hats, plume smugglers, grave robbers, and, at the heart of it all, a flute-playing thief—had been a welcome diversion from the unrelenting pressure of my work with refugees.

I had regarded it as an amusing puzzle, doing research here and there and reaching out to members of the fly-tying community in my spare time. But something changed after my visit to the Tring, once I realized the true scope of the theft and the loss it represented to scientific understanding, and once I learned that so many skins were still missing. The side hobby turned into a mission, a quest for justice in a crime where none had been served.

As soon as I got back to my apartment in Boston, I taped the Tring's spreadsheet and Adele's interrogation notes on the wall next to my computer.

Soon a strategy began to emerge. So long as Edwin continued to

ignore the requests I periodically sent for an interview, I would circle him, talking to those who had bought his birds, teasing out the
names of other customers, cajoling them into forwarding incriminating e-mails, and exploring whether he had worked with an accomplice. If Edwin thought I had the goods on him, I figured, he
might feel it was in his interest to tell his side of the story.

Until this point, those in the fly-tying community who had
bought Tring birds had no reason to talk to an outsider like me. But
now that I could confront them with the evidence from the police
interrogation notes, some started to sing.

Of the four individuals Edwin had named, two of them immediately started telling me everything. They forwarded e-mails that
Edwin had sent them and they shared photos of the birds they'd
bought, and they provided letters from the Tring's curators to prove
to me that their skins had been among the nineteen that were returned to the museum. They also named other buyers.

The third individual, Mortimer, the dentist who had inspected
several skins during a layover in London prior to placing a seven-
thousand-dollar order, reluctantly answered some questions before
going silent.

The last person mentioned by Edwin in the interrogation was a
Dutchman by the name of Andy Boekholt, the man who was unwit-
tingly responsible for Edwin's downfall. At the 2010 Dutch Fly Fair
in Zwolle, Holland, Boekholt had bragged about the Blue Chatterer
he purchased from Edwin to "Irish," an off-duty detective. He never
replied to my messages.

I pressed on nevertheless, confronting those who had been named
by the first two men on the list, who in turn coughed up more evidence and more names.

One of those names was Ruhan Neethling, chief financial officer of
the Montagu Dried Fruit & Nuts Trading Company, which was

based in a small town on the Western Cape of South Africa. Soon after hearing that he'd bought thirty thousand dollars' worth of Birds of Paradise from Edwin, I found myself on the phone with the South African.

It was late in Montagu, but Neethling was generous with his time. He'd been a professional hunter, he told me, guiding Americans and others throughout his country looking for springbok, impalas, wildebeests, and kudu. In the early 2000s, he helped set up two game farms next to the Karoo National Park a couple of hundred miles from the coast, where hunters come to shoot stocked game. More recently, he'd worked as a financial controller for Coca-Cola in Papua New Guinea.

Neethling had developed a passion for salmon fly-tying much later in life than Edwin, but he quickly became obsessed. In his first year, 2009, he tied fifty-five flies. (A typical fly takes ten hours; this meant he'd spent nearly twenty-three full days sitting behind the vise). He excelled in creating "freestyle" flies that didn't adhere to traditional Victorian recipes: his Elvis Has Left the Building fly sported the emerald coin-shaped feather of the King Bird of Paradise. Another, the Blue Uncharmed, was inspired by the mating display of the Blue Bird of Paradise. Both species were on the Tring's list of missing birds.

While most tiers were wary of me and immediately became defensive, either insisting that they had nothing to do with Edwin's crimes or requesting anonymity before agreeing to speak, Neethling didn't seem the slightest bit concerned. When I mentioned that I'd heard he bought tens of thousands of dollars' worth of Bird of Paradise skins from Edwin, he laughed warmly.

"No no no no no. . . . Why would I? I lived in Papua New Guinea! That's exceptionally funny," he said, like a father amused by his child's confused question.

He claimed he'd gotten the feathers from hunters and Papuan tribal headdresses, after hopscotching around the smaller islands off the coast in search of skins and forging personal contacts with the Papuan community. "I actually had to look very hard to find people that knew people that could hunt them for me!" he said.

That's not to say he didn't buy some of the Tring's birds. He readily admitted that Edwin had sold him a patch of Indian Crow for three thousand dollars and a full Blue Chatterer skin for six hundred. In late 2010, he told me, he placed an order for individual feathers but never received the shipment—he presumed Edwin was arrested before he had a chance to drop them in the mail.

"You must have been shocked when you found out," I offered, referring to the theft.

"The fact that it happened, I don't think is shocking at all," he said. "Where something is scarce, people are creative."

When I asked if he thought it was a pretty outrageous thing to do, it became clear that in his view, the crime wasn't all that serious. "Right is right and wrong is wrong," he said, but "it's no more or less wrong than someone walking into a shop and stealing a pair of trousers."

I asked what he'd done with the Indian Crow and the Chatterer.

"I probably still have some of his stuff," he replied nonchalantly. But since he had already stripped the feathers from the skins, he said, he figured the Tring wouldn't have much use for them.

Quoting him back to himself, I asked, "But if right is right and wrong is wrong, shouldn't you return them to the museum?"

"I would, if the museum could tell me what they're going to do with them and how it's going to benefit the scientific community. I would return them."

After a long pause, he added, "I'd want them to explain very clearly what they were going to use the feathers for."

I was a bit taken aback. Why should the rightful owner need to prove to someone in possession of stolen goods that they deserved to get them back?

Having spent some time on Neethling's Facebook page in preparation for our interview, I knew that he regularly posted messages from a strange millenarian group called the Second Eighth Week Ministries. When I asked whether his religious beliefs shaped his relationship to the natural world, he responded enthusiastically, "Oh! Yes! Definitely! Definitely!"

"So, does the concept of extinction of species trouble you?"

"Nope, not at all."

"But why not?"

"Everything is going to go extinct in any case."

"But isn't this just nihilism?" I pressed. "Doesn't it take away our responsibility to take care of what God gave us, if we think our planet will eventually be wiped out in the Rapture?"

"It *totally* takes it away!" he cried, as if I were finally seeing the light.

"And you're fine with that?"

"Your responsibility is to align your world with God's world. His will is not for this dimension to exist into eternity. His will is not for this dimension to survive the next fifty years or whatever it is."

Anticipating the answer, I asked him if he believed in evolution.

"Nope, not at all. Not even a single bit. The fossil records do not confirm evolution. You want to talk about belief systems? Evolution is a religion! It's nothing more than that. It's been conjured up! It's a knowledge base that was given to man by the Fallen Watchers, which is a group of angels that did not agree with God."

I asked him how he thought these birds had become so unique, if not through evolution.

To him, the answer was obvious: "God created them that way!"

It was after midnight in Montagu. I could hear South African crickets sawing away in the background. One last time I pleaded the Tring's case, trying to convince him of the various ways their collection had helped humanity, such as confirming the rising levels of mercury in the oceans.

"Man is not going to save this earth," he cut in. "He's got no chance of saving this earth because God has written it to be destroyed. What these scientists are doing is, they are playing God. They are refusing to acknowledge that what preserves this earth is the power of God. Not the ability of man to read mercury levels!"

So Ruhan the hunter and dried fruit executive wouldn't return anything to the Tring because the planet is already screwed, and museum curators are doing the work of fallen angels. I added his name to the Tring's spreadsheet and crossed off two birds from the missing skins column: only sixty-two to go.

After locating another tier who admitted to buying a Blue Chatterer, a Dane by the name of Flemming Andersen, I thought I'd whittled it down to sixty-one—until he forwarded proof that it was among the nineteen birds returned to the Tring. I pressed on, convinced that someone out there was sitting on the main stash of the missing skins. I kept transcripts of my interviews, forum posts, and other scraps of information in a stack on the corner of my desk, but despite occasional discoveries, I knew the trail was going cold.

After all, Edwin had somehow managed to wipe all traces of his website from existence. I knew the ClassicFlyTying.com forum had been a hotspot for buying his birds, but the site had enforced a "No Tring Discussion" policy since Edwin's arrest, deleting anything remotely incriminating.

As the weeks turned into months and the months into years, my search for the missing skins grew into something like a separate, submerged identity.

By day, I fought to keep the United States' doors open to Iraqi refugees, managing a small staff and working with hundreds of pro bono attorneys representing the refugees on my list.

By night, I befriended heavyweights in the fly-tying community on Facebook, riffling through their photo albums in search of any hint of the Tring's birds. I talked my way into private groups on the social networking site dedicated to buying and selling rare feathers, and I started taking screenshots. When the stack of evidence on my desk began to teeter, I organized the papers into manila folders. When the folders grew too numerous, I bought an accordion file.

At some point, the accordion file began to burst at the seams, now with additional notes about Wallace, Kelson, Rothschild, and the Victorian era, which I'd started reading about in an effort to understand this strange obsession. Finally I bought a filing cabinet.

Even as I drew a large net around him, Edwin remained dispiritingly out of reach. I'd obsessively accumulated details about his background and the price points for each species of bird he'd stolen, and I'd developed an intimate understanding of who was who in the feather underground, but with the exception of Ruhan, I still hadn't located any of the missing skins.

I still didn't even know whether Edwin had acted alone.

Whenever the well of leads ran dry, I found myself returning to the forum. Though I knew that most of the incriminating posts had been deleted in the chaotic days after Edwin's arrest was made public in November 2010, I spent dozens of hours searching for anything that the administrators might have missed. Occasionally, I'd find something that raised an eyebrow, such as a post from July 26, 2010—a year after the burglary but a full four months before the arrest was announced. In it, Bud Guidry, the administrator of the forum, uploaded a photo of Indian Crow feathers he'd just purchased, commenting, "This picture always gets my heart racing." In response to Guidry's claim that the plumes were originally owned by a turn-of-the-century tier, a well-known feather dealer named Aaron Ostoj quipped: "Well, it was that or stolen from a natural history museum and sold at 3000% profit :)"

"A tad more profit than that Aaron," replied Guidry, "just a tad more."

It felt as though I was barging into a speakeasy that had already been tipped off: they had done a frustratingly good job cleaning up any trace of their connection to the Tring heist.

But then I found a time machine.

In October 2001 the Internet Archive launched the Wayback Machine, which dispatches web spiders to crawl through the Internet and take snapshots of pages for posterity. By 2009, the year of the burglary, the spiders had taken three petabytes' worth of screenshots of constantly changing websites, enough to fill three thousand iMacs.

I stumbled across the Wayback Machine while poring through the Internet Archive's scans of the 1874 twenty-seven-volume *Catalogue of Birds in the British Museum* late one night in July 2013. I excitedly typed in EdwinRist.com, hoping to exhume the site I'd heard so much about, but came up empty-handed: "Hrm. Wayback Machine doesn't have that page archived."

My luck changed when I plugged in the link to the ClassicFlyTying .com Trading Floor: on four separate dates throughout 2010, the Wayback Machine's spider crawled through the forum, snapping screenshots of the fly-tying community's transactions.

I clicked on the November 29 snapshot, and my eyes bulged. It was like peeling back a layer of earth to find a perfectly preserved fossilized skeleton. There were dozens of posts about Indian Crow, Blue Chatterer, and Resplendent Quetzal skins for sale, listings that no longer appeared in searches on the forum. I could see the title and author of each post and the number of views.

There was a listing for a full Blue Chatterer skin from November 28, 2009. An Indian Crow breastplate posted on April 19, 2010. A full Flame Bowerbird skin on May 7, 2010, and packs of Resplendent Quetzal feathers on May 8. "Exotic bird skins for sale" on July 17, and "Packs of feathers/birdskins" on the twentieth. More Indian Crow and a Purple-Breasted Cotinga skin on August 31.

Heart racing, I clicked at random on one of the listings, from April 21, 2010, entitled "Crow anyone?"

I understood why the listing had vanished from the website. At the top was a link to an eBay auction: "VINTAGE FLY TYING FEATHERS—INDIAN CROW SKIN—NON CITES." Members of the forum, upset by the high price—over one thousand dollars—lamented the rising cost of feathers: "We do it to ourselves by creating the demand."

I wasn't sure it was a Tring bird, but when I scrolled to the bottom of the page, I found my smoking gun, confirming the identity of seller. "It's not Edwin who's the crook," wrote one member, "it's the silly fuckers with more money than sense who'll pay that." I raced over to the timeline hanging on my wall and added the transaction. Over the course of the next hour, with the help of the Wayback Machine, I exhumed another fifteen sales.

My excitement mounted when I realized that all the posts had been made by the same person, seemingly working on Edwin's behalf. Under the screen name Goku, this person created the forum posts, uploaded photos of the birds, fielded orders, and appeared to be handling the financial transactions.

"Have a friend in need that sadly have to sell his IC . . . as he can't afford to keep the feathers and really need the money for the family," Goku wrote in late August 2010, referencing the particular subspecies of Indian Crow the feathers came from. "This cape is a top cape, one of the best I've seen in person, still very full . . . please send mail for price."

Elsewhere Goku posted links to Edwin's eBay.co.uk offerings, trying to drum up bids before time ran out on the auctions.

Edwin even commented on some of Goku's listings. On October 6, 2010, a month before the arrest, Goku announced a new sale of a Blue Chatterer skin but declined to reveal a price, insisting that only "serious bidders should inquire." When a number of members complained about his high-handed tone, Edwin rallied to his defense. "Personally I do not find Goku's tone condescending here, nor do I think there is any problem with him not wishing to display the price," he wrote. "Everyone knows these items are expensive."

On November 11, Goku announced a "Mix pack" of feathers for sale, including three species of Blue Chatterer and three subspecies of Indian Crow. After a Belgian named Geert Werbrouck placed an order, Goku replied: "Thank you so much! The money goes to a student friend of mine :) I'll need your addy, could you send me that on PM?"

The next morning, Adele and her deputies descended on Edwin's apartment. Goku never posted feathers again.

Who the hell was he?

21

DR. PRUM'S THUMB DRIVE

In September 2013 my memoir about the war was published. That same month I fired myself from my nonprofit, which was chronically low on funding. Though over two thousand refugees had made it to the United States through the List Project, many more never would, and it was hard not to feel that I had failed.

I set off on a book tour, speaking on campuses and encouraging students to tackle global problems while trying to mask how burned out I was. When they asked what I was planning to do next—go to Afghanistan? take on Syrian refugees?—I didn't know how to tell them that I had become obsessed with righting a different kind of injustice and dreamed of chasing down a feather thief.

On a trip to Yale, I visited the Peabody Museum of Natural History to meet with Dr. Richard O. Prum, the William Robertson Coe Professor of Ornithology and head curator of vertebrate zoology at the museum. I knew Prum was a MacArthur genius and Guggenheim fellow, head of his own prestigious lab, and the world's leading expert on Cotingas, which constituted nearly a third of the birds stolen from the Tring. But before I stepped into his cluttered office,

I had no idea he had also been trying to solve the mystery of the missing skins.

In 2010, the year before I went to the International Fly Tying Symposium in Somerset, New Jersey, Prum had driven down from New Haven to that year's symposium, pacing the aisles, talking with vendors, gathering business cards, and identifying the various species of exotic birds for sale.

"I was trying to get Fish and Wildlife to bust these fuckers!" he told me. He'd called the agency in charge of enforcing anti-trafficking statutes, urging them to attend the show, but one of its officers had recently been killed in the line of duty by a drunken deer hunter in Gettysburg; all the agents in the region were headed to the funeral that weekend.

"I'm running around with my hair on fire trying to get somebody interested that these wildlife crimes are happening all around us," he said. "They've got tropical birds from numerous continents for sale in New Jersey, and nobody seems to be doing anything about it!"

Before the demands of his academic life put a stop to it, he'd briefly become obsessed with Edwin Rist, pressing the Tring for details about the affected species and looking for a journalist willing to shine a light on a hobby that he wanted to stigmatize into oblivion.

"I've been waiting years for you to walk through the door," he said as he riffled through his desk, an accretion of many years' worth of memos and journals, a decommissioned computer monitor, manila interoffice envelopes, large Ziplocs stuffed with Golden Parrot feathers, at least seven coffee mugs, and a Darth Vader bobblehead. At last, he uncovered his notes from the symposium.

I recognized most of the names of the dealers—there was John McLain of FeathersMc.com and Phil Castleman of Castle Arms.

"Nine or ten vendors were displaying tied flies with feathers of non-US Neotropical, Asian, or European bird species. Three or four vendors were selling flat skins, scientific skins, or taxidermy mounts of non-US tropical birds," he'd written. The ornithologist had spotted skins of Black-Collared Barbets, Golden Tanagers, Black-Backed Grosbeaks, Bronzed Sunbirds, Bamboo Partridges, Indian Rollers, Eurasian Jackdaws, Dusky Parrots, Yellow-Tailed Black Cockatoos, and Scarlet Ibises.

"But they all say that their birds are from the Victorian era," I replied, "before the CITES laws came into effect."

"All of these birds are protected by laws!" Prum shouted, his indignation palpable. "None of them is importable without special permits. Most of them were prepared in ways that indicated they could not have been nineteenth-century birds that they'd received from Grandma." In his opinion, the skins were obviously being trafficked, an orgy of conspicuous consumption of the birds he'd spent a lifetime studying.

"This material is criminal," he said, pausing between each word for emphasis. "You can't possess it and not have broken numerous laws."

"Did any of them have biodata labels attached to them?" I asked.

"No. There were no labels, but there *were* price tags! It's a fuckin' outrage!" he thundered.

"Even after all this time," I said, referring to the many sales I'd seen of protected species, "I don't understand why they would take such risks in the pursuit of their hobby."

"People don't actually fish with this shit, right?!" Prum said. "So what is it about? It's about this fixation, this obsession with originality. Well, there's no fuckin' originality in the world! Who are these guys? They're dentists from Ohio! What claim do they have to originality in anything?!"

When I told him that one of Edwin's customers was in fact a dentist, Prum laughed. Calming down a little, he went on. "What I see is a story of the struggle for authenticity . . . to try to make what people are doing meaningful. What they've done is enshrined this in a period where English fishermen were members of a colonial power that ruled the entire globe and could extract fascinating things from it, then sell them in commercial markets.

"But that dream is extinct," he said. "That world is gone.

"When *I* work on feathers," he added, "knowledge is a consequence. When I pluck a feather and destroy it, we discover things about the world that nobody knew before." By contrast, Edwin and the feather underground were a bunch of historical fetishists, practicing a "candy-ass, ridiculous, parasitic activity" that Prum would be glad to see go extinct.

Before I left, he told me he had something for me. Rummaging through his desk drawer, he pulled out a small USB drive.

Out in the parking lot, I got my laptop out of the car and plugged it in, gasping when I discovered that Prum had taken meticulous screenshots of Edwin's website, seemingly the only record of it in existence.

As I clicked through each file, I could see why Edwin had wiped it from the Internet. On the "Exotic Materials Photo Album and Sale Page" were links to thirty-one different listings, using the Latin binomial nomenclature for each species and subspecies.

Each link jumped to a high-resolution photograph of the bird. Although the tags were hidden, the birds displayed the telltale cotton eyes and unique preparation of museum specimens. Skins prepared for research have the wings and legs drawn close to the body, unlike birds that have been mounted on hats with outstretched wings.

Above each listing, Edwin had added some showroom descriptions: "The Masoni subspecies of Indian Crow is by far the rarest, and is very rarely seen in collections. The feathers are a deep brown, with blood red tips and a pronounced crimp." Introducing a species of Blue Chatterer, he wrote: "Cotinga maynana is the most colorful species of blue chatterer. It is very rare, but is exceptionally bright." On the page featuring the birds collected by Wallace 145 years earlier, Edwin wrote: "King Bird of Paradise is a bright little bird of paradise, with vibrant iridescent underwing coverts. Please contact me for availability of full skins and prices." He marveled at the "exceptional" neck feathers of his Flame Bowerbirds: "their shiny translucent nature is unmatched."

Elsewhere on his site he added, "I also sell birds on consignment, so if you have a bird you want to sell, I can help!

"Don't worry," he reassured his buyers: "unless you want me to, I will not say where any given bird is from."

In Edwin's sentencing hearings at the Crown Court, the prosecutors had tried to focus the judge's attention on the financial motive behind the theft: these birds were stolen so that they could be sold. But his defense attorneys had won the day, thanks to Dr. Simon Baron-Cohen's report, which, beyond diagnosing Asperger's, asserted that Edwin "had not been motivated by money."

Although I'd never seen his website until now, I knew that he had registered EdwinRist.com only fifteen days after the Tring heist. It was unmistakably designed to sell birds. On the "About" page, he even wrote: "I have become interested in retailing flytying materials, a venture that started as an attempt to help fund a new flute purchase, but soon turned into a larger, more extensive hobby."

As I scrolled down the page, I found Edwin in his own words, making lists of his favorite fly-tying books and friends and providing a mini-autobiography. "I am currently working on a book about salmon flies, both modern and classic," he wrote. "This work will include details on dozens of patterns. . . . In addition, a large variety of exotic feathers and birds will be featured, along with magnificent artwork by Long Nguyen from Norway. Check back here often for progress updates and photos!"

Who was Long Nguyen? I thought I knew everyone in Edwin's inner circle by this point.

From the parking lot, I found a faint campus Wi-Fi signal. I asked Spencer Seim, who was friends on Facebook with Edwin, if I could log into his account for a glimpse of his page, which was otherwise walled off to strangers. I found Long Nguyen everywhere. There were photos of Long and Edwin together on rooftops in Norway, mimicking the Scream in front of the Munch Museum, complimenting each other's flies. Long had tagged Edwin in a photo album of a trip the two of them took to Japan together in the spring of 2010, showing them in the Asakusa Kannon Temple, strolling through parks beneath *sakura* blossoms, ordering raw fish, shopping at the Harajuku market.

And then I found the painting. Long had uploaded a photo of an oil painting of three birds—a Banksian Cockatoo, a Malayan Peacock Pheasant, and a Flame Bowerbird—which he announced as a gift for Edwin. In the comments section, Edwin replied in Japanese: "Oi! lonngu sama!! kore wa sugoi desu ne!! [Hey! Mr. Long! That is so amazing!]" before reverting to English to ask "Did your box arrive?"

"I've to check the mailbox today Edwin-aniki," answered Long: "I'm so excited!"

I had seen this painting, during a late-night trawling of the forum a year earlier, but thought little of it. I rushed back to the forum, searching for the handle of the person who had posted the painting.

It was Goku.

Goku, who had posted numerous links to eBay auctions of Edwin's stolen birds, was, in fact, Long Nguyen. Goku, who sold packets of feathers, and breastplates of Indian Crow. Goku, whose sale of a "Flame bowerbird, male, full skin" had been deleted.

How had I missed it? Long was everywhere.

I hopped in my car and bombed up I-95 back to Boston, the revelation setting my imagination on fire. Long was the accomplice. Had he been there the night of the theft, to help hoist Edwin into the museum?

Or had he been the mastermind? Maybe my vision had been clouded from the beginning, and Edwin was just a patsy, an impressionable, innocent kid who had been dragged into something and then set up as the fall guy.

A few weeks after Prum gave me the memory stick, I boarded a flight to Chicago for another leg of the book tour. As the flight attendants droned their way through the safety presentation, I opened my Facebook app and navigated to a private group of Victorian salmon fly-tiers.

A fight had just erupted after a member posted an old article about Edwin's arrest. "I know this happened back in 2010 but never heard about it and it is kind of amazing," he said, unaware that he had just touched the third rail by bringing up the topic of the Tring heist.

The conversation quickly turned to the missing skins. "His mate is still out there," replied a British tier named Mike Townend.

Jens Pilgaard asked, "Does anyone have an idea of who it could be that holds the feathers?"

I snapped screenshots, hoping to preserve the thread before it was deleted. As the plane taxied, the flight attendant announced it was time to switch our phones off, but there was no way I could miss this.

"His partner in crime, who I believe was the mastermind of this crime . . . thinks he is immune from prosecution," wrote Townend.

"He goes by the name of Long. Your days are numbered."

This was, to my knowledge, the first time Long had been called out publicly. He entered the thread to deny any involvement. "I heard people going around with rumors about me, and couldn't care less," he wrote. "It's not like I'm going to live by fly-tying, it's JUST a fucking hobby to me."

Noticing the flight attendant standing over me with a cross look,

I guiltily shut my phone off. By the time we landed a couple of hours later, the moderator had deleted the entire thread.

I wrote Long to see if he'd be willing to tell me his side of the story, but he declined.

If anyone had the missing skins, I was sure it was Long.

And then Edwin, who was performing in ensembles and chamber orchestras throughout Germany, broke his silence. For the first time since the arrest, he returned to the forum with a post entitled "Long Nguyen."

"Ladies and Gentleman of the Flytying world," he wrote, "most of you have heard of me, and for obvious reasons I have chosen to remove myself from mainstream flytying. However, I have found a need to address something that has been disturbing me for some time.

"My friend, Long Nguyen from Norway, has been . . . publicly slandered for his supposed involvement in the museum theft I committed alone in 2009. Two people, one from Denmark and another from the UK, even went so far as to go on a rumor spreading vendetta that Long was the 'Brains behind the operation.'

"I am more appalled at the behavior of . . . the flytying world towards Long, than the flytying world is at my own actions," he declared.

Bud Guidry, who had banned all discussion of the so-called "Tring incident," was not happy. "I'm done with this bullshit. I've tried to keep this away from members for years, and you still are like a bad weed: rid yourself of it, and it just keeps coming back uglier than ever.

"You wanna defend Long," he added, "by all means do so . . . what I fear most is you have only driven the nail deeper into Long's back." Turning his attention to the community, he wrote: "You have no clue of the time and effort I have spent trying to keep this one subject out of this forum over the years. Been a struggle to say the least."

For three years, I had been periodically nudging Edwin with inter-view requests, without luck. But now that he'd spoken about details of the case publicly for the first time, I had to try again. I wrote to him saying it was time to speak.

Surprisingly, he responded. "I hope you understand that talking about my story and addressing this publicly is a bit like rubbing salt into an old wound, and I've needed time to think about your re-quest," he wrote.

I excitedly replied to ask him for dates when we could meet, then waited impatiently for a reply. Twenty-four hours turned into a week, then two weeks, and still none came. I read and reread my e-mail. Had I been too eager? Had I said something that scared him off? Did he spook easily?

When at last he offered me a window, it was less than a week away. Feeling I was on the brink of solving the mystery, I booked a ridiculously expensive flight to Düsseldorf without hesitation.

"Is there any reason we should be nervous for our safety?" my wife, Marie-Josée, asked as we packed.

We were newlyweds. She had been a lawyer at one of the firms that partnered with the List Project, helping twelve Iraqis navigate to refuge in America. While we knew each other over e-mail, we had never met in person until she came to one of my book tour events in Los Angeles. I moved to L.A. ten days later, bought a ring within two months, proposed at four months, and married her ex-actly a year later.

If this interview had happened a couple of years earlier, I wouldn't have given the question of security a second thought, but a lot had happened since then. We'd just bought our first home and were hop-ing to start a family. I was calculating risk differently these days.

I tried to brush the idea off. "He's a flute player!" I said. "He stole feathers. He's not gonna do anything!" But with the interview only days away, I wondered if I was being reckless. What kind of person was Edwin really? For all the time I'd spent investigating his crime, I didn't know much about his personality. How much could you really know about someone from their online persona? I realized I'd never even heard his voice before. Would he only give one-word answers? Was he quick to anger? How would he react when I confronted him with all the evidence I'd gathered?

I could hire a bodyguard but didn't know how I could do so without ruining the interview. Would it be possible to have Edwin frisked before he came into the room? Could I just put an armed goon in the corner without explaining who he was?

I found the highest-rated security service in Düsseldorf on Yelp and got one of its partners, Jan, on the line. He was comfortingly true to Germanic stereotype: a deep, flat voice, all business, dispassionate. A bodyguard cost fifty-two euros an hour, available for six-hour blocks. It seemed foolish to haggle with someone you were hiring to protect you, so I agreed.

"Tell me about this guy," Jan said, the sound of a retractable pen clicking in the background.

"He was born in New York and moved to London a few years ago before coming to Düsseldorf to play the flute—"

"Not biography," Jan interrupted. "How big is he?"

I'd spent years tracking this person and didn't even know how tall he was. "Six feet, maybe?"

"How old is he?"

"Twenty-six."

"Uh-huh," Jan said. "Have you met him before?"

"No. And to be honest, I don't even know if he's going to show."

"When and where is the meeting?"

"May twenty-sixth, at the Stage Forty-Seven Hotel in Düsseldorf."

"What is this guy's name?"

"Edwin Rist."

"What'd he steal, again?"

"Feathers."

There was a lengthy pause. He said Edwin would probably be intimidated if a bodyguard were in the room; better to have one wait in the hallway with a room key. I could hold on to a walkie-talkie and squawk it if we needed him.

I agreed to the plan.

"Okay," said Jan. "We'll send Klaus. Bring cash."

In the days leading up to the interview, I prepared an exhaustive list of questions with manic intensity. I knew I couldn't start out by asking where the missing skins were, but I also didn't know how much time he would give me. I sequenced the questions in a way that I hoped would back him into a tighter and tighter corner. I would feign ignorance about certain parts of the story, to see whether he would tell me the truth or lie. I would find out Long's true role.

As I rehearsed, I couldn't escape the nagging question: What if Edwin didn't show up? What if he was just toying with me, summoning me across the world to sit in an empty hotel room? I had just plunked several thousand dollars down for flights to a German city I'd never been particularly eager to visit, and another few hundred for a German bodyguard, but I didn't even have Edwin's cell phone number. It was not the most considered step I'd taken.

As we inched our luggage through the security line at LAX, Marie-Josée asked a question I couldn't answer: "Remind me why he agreed to talk to you?"

22

"I'M NOT A THIEF"

The night before the interview, jet lag and jittery nerves kept me up. While Marie-Josée slept, I watched the German version of the Home Shopping Network on mute, where Hausfraus peddled a Spanx-type shirt called the *Schlankstütz*. It had taken me years to get Edwin to speak to me, and now I would stumble into it half-asleep. What if I failed to notice some key revelation? What if I forgot to confront him with a critical piece of evidence?

When the northern sun rose and light began to filter through the pewter sky, I was still awake. As Marie-Josée slept, I tiptoed into the separate sitting room, where I had mounted a shotgun microphone on the coffee table. Stashed beneath a nearby ottoman was a second recorder; a third was hidden behind the TV. I wasn't leaving anything to chance.

Klaus the bodyguard showed up at ten, an hour before Edwin was scheduled to arrive. Looking every bit the part, he was a behemoth, six-four and 250 pounds, crammed into a tracksuit. He had a buzz cut, looked as though he'd shaved with a knife, and barely spoke a word of English. He gestured at a chair in a dark corner of the hallway outside our room, produced two walkie-talkies from his jacket, and handed me one with a reassuring glance.

Back in the room, I stretched out on the sofa and stashed the walkie-talkie behind one of its cushions. As I pored through the pages of questions I'd prepared, the many versions of Edwin Rist that had appeared throughout the investigation thrummed through my mind. Edwin Rist committed the natural history crime of the century. Edwin Rist was a genius, masterminding a heist that netted him hundreds of thousands of dollars. Edwin Rist was a virtuosic flautist. Edwin Rist just did something dumb, like a lot of teenagers. Edwin Rist had some kind of disorder, maybe Asperger's. Edwin Rist was desperate for money to provide for his needy family. Edwin Rist was the future of fly-tying. Edwin Rist was a black mark on the community of fly-tiers. Edwin Rist was impulsive. Edwin Rist was the best anyone had ever seen. Edwin Rist was a narcissist. Edwin Rist was a felon. Edwin Rist didn't work alone. Edwin Rist was just a mastermind's pawn. Edwin Rist still had a lot of the stolen loot, to be sold decades down the road. Edwin Rist beat the system—

A ringing phone startled me out of a deep sleep. "Edwin Rist is waiting for you in the lobby," the receptionist said. Marie-Josée groggily entered the sitting room as I nervously started the recorders. I showed her how to operate the walkie-talkie, returned it to its hiding place, and made my way down to meet him.

Out in the hallway, I shot Klaus a readying glance. He took a step back into the shadows as I turned to go down the steps.

It was May but still chilly enough for Edwin to be wearing a peacoat. He was taller than I expected, over six feet. He had a three-day stubble and wore designer lenses and a thin silver chain around his neck. He extended his hand with a wan smile.

Five winters had descended since the crime, four since the arrest, and three since the sentencing. I wondered if he realized how consumed by his actions I'd become. As we approached the room, I wondered why he had shown up. What did he stand to gain from speaking to me? Did he think he could outsmart me? Would he outsmart me?

"Edwin, meet my wife, Marie-Josée." She greeted him as we entered the room, and I could see his eyes settle on the imposing microphone and audio equipment. "She's going to take care of the recording today," I said, even though we'd never discussed whether the interview would be recorded. To my relief, he agreed. Sirens wailed in the distance as I offered to take his coat, patting it down lightly as I guided him toward his chair. Marie-Josée poured him a cup of tea, took a seat on the sofa, and donned an oversize pair of headphones to monitor the recorder's audio level.

"How much time do we have?" I asked.

"We could be done in two hours, or we could be here till the evening," he said with a smile. "Depends on you."

I looked down at my questions. Of the 284, there were really only two fundamental questions that I'd come to Düsseldorf to answer. The first: Did he really have Asperger's, the diagnosis of which kept him from prison?

The second: Was Long sitting on the missing skins?

For the first two hours, I peppered him with questions about his life. He spoke happily about his childhood, the flute, Germany, and learning to tie flies. I liked him—he had a wry sense of humor and was thoughtful, often pausing to gather his thoughts before responding in full paragraphs. In another life, we might have been friends.

When I felt he was comfortable enough to discuss the events of

June 23, 2009, I asked him if he had known much about the historical importance of the skins he had taken.

He knew Alfred Russel Wallace's birds were kept at the Tring, he said, but he didn't realize that he'd taken any of them until he got back to the safety of his bedroom, the morning after the heist.

"What'd you do with the tags?" I asked casually.

"It depends," he said. "Some of them I took off. I didn't take them all off." If he had known Wallace collected them, he said, he "probably would have treated them with a little bit more respect."

Doing my best to appear nonchalant, I brought up the opinion I'd heard from so many tiers over the years—that museums didn't really need so many birds to do their research, and that they ought to sell them to the community, where they could be truly appreciated.

"Did you resent the Tring for having all these beautiful birds?" I offered.

"Em . . ." His diction reflected his many years spent abroad— American *ums* had become British *ems*; his *ands* now sounded more like German *unds*. "I wouldn't say I *resented* it. I mean, it was a shame."

He took a sip of tea before saying that with museum specimens, "after a certain period of time—I think about a hundred years— technically speaking, all of the scientific data that can be extracted from them has been extracted from them. You can no longer use DNA, because what you would want to do it for is to prolong and help living birds, which hasn't really worked anyway, because they're still going extinct, or will go extinct depending on what happens with the rainforests."

This was absurd, of course—scientists had recently extracted 419-million-year-old bacterial DNA from salt deposits on an old buffalo skin in the Michigan Basin, but I didn't interrupt.

"As far as measurements and things," he said, "they were taken *ages* ago." He believed their only real value was historical. "I understand that they're preserved because if they're not, they might fall apart after fifty years in the sunlight or something like that, but they are collecting dust, so to speak. I didn't have a problem with that because I know this is how museums operate. I *do* actually think it's a shame that this is how it is. . . .

"Again, I'm not a scientist," he acknowledged, "but I do view it as a shame that they're in a box in the dark, where an idiot with a rock can go in and take them."

It was a curious stance: he almost seemed to blame the Tring. I relayed the anguish that Prum and the museum's curators had expressed over the fact that these skins might have held answers to questions that hadn't even been asked yet, but Edwin was unmoved.

He told me he'd feel bad about it if it were true. "But at the same time, I'd say 'If you haven't made the breakthrough yet, *when* are you planning on doing that?!' Because as far as preservation is concerned, em, aren't we *kinda* running out of time, ever so slightly? You know?!"

"I dunno," he chuckled. "I think that things such as illegal poaching are probably hurting more. I think that, technically speaking, *had* the museum just put all those things up for sale, you would have nullified fifty Indian Crows' worth of demand, which is fifty Indian Crows that would probably still be alive in the wild."

"Whoa," I said, my poker face slipping for a moment. "You're making the case that by taking the Tring's birds, you *saved* live birds in the wild?"

"Well, that's a flowery way of putting it, and I wish that that were true." He grinned, then added: "Maybe in a sense it technically *is* true."

I glanced over at Marie-Josée. Her eyelids were heavy, but she was making a valiant effort to stay alert. I wondered if Klaus was awake in the darkness of the hallway outside. As soon as I met Edwin, I had realized our bodyguard was unnecessary, but I wasn't about to interrupt the interview just to send him packing.

Edwin sat there patiently, his posture perfect. Annoyed as I was by his self-serving misreading of the state of modern scientific research, I wasn't there to debate him, at least not yet. I steered the conversation to the matter of his sentencing.

If the search for the Tring's missing birds had unexpectedly become my mission in life, it was fueled by a sense that justice had been thwarted: eighteen months of advance planning, at least tens of thousands of dollars in profit, irreparable damage to the Tring's collection and future research, and not a single night behind bars for the perpetrator. For that, he had a diagnosis from Dr. Baron-Cohen and the precedent of the Bristol grave robber with Asperger's to thank.

In his report to the court, Baron-Cohen based his diagnosis in part on Edwin's scores on the Adult Asperger's Assessment, a diagnostic tool that he had developed. The assessment, which Edwin had taken on the advice of his lawyer, searches for symptoms like a "marked impairment" in eye contact, "stereotyped and repetitive motor mannerisms" like twisting one's hands, and a failure to develop friendships. The questions in the assessment are meant to tease out whether the patient has a lack of "theory of mind"—an inability to infer the beliefs, emotions, and desires of others. People with Asperger's generally have difficulty understanding social situations or predicting other people's thoughts.

Over the years, I'd spoken with a number of people who knew Edwin who thought the Asperger's diagnosis was bullshit. Until his arrest, he'd been in a three-year relationship with his girlfriend at the Royal Academy. He seemed to have no shortage of friends, at school and in the fly-tying community. Those who mentored him in his early fly-tying years uniformly described him as charming. I had always maintained a healthy measure of deference to clinical experts, but now, as we entered the fourth hour of the interview, I was having some serious doubts.

Edwin was a formidable interviewee. He didn't seem to exhibit the classic symptoms of the disorder. In fact, he struck me as quite intuitive and empathetic. He seemed capable of sensing where my questions were headed, several steps in advance. If my brow furrowed even slightly in the middle of a questionable response, he would adapt on the fly and try a new approach. He was disarming and likable, but read me masterfully, rarely letting his guard down.

"I'm just thinking about your master plan, gaming out all the possible scenarios in the months leading up to the break-in," I said. "And now here you are, your fate depending on Sacha Baron-Cohen's cousin."

"I mean, you can't make this stuff up!" he laughed. "Like really! It's not possible! It's unbelievable. And at the time, you don't see it as 'Borat's cousin is interviewing me to see if I'm retarded.'"

"How did you see it then?"

He hiked his voice up into a nasal register, as if to poke fun at his frame of mind during the diagnosis: "'Ohhh . . . maybe I have a problem, and this guy's a professional, okay, yeah.'

"You go along with it," he said, his voice returning to normal. "I mean, it's not really scientific or medical in terms of the approach."

"It's weird to say this in front of you," I ventured, "but it doesn't seem like you have Asperger's. You're making eye contact, for example."

"Em . . . ," he started, shifting in his seat, "I mean, it's been a question in my mind for a very long time. Because I *have* a diagnosis, apparently, by this renowned, knowledgeable individual, great professor and specialist in this stuff. . . .

"I don't want to say I'm *grateful* for it," he continued, "but I *am* grateful for it, because without it, I probably would've spent two years or more in prison. I spent ages trying to recover from this, because I thought I had Asperger's. Well, maybe I do. But I thought I was really, really mentally disabled for a while, and when you think these things, you become it."

"What do you mean?"

He told me that before the arrest, he'd never had any problems maintaining eye contact. And now, years later, he said, "I don't have problems with eye contact. . . . It's not an issue, I don't actively think *Eyes! Can't do that!*" But in the lead-up to his sentencing hearing, "I started thinking *Eyes! I can't look there!*" He bulged his eyes and waved his hands comically.

Before I could say anything, he said: "The other one was *Ohhh autistic people, they sort of have tic*s, so I was sort of sitting in chairs, rubbing my hands together."

He made a strange panting noise and started rocking in his seat. "Just some body motion which is repetitive and autistic, and before you know it, you're sitting in a chair rocking back and forth, not making eye contact . . . because those are symptoms."

He was smiling slightly. I leaned back, trying to mask my reaction to the statement that, with the prospect of prison looming, he'd become what he needed to be.

My eyes darted down at my notes and then over at Marie-Josée, who had lost the battle against jet lag and was fast asleep. The antenna of the walkie-talkie was poking out from behind the couch cushion. I wondered if Edwin could see it from his vantage point. If her hand accidentally squawked the receiver, Klaus would burst in and ruin the interview.

"With the Asperger's diagnosis," I asked loudly, hoping to wake her, "do you think you had a less-developed sense of right and wrong?"

"Em . . . ," Edwin replied, as Marie-Josée pried open an eyelid and noticed the walkie-talkie. "The thing is, anytime I say I have a less-developed sense of right or wrong, sounds sort of like I'm trying to weasel out of something. Em. I was young."

He caught himself: "Of course, *many* people have very, very strongly developed senses of right and wrong, even when they're young, and others have to work on it. I think . . . I hadn't been in situations to experience that." He blamed homeschooling, in that when he misbehaved, he was in trouble only with his mother. "Let's face it, everybody gets in trouble with their parents, and then it's okay."

I struck a line through the rest of the Asperger's-related questions on my list. I had my answer.

"This is the way the legal system functions," he said, sensing that I was a little jarred by the discussion of his diagnosis. "It's the way that justice functions. Sometimes it's very unfair for either the victims or the person who is guilty."

We stopped to eat the sandwiches I'd ordered; I hadn't wanted there to be any excuse to leave the room. I didn't want him to bump into Klaus or to admit something when the recorders weren't running. I'd waited three years to get him in that room, and I was going to do everything I could to keep him from leaving until I found out about Long.

The sun, with all the strength of a streetlamp in fog, gave out sometime around three in the afternoon. I jabbed a pen into my leg to wake myself up and decided it was time to talk about his friend in Norway.

I began by saying that there were a lot of people who didn't think he acted alone.

"Before you say anything," he cut in, "I have said this many, many times. . . . Long was not involved. In any way, whatsoever. I had sent him birds. He was the one who showed the birds at the fair. Which is why I think he was implicated in this. He didn't sell anything. I didn't sell him anything. He was not involved in planning. He was not the mastermind."

It was as though he'd read my mind. "How many birds did you send him?"

"Three."

"How many?" I started sifting through a thick pile of pages, searching for the Tring's spreadsheet listing the tally of missing skins.

"Three. Two or three." He was watching me intently. "I can't remember if it was two or three."

"And how many did you sell yourself?"

"I only sold two Indian Crows and two Chatterers." His answers were becoming choppier. He corrected himself. "Three Indian Crows and two Chatterers, so five things in total, plus feathers."

This was, of course, wildly false: under interrogation, he had admitted to selling nine birds. Nineteen had been returned by his customers to the museum following his arrest.

"The British Museum of Natural History says two hundred and ninety-nine birds were stolen," I said, searching through my papers, "and that there are sixty-four skins still at large."

"I find it impossible to believe the museum knows exactly how many birds they have at any given time regardless of how well they inventory them!" he interjected. "Maybe the Darwin finches . . . and possibly the Wallace birds. But the other birds, which are scientifically less interesting, I can't believe they're that focused on them!"

"But isn't that their whole raison d'être? Why is that so hard to believe, that they would have a list?"

"Because once you make a list, why would you update it?"

"What do you mean?" I asked, momentarily flummoxed.

"Why would you update it before you get burgled?" he asked.

"But if they knew that in 2005 they had seventeen Flame Bower-birds, and now, in 2009, there are none, why is that number in doubt? Are you suggesting someone else took them?"

"I can't suggest that because I have no proof, but I don't find it improbable that people didn't take things previously," he told me. "It could be anyone who works there. The only reason they probably realized I was there was because I broke a window. . . . Had I taken two of each, I doubt they ever would have noticed."

I knew that Edwin hadn't disputed the numbers when confronted with the list during the interrogation at the police station. I held up the Tring's spreadsheet, and a wave of recognition flashed across his face.

"This doesn't strike me like a haphazard list," I said, reading aloud the column headings of the spreadsheet: "'Number of Specimens Missing in July 2009,' 'Intact Specimens with labels, without labels,' 'Number returned by Post,' 'Total Outstanding.' They seem to know exactly what's missing," I said with a stern look.

His voice, brashly confident a moment earlier, was now muted. "I would agree, it looks very, very thorough, and it looks very, very calculated, I guess."

Now that we could dispense with the attempts to muddy the numbers, I began to reveal all the evidence I had on Long, reading from printouts of their Facebook exchanges and forum posts where Long personally attested to the quality of certain skins, and laying out the timeline, which reflected a spike in sales shortly after the two returned from Japan.

"Can you see why I don't believe what you're telling me about Long's involvement?"

"I see what you mean," he said, wilted. "And. Und. Yeah. I. You know. It looks bad. Basically."

"So here's the thing," I continued. "If there are still sixty-four skins missing, shouldn't they be returned? Where are they?!"

"If someone has them, I really don't know about it. And the question is, does one individual have them?"

"But"—I paused, exasperated by his response—"aren't *you* the person most uniquely positioned to answer that?"

"In what sense?"

"That *you* were the one who took them!"

Edwin told me he'd never spent much time thinking about the missing birds. "I don't have them," he insisted. "And Long doesn't have them. I don't know who has them."

I was obviously annoyed: I didn't see how this could be possible.

"I think that detective woman was looking for my accomplice, or my driver," he continued, "because she couldn't believe the fact that I had taken a train." He toyed with his tea bag as he spoke. "They had a very hard time believing the fact that an eighteen-year-old idiot with a suitcase and a rock could steal a suitcase full of birds from the Natural History Museum, walk out, walk forty-five minutes, get on a train, and leave."

"Which," he added, "even as I think about it, *is* absurd!"

"Do you think Long would talk to me?" I asked.

"I mean, you can try. I can talk to him, and I can suggest that he meets with you."

I looked down at the recorder—its counter was approaching eight hours. Marie-Josée looked as though she was down for the night. It was time to call it quits. While Edwin seemed as alert as ever, I was drained.

As he gathered his things, we made small talk about his life in Germany. I jokingly asked if his friends teased him for being a feather thief, but his face clouded at the word *thief.*

"I try to refrain from certain words," he said. "*Thief* is one of them. This is going to sound very strange, but I don't feel like a thief. You know, to me, a thief is somebody who is down by the Rhine, waiting for you to look the other way, and picks your pocket, and the next day is back, looking for the next victim. Or somebody who makes a career out of breaking into homes, or who walks around and steals things from the school."

I decided against reminding him that he stole a TV from his school.

"Personally, I don't view myself as a thief. . . . I'm *not* a thief. In that sense. People can leave their wallet with me. I'm not going to take it. I can find somebody's wallet, and if there's an ID in it, I'll give it to somebody who can look after it and return it later."

On his way out the door, he told me I could e-mail him with follow-ups anytime, but we both seemed to know that this was the first and last time we'd talk.

After he left, I paid Klaus and collapsed into a coma-like sleep.

Early the next morning, a light rain was falling as I shuffled down to the hotel's breakfast buffet. Across the street, the proprietor of the Dene & Gör Döner kebab shop readied his place for a morning crowd that never materialized. He heaved the meat onto the spit, and I watched it spin until its color changed from pale flesh to rusty red. The sign in the rain-streaked window read IT'S BETTER THAN YOU THINK.

I cycled through the highlights of the interview in a state of disbelief. I wondered if he had truly duped Dr. Baron-Cohen. Had he duped me? Edwin had told the truth about some things and lied about others. He didn't seem very remorseful. Even though he'd sat through hearings in which museum curators spoke of the catastrophic blow to scientific research, he remained skeptical about the mission of the Tring, at one point laughingly referring to it as a "dusty old dump." He compartmentalized, drawing a distinction between stealing from another person and robbing an institution like a museum.

He spoke like someone who knew he had got away with it and who had help doing so.

My phone buzzed with an e-mail.

Hi Kirk. Got words from Edwin now. Interesting case, and interesting story about me. If you want an interview, then I'll be available this summer.

Best regards, Long.

23
THREE DAYS IN NORWAY

"I keep thinking about one of Edwin's answers," Marie-Josée said after we got home to Los Angeles.

"Just one?"

"When you asked what color his suitcase was, he didn't remember."

I paged through the transcript to his response: "I dunno. Suitcases are black, normally." It did seem a little off.

"Didn't the police say the birds could fill up to six garbage bags?" Marie-Josée asked.

"Who doesn't remember the color of their suitcase?!" I exclaimed, still a step behind my wife.

"Do you think two hundred ninety-nine birds would've fit in just one?" she continued.

Seeing where her questions led—that multiple suitcases would suggest multiple people—I got out a medium-size suitcase. Having seen the window at the Tring, I knew he couldn't have fit one much larger through it. Working together, we spent the next hour building a pile of fake birds. A rolled-up pair of dress socks formed a

Blue Chatterer. She folded several dozen T-shirts and dish towels into the approximate size of an Indian Crow, and used her leggings to fashion Resplendent Quetzal tails.

We started packing. Marie-Josée, consulting the Tring's spreadsheet, counted off each species. When the suitcase was halfway full, we were already at eighty birds. Of course, our experiment was hardly scientific—my washcloth Flame Bowerbirds might have been a bit large—but it seemed as though it would've been difficult to fit all of them in a single suitcase. I'd heard rumors that Edwin also used a backpack, but I had forgotten to ask him during the interview, and he was no longer replying to my messages.

I looked up at Marie-Josée.

"Do you think Long was there that night?" she asked.

———

I'd never been so impatient for a plane to land. As the Norwegian Air flight inched across the ocean toward Oslo, the bloodhound in me ranged impatiently. I had him. Four years after I'd first heard of the theft, I would get the Tring's birds.

In the two years since I'd discovered he was Goku, Long's involvement in the Tring heist had taken on almost Kurtzian proportions in my mind. After Edwin's underwhelming defense of him during our interview, I had just about convinced myself that Long was behind it all, reimagining the key moments in the theft, this time adding the mysterious Norwegian to the mix. Had he cupped his hands to hoist Edwin over the wall? Had he followed him in with a second suitcase? Was he crouched in a bush with a walkie-talkie, updating Edwin on the security guard's movements? Was he idling out front in a tinted BMW? Or had he called all the shots from some manor in the Norwegian countryside?

Adele, who knew of my suspicions about a Norwegian, was waiting for my report. In the weeks leading up to the trip, I assembled

Sketches of beaks of various birds, including the Chestnut-breasted Malkoha and the Black-and-yellow Broadbill, from one of Wallace's specimen notebooks, dated 1854.

A Yellow-crowned Barbet bearing one of Wallace's specimen labels, noting the date and location of its collection. His inclusion of such data and argument for its importance led to him being hailed as the father of Biogeography.

The naturalist Alfred Russel Wallace in 1862, shortly after his return from an eight-year expedition throughout the Malay Archipelago, where he gathered over 125,000 specimens. Wallace independently arrived at the theory of evolution by natural selection now attributed to Charles Darwin.

The Red-ruffed Fruitcrow, known to contemporary practitioners of the Victorian art of salmon fly-tying as Indian Crow. Its black and orange breastplate feathers are among the most coveted plumes in the community. A single museum-grade skin can sell for $6,000.

The Spangled Cotinga, one of the seven species known to fly-tiers as the Blue Chatterer. Its turquoise feathers are called for in many salmon fly "recipes."

The Resplendent Quetzal, another bird whose colorful feathers are prized by fly-tiers. Though the species is protected by CITES, an international treaty, making it illegal to buy or sell, packets of its feathers are routinely sold on eBay.

An adult male Greater Bird of Paradise, perched on the treetops of the Aru Islands, where Alfred Russel Wallace became the first Western naturalist to observe the bird's courtship display. Wallace worried that mankind's need to possess such beauty would eventually lead to their extinction. Little did he realize that a burgeoning fashion trend would soon send plume-hunters into those very forests.

A woman with an entire Greater Bird of Paradise mounted on her hat, ca. 1900. In the late 19th century, a "feather fever" in fashion swept through Europe and the United States. As a result, between 1883 and 1898, bird populations in twenty-six states had dropped by nearly half. Historians have described the craze as the greatest direct slaughter of wildlife by humans in the history of the planet.

The January 1907 cover of *The Delineator*, a popular women's fashion magazine.

Sixteen hundred hummingbird skins sold for two cents apiece at a London millinery auction in 1912. In the final decades of the nineteenth century, one hundred and forty million pounds of plumage were imported into England and France alone. By 1900, millinery was a booming industry, employing nearly one hundred thousand New Yorkers.

THE "EXTINCTION" OF SPECIES;
OR, THE FASHION-PLATE LADY WITHOUT MERCY AND THE EGRETS.

Sandwich-board men protesting the widespread slaughter of egrets in the streets of London in July 1911 as part of a campaign by the Royal Society for the Protection of Birds, founded by Emily Williamson and Eliza Phillips.

Around the turn of the century, some began speaking out against this widespread slaughter. This cartoon from an 1899 edition of *Punch* depicts a woman with a bird mounted on her hat above the caption: "The 'extinction' of species; or, the fashion-plate lady without mercy and the egrets." The magazine played a key role in stigmatizing feather fashion throughout the U.K.

Here U.S. federal agents pose with confiscated egret skins in the 1930s. After the passage of a series of conservation laws, the protection of birds became a high-stakes battle between wildlife agents and poachers. By 1900, a kilo of Snowy Egret feathers was worth nearly twice its weight in gold.

An illustration from the frontispiece of *The Salmon Fly* (1895) depicting George M. Kelson, the English lord whose pseudo-scientific book of fly "recipes" popularized the art form. "We have here a well-bred hobby noteworthy of the attention of the greatest amongst us . . . Divines or Statesmen, Doctors or Lawyers," Kelson wrote.

Plate 1.

THE BLACK RANGER.

THE INFALLIBLE

BRITANNIA.

JOCK SCOTT

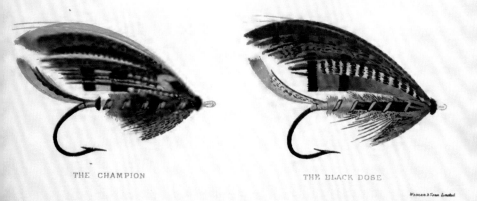

THE CHAMPION

THE BLACK DOSE

Six salmon flies depicted in *The Salmon Fly*. As the art form progressed, flies took on increasingly lofty names like the Infallible, Thunder and Lightning, and Traherne's Wonder, named for its creator.

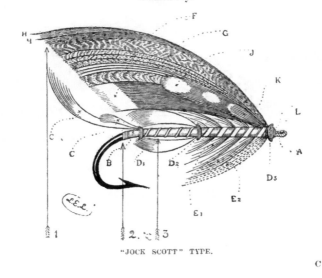

"JOCK SCOTT" TYPE.

An "analytical diagram" from *The Salmon Fly* illustrating the various parts of a Jock Scott salmon fly. Although salmon cannot tell the difference between a tuft of dog fur and an exotic bird feather, Kelson's book argued that rare and expensive plumes were more effective in attracting the "King of Fish."

The Jock Scott fly, tied according to Kelson's 110-year-old recipe by Spencer Seim, the fly-fishing guide who first told me about Edwin Rist and the Tring heist. Instead of using costly and illegal feathers from exotic species, as many tiers do, Seim uses dyed feathers from ordinary game birds like turkeys and pheasants.

Edward "Muzzy" Muzeroll, with the Victorian salmon flies that first caught the attention of thirteen-year-old Edwin Rist at the Northeast Fly-tying Championship. Before long, Edwin's father had arranged for his son to take private fly-tying lessons with Muzzy.

Edwin Rist in the summer of 2004, learning to tie his first salmon fly under Muzzy's supervision.

Tied by Edwin Rist

Durham Ranger

The Durham Ranger, the first salmon fly Edwin tied, following George Kelson's 1840 recipe. Edwin used cheaper substitute feathers, but at the end of the session, Muzzy handed him a small envelope filled with $250 worth of rare feathers and whispered, "*This* is what it's all about."

Lord Lionel Walter Rothschild was born into a family of legendary bankers but was drawn to the natural world. By the age of twenty, he had obsessively collected over 46,000 specimens. For his twenty-first birthday, his father built him a private museum in the corner of the Rothschild estate at Tring Park outside London. Upon his death in 1937, Rothschild's museum was bequeathed to the British Natural History Museum.

The Tring Museum today, now home to one of the greatest ornithological collections in the world. Late one evening in June 2009, twenty-year-old American virtuoso flautist and Royal Academy of Music student Edwin Rist broke through a rear window and pulled off one of the largest specimen thefts in history.

Inside one of Tring's corridors of specimen cabinets, like the one Edwin walked down the night of the heist.

A tray of Scarlet Minivets in one of the Tring's cabinets. Over the course of several hours, Edwin filled a suitcase with birds from sixteen different species and subspecies, selecting only the brightly plumaged adult male specimens.

The Tring Museum's press release calling on the public to come forward with any information regarding the theft included this photo of the species the thief had targeted: Red-ruffed Fruitcrow, Resplendent Quetzal, Cotingas, and Birds of Paradise, several of which had been collected by Alfred Russel Wallace.

Over sixteen months, Edwin sold feathers and skins obtained during the heist on eBay, through his personal website, and on an online forum popular with fly-tiers, ClassicFlyTying.com. This "mix pack" of feathers plucked from the stolen birds, including several species and subspecies of Indian Crow and Blue Chatterer, was posted to the ClassicFlyTying.com trading floor the night before his arrest.

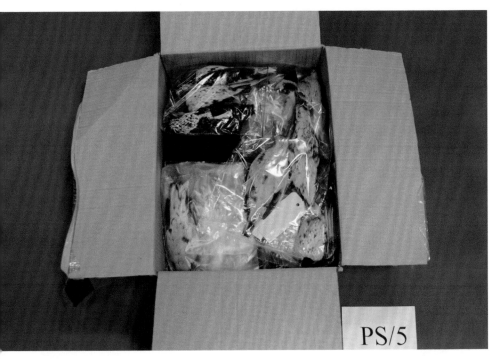

A box of Cotinga skins stored in Ziploc bags that was recovered from Edwin's apartment on the morning of November 12, 2010. Curators were dismayed to find that many of the specimens were missing their labels, without which they were of little to no scientific value.

Twelve Resplendent Quetzals, some missing their tail feathers, also recovered by the police. Bags stuffed with hundreds of iridescent green-tipped feathers, intended for sale on eBay or the forum, were also seized.

Detective Sergeant Adele Hopkin, who received the tip that led to Edwin's arrest; Mark Adams, senior curator of ornithology at the Tring Museum; and Detective Inspector Fraser Wylie of the Hertfordshire Constabulary *(l. to r.)*, with some of the recovered bird skins.

Edwin Rist, twenty-two, arriving at the Hemel Hempstead Magistrate's Court for his initial sentencing hearing on November 26, 2010. The case was referred to the Crown Court after prosecutors argued that the sentencing powers of a magistrate judge were insufficient for such a serious crime.

A decadent display of exotic plumes, including Indian Crow, Blue Chatterer, Resplendent Quetzal, Jungle Cock, Argus Pheasant, and the Banksian Cockatoo. Fly-tiers frequently show off their materials in what is sometimes referred to as "feather porn."

A series of Indian Crow flies, resting on the breastplates of the bird skins from which the feathers used to tie them were harvested. Among these are flies tied by the Québécois Luc Couturier, a master tier who was the first to encourage Edwin to pay a visit to the Natural History Museum in Tring.

An 1849 color plate of the Wheatley no. 8, an 1849 salmon fly whose recipe calls for King Bird of Paradise and Resplendent Quetzal feathers. Several Victorian flies call for such expensive and rare materials that it is considered an achievement just to tie one.

A pair of Wheatley no. 8 flies tied by Long Nguyen, one of Norway's greatest fly-tiers.

Long Nguyen at work on a Thorndyke Fly, designed for use in the rivers of middle Norway.

more questions, each carefully crafted to pierce through any deception. I would nail him to the wall with a meticulously organized folder of printouts of the Wayback Machine forum posts, screenshots of his various sales, the transcript of my interview with Edwin, and Facebook comments and photos tying him to critical points in the timeline.

While my fellow passengers slept, I batted around fantasies of tripping him up and getting him to admit to having the missing skins, then waving Interpol agents in from the woods.

There was another image in my folder: an ultrasound. Only days before my flight departed, we'd learned that Marie-Josée was pregnant.

Somewhere over Greenland, my seatmate, an American woman in her forties with a hot pink pillow sausaged around her neck, turned to me with an eager smile and asked, "Do you *live* in Sweden?"

"No." I stared at the in-flight map tracing a red line between Los Angeles and Oslo, searching for an appropriate response. "I live in L.A."

She nodded her head and said, "I am *so* excited!"

The Norwegian countryside looked familiar to my midwestern eyes—barns painted tomato red, hay baled tidily before winter, Christmas-green forests of spruce spotted with faded-gold clusters of birch. I had pressured Long into letting me interview him at his home in the small village of Asker, some thirty minutes by train southwest of the capital down the Oslofjord. I didn't want to confront him in a crowded café, and I had the outlandish hope that he might leave an incriminating piece of evidence in plain sight—a wing poking out from a box in the closet, or an iridescent glimmer under the couch.

It was late morning when the conductor announced our arrival at Bondivann, a secluded station tucked between a sliver of forest and a teardrop-shaped lake.

My phone buzzed with a text from my brother: "You're in Jo Nesbø country . . . watch out!"

Long Nguyen greeted me with a broad, toothy smile and twinkling eyes. He had a bowl cut of tousled jet-black hair. Edwin had told me that Long, like all Norwegians, was "basically a millionaire" as a result of the country's oil wealth, but as I shook his hand, I saw a modestly dressed student: Chuck Taylors, tattered jeans, a flannel shirt, and a thin winter coat. He was in his last year of graduate studies in landscape architecture, but apart from that, I knew very little about him.

As he led me through a forest path toward his home, we made nervous small talk about the weather, my hotel, and how expensive things were in Norway. I thought of my brother's text and half expected Edwin to jump out from behind the pines. At last we emerged into a complex of four-story apartment buildings that looked like they had been built in the sixties. Thick paint the color of sockeye salmon coated the balconies.

As he fidgeted with his keys at the front door, I could hear a bird chirping with joy at the sound of his master's return. His back turned to me, I dropped a pin on Google maps on my phone and sent it off to Marie-Josée, just in case.

I scanned the dimly lit apartment he shared with one of his sisters. Various unframed paintings and charcoal sketches of birds adorned the walls; vases and jars filled with peacock feathers were wedged into bookshelves; and neon-colored fish flitted about in a hundred-gallon aquarium.

Before my eyes could fully adjust, a bright flash of emerald exploded from another room and headed right at my face. A Green-Cheeked Conure flapped like a heat-seeking missile onto my shoulder, where it began shrieking in my ear.

"Meet Rin," Long said with a laugh, as he went off to the kitchen to prepare tea.

As I stroked the parrot's cheeks, it closed its eyes like a kitten and nuzzled against my finger. Rin and I wandered over to the bookshelf, where I found piles of manga on the lower shelves, beneath a carefully arranged collection of early-edition classics of the fly-tying genre. On top was a small bamboo picture frame with a photo of Long and Edwin in Japan.

I turned a corner and found myself directly in front of the painting of exotic birds I'd seen on his Facebook page, which had led me to link his identity to Goku's. He'd said online that it had been a gift for Edwin, but he'd obviously changed his mind since then.

"I guess you'll want to see my fly-tying desk," a voice said from behind me.

My heart accelerated as I entered his bedroom, which wasn't much larger than a closet. His bed was a narrow twin mattress without a frame. The rest of the cramped room was dominated by a large desk at which he tied his flies. I'd seen a number of workstations before, but never one this messy.

"How do you find what you need?" I asked.

"Every fly just takes twice as long," he replied slowly, and I realized he was watching me scan his room. I suddenly felt like an intruder. I'd traveled thousands of miles after convincing this person, who was wary of me for obvious reasons, not only to let me into his inner sanctum but to allow recording equipment so that I could capture every uncomfortable moment of the conversation.

We decided to talk in the kitchen, where Rin's refrigerator-size cage claimed a third of the room. With his bird on my shoulder, I found a seat at the table, which was cluttered with business cards of various fly-tiers and coils of silkworm gut. Another fish tank sat on the countertop, only this one was dank and nearly empty of water, sporous growth streaking up its sides like smoke. If Long was a millionaire, he certainly hadn't let it affect his lifestyle.

Long poured some tea, set out a loaf of bread, some butter, and slices of brown caramel-flavored Norwegian cheese, and began to unfurl the story of his life.

He was the same age as Edwin, born in 1988 in Trondheim, the old Viking capital of Norway. His parents had fled Vietnam during the Boat People Crisis of the mid-1970s, reaching Norway after a protracted spell in Malaysia. Long was the third of four children. His dad worked long hours in restaurants and liked to fish for salmon in his downtime—his tackle box was filled with brightly colored lures.

Long began drawing birds when he was three. He was interested in little else, sketching what winged overhead and copying what he found in books. When he was six, his mom died of lung cancer. As the family gathered around her bedside in the final moments, Long didn't understand what was happening. His father, nearly destroyed by the loss, withdrew into himself, spending less and less time with his children and succumbing to a gambling addiction. Social workers were soon dropping by the house to check on the children, taking them to doctors' appointments and school functions.

When he was ten, Long and his brother were sent to live in what he called "the institution," a home for boys in troubled circumstances. He still attended the same school, but because he never felt comfortable inviting classmates over, he didn't develop deep friendships.

In his solitude, he began to tie flies, trying to replicate what he could remember of his dad's tackle box. He found a magazine on salmon flies and immersed himself, tying as soon as he got back from school, sometimes missing dinner, huddled over the vise until it was time to sleep, tuning out the rest of the world. Sometimes a single fly would take months to finish: he'd get a third of the way through and realize the pattern required a feather he didn't have or couldn't afford. He took an after-school job in a local pet shop and began to save up so that he could buy the materials he needed.

One of his teachers, a kind woman named Greta, recognized that the precocious boy needed attention and affirmation. When she learned of his fly-tying talent, she and her husband, who had become like parents to Long and his siblings, took him on a special trip to Denmark, where he met Jens Pilgaard at his Fugl & Fjer Fluebinding feather shop. For the first time, Long saw full skins of Indian Crow, Blue Chatterer, and other exotic birds. Jens, who ensured that all his materials were legally sourced with CITES permits, took him under his wing, tutoring him in fly-tying techniques and gifting the occasional feather. Over the years, they grew close.

By his late teens, he was already one of Norway's finest fly-tiers. He joined the ClassicFlyTying.com forum and collected admirers and friends throughout the globe. Adults asked him for tips on certain techniques and complimented the pictures of flies and paintings of birds he occasionally shared online.

But nothing made him as proud as when he caught the eye of the great Edwin Rist. Long had read about the American tier in magazines, marveled at his flies, and couldn't believe that he was now trading messages with the "future of fly-tying" himself.

I tried to summon a hard edge, hoping not to be swayed by the obviously earnest and fractured soul pouring me tea in his modest kitchen, but Long was clearly not the person I'd imagined.

"What birds did he send you?" I blurted out.

"I had a couple skins he sent me," he replied calmly. "I wanted to trade that painting, actually . . ." He trailed off.

"The skins of what?"

"He sent me some Cotinga, and I think he sent me one golden . . . what's it called?" He searched for the word in English. "The Flame Bowerbird."

"He didn't want me to know about the truth behind the birds, that they were stolen," he continued, as I rooted through my backpack for the folder of evidence.

"How many birds did he send in total?"

"I really can't remember, but I think it was like three, maybe four."

The story hewed suspiciously close to what Edwin had told me. It wouldn't have been difficult for them to coordinate their story—but then again, they might have overlapped because they were both telling the truth.

I pulled out all the screenshots I'd taken of Goku's activity and began to read the exact date and time of each post: "Flame Bowerbird, male, full skin," "Indian Crow cape for sale," "Purple-Breasted Cotinga skin for sale." Long interjected to say that he'd never physically held those items—that he'd only been creating the posts on Edwin's behalf, but I reminded him that Edwin already had an eBay account, a website, and knew how to make posts on the forum.

"Why on earth would he need your help?" I asked.

"It doesn't make sense, I think," he said in a chastened tone.

I battered him with questions about each sale, asking who bought what, but Long said he couldn't remember anything, including whether it had been he or Edwin who received the money.

"You *would* remember, though, wouldn't you?! I'm not trying to be an asshole, but you would remember. These things were thousands of dollars! Don't you think you would remember?"

Rin, still perched on my shoulder, was getting agitated.

"I don't think I sold things for thousands of dollars," he said. "What I remember most is selling small amounts, like packages of feathers."

"Did he send you those to then mail to buyers?"

"I don't remember."

Rin started shrieking so loudly, my ear began to ring. I was getting frustrated. Long's reputation had been grievously tarnished by his association with Edwin. Jens, his erstwhile mentor, had shared with me the e-mail in which he cut ties with Long, whom he viewed as a son, over his involvement with the stolen birds. He'd been called everything from Edwin's fence to the mastermind behind the heist. How could he have forgotten the details about the event in his life that had cost him so dearly?

"I spent four years trying to forget all this," he said, sensing my mood. "You're trying to bring it all to the surface. It's really hard, though, because I'm trying for so long to just put this behind me. The details are quite unclear to myself because I'm trying to close this case."

"Yeah, me too," I muttered.

"Edwin told me that you were one of the first calls he made after he got arrested." Searching for a different way in, I asked, "What did he say to you?"

"He told me everything. Then I realized everything I've been doing. . . . I thought I was helping a friend! Instead, I was really shooting my own leg. I thought I should be nice to Edwin, being very naïve. But it was like totally backstabbing a friend . . . the worst thing you can do. What he did was horrible."

Long told me he mailed the few skins he had back to the Tring shortly thereafter. After realizing how his posts might be construed, he panicked and began to erase his digital tracks. "That's why I deleted all the posts on the forum, because it seems like I've been behind the whole scenario," he said, but now recognized that it only made his involvement more suspicious. He had a forlorn look. "That was totally idiotic."

Bit by bit, over the subsequent hours of the interview, his memory yielded small confirmations: he remembered receiving money through PayPal, which he would then forward to Edwin. I asked if

Edwin paid him for this service, and he admitted that he'd received some feathers as payment. Just as the community of fly-tiers engaged in bidding wars over exotic birds, he too fell under their spell: he wanted Blue Chatterer and Indian Crow feathers so badly that he hadn't stopped to think clearly about how a student flautist had come to possess so many rare skins.

I read from the transcript of my conversation with Edwin, in which he blamed his arrest on Long, blaming him for talking indiscreetly about the birds he'd received. I hadn't yet discovered that Edwin was mistaken—that it wasn't Long who had blown his cover but rather the Dutchman Andy Boekholt, who had shown a suspicious bird to Irish. I glanced up to find a wounded look on Long's face.

"What should I feel? I didn't know this until now. He never mentioned that it was because of *me* that . . ." He trailed off. "I don't feel bad," he said, as though he were trying to convince himself. "I feel sorry for him. I don't support his actions, but I support him as a friend." He spun in circles, alternating between anger and hurt.

In his wounded state, I brought up the topic of the missing skins once again.

"Many people would probably think that I possessed those skins," he said quietly.

"Why?"

"Because I was closely related to Edwin. . . . That would be a natural thing to assume."

"Do you have them?"

"No."

"How can you prove it?"

"I can't prove it."

"Then the question becomes, where are they?"

"I don't know."

"But how is that possible?" I said in exasperation. "How do you not know?! You and Edwin."

"I don't know because only a tiny part was sold through me. . . . The rest, he was selling not through me."

We sat in silence. The sun had set hours ago, and the groceries he'd purchased—pasta, a bottle of wine, vegetables, and ingredients for a Norwegian brown sauce—were all still in grocery bags. The last train back to Oslo was imminent.

Ten hours after I'd arrived, we shuffled down to the station, my head aching, my voice hoarse, and my stomach racked with hunger. As the train charged noisily into the station, he turned to me with a serious expression and said, "Look, I know the hand I played." The doors slammed shut before I had a chance to follow up. I had no idea if I'd ever see him again.

On the way back to my hotel in Oslo, I mulled over what he'd said. If this was an admission of guilt, it wasn't cathartic, either for him or for me. If it was a declaration of innocence, it wasn't very convincing.

I made quick work of the hotel's unfortunate minibar—cans of chili nuts, chocolate bars, and vinegar potato chips—chased the ensuing stomachache with Ambien, and went to sleep.

I was roused from my slumber by an early-morning phone call from the front desk informing me that a Mr. Long was waiting for me in the lobby. Bleary-eyed, I descended to find him perched on the arm of a sofa with a concerned look on his face.

As we headed out in search of caffeine, I realized how shaken he had been by the interview. He said he was thinking about giving up fly-tying but was worried that the friends he'd made through the hobby might not like him anymore. He kept asking me questions about how to live an ethical life, and whether it was possible to be both environmentally conscientious and a citizen in the modern world. Hadn't I negated a lifetime's worth of recycling simply by flying to Oslo? he asked. Hadn't the animal that yielded the leather in my belt suffered? What about eating meat?

"Long, I'm not sure this is a question of animal welfare. . . . We're talking about a felony heist of dead birds."

He nodded gravely.

As we wandered around Oslo, I sensed he felt that now that the interview was behind us, we could just hang out, maybe even strike up a friendship.

Given our discussion of animals and skins, I couldn't resist ducking into a storefront that had a decadent display of furs. Inside, a large taxidermy polar bear was frozen on its haunches in a menacing posture. A mounted baby seal stretched out on a nearby table. The manager, an elegant woman with ink-black hair, looked at the two of us skeptically: we didn't appear as though we could afford what she was selling.

In the corner of the shop were eight shelves stacked with polar bear skins, ten in total. The smaller females were $25,000 each; the larger males started at $50,000. I stood in front of the largest skin, the bear's jaw opened wide, teeth flared. As a rug, it would take up fifteen square feet. When I told the woman that I was an American, she scoffed and said there was no way I could bring a polar bear home now, thanks to Walter Palmer, the American dentist who had paid $54,000 for a guide in Zimbabwe to help him find a lion. When news broke that Cecil the Lion had been lured out of a sanctuary, shot, decapitated, and skinned, Palmer became the most hated dentist in the world. "You'll never get it through customs," she said, pronouncing *customs* with a sneer.

Back on the street, I was annoyed. Between Long's question about the environmental impact of the flight I'd taken and the discussion of Palmer, there seemed to be endless ways to rationalize bad behavior. Palmer had blamed the guide for luring a protected beast into the sights of his bow. Edwin had said he stole from an institution and not a person, an institution that he had concluded was no longer participating in any meaningful scientific research. Long had said he simply trusted a friend, never questioning how a fellow student suddenly came into possession of such priceless skins; now he was wondering whether meat eaters inflicted greater ecological damage than fly-tiers. If any fly-tiers had doubts about whether the feathers and skins they had were from the Tring, they eased their consciences by deciding that the museum's tally of missing skins was only a guess and an incorrect one at that.

I wanted someone to step forward and claim responsibility, to own up to their actions.

We walked around the Aker Brygge neighborhood, at the heart of which is the Thief Hotel. Even though he clearly hoped the interrogation was over, I couldn't resist reopening the topic.

"What was so great about your friendship with Edwin that you decided to stand by him after everything? At such a huge cost to your reputation?" I asked, referencing the public allegations on Facebook.

He shot me a pained look. "I thought that's what being a friend meant."

At the same time, Long admitted he didn't know Edwin all that well. When I asked why he would risk so much for someone he wasn't even all that close to, he exclaimed, "I idolized Edwin! He was the best tier of our generation. So when he asked me to help with raising money for a new flute, I was proud."

"You saw it as an honor," I volunteered.

"Yes, very much."

That night we went to a dinner party with four Norwegian fly-tiers, feasting on fresh-killed venison, clams, and aquavit. The more time I spent with Long, the sorrier I felt for him, and the angrier I grew toward Edwin, who must have sensed his friend's vulnerability and exploited it. He had involved Long in a crime without his knowledge, asking him to handle stolen goods, to accept and forward payments for illegal materials, at a time when he knew that British law enforcement was searching for them. Even during our interview in Düsseldorf, long after he'd escaped the grip of the law, Edwin still seemed content to let clouds hover over his friend.

On my last day in Norway, though, I woke up in an ornery mood. Somehow the purpose of the weekend seemed to have slipped from my grasp. Over some twenty hours of interrogation, Long's role had shrunk from mastermind of the Tring heist to unwitting victim, a vulnerable kid with abandonment issues whose ultimate crime had been to trust someone he shouldn't have. But I hadn't made any progress on the question of the missing skins. Even if Long had been naïve enough to believe Edwin's various fictions about the origin of the skins, he seemed frustratingly forgetful about the precise number of birds and feathers that had passed through his hands.

Had I been played? Had he preyed upon my empathy, supplying me with another version of events that I was all too ready to believe? I liked him. I wanted him to succeed in life, to emerge from this mess a better person. I didn't want to unleash Adele or Interpol agents on him. But I had a nagging feeling that something had gone unsaid, and I wouldn't be content until I knew what it was.

He offered to meet me on the front steps of the National Gallery. Twenty-one years earlier, on the first day of the 1994 Winter Olympics, when the nation's attention was on Lillehammer, thieves had leaned a ladder against the gallery, climbed through a window, and made off with Edvard Munch's *The Scream*. In its place, they left a postcard with a handwritten note: "Thanks for the poor security!" For years, Pål Enger, the ringleader, hid the masterpiece in a secret compartment in his kitchen table.

Long was in a chipper mood and made small talk as we headed down the street in search of lunch. I listened halfheartedly but eventually lost patience and erupted: "I think you've been honest with me, Long, but it feels like you're still holding something back. There were so many steps to this! He sent you the birds, skins, he sent you feathers already prepared in bags! He sent you the photos! He asked you to mail them! He asked you to take the payments and forward the money to him!"

I stole a glance at him. He was looking down at the pavement, hands in his coat pockets, as cars and strollers whizzed past.

"Even if you were a trusting person and looked up to Edwin," I continued, "it seems like there were so many steps where a reasonable person would say 'What is going on here?!' And you're not a dummy! You're a very bright, talented person."

After a pause as long as a city block, he spoke. "I feel like there shouldn't be any reason to believe me, because it sounds too . . . too illogical."

His voice was soft. "I feel like just being in that situation is so hopeless. I'm not holding anything back, but it feels like being trapped inside this cage. It doesn't matter what I tell."

"No!" I shot back. "Nothing's hopeless. It *does* matter what you say. I've heard from two people in the last year, for example, that you've told them that you have tons of Indian Crow . . . and I don't know what to make of that, whether to doubt what they're saying or doubt you. I'm just trying to—"

"Extract the truth," he offered quietly.

"So what am I supposed to do with that knowledge?" I asked.

"You do whatever you need—"

"But is it true?"

"Yeah." He seemed to be shrinking before my eyes, his voice growing fainter, his pace slowing.

"You have a lot of Indian Crow?"

"I have . . . I still have some of the packages of the ones I was supposed to sell."

He had opened the door a crack, and I came barging through.

"How many?"

"Um . . . a hundred and ten maybe?"

"Birds?!" I exclaimed.

"No, just feathers."

"What are the species?" I asked, trying to keep my composure.

"*Granadensis. Pyroderus scutatus scutatus. Pyroderus scutatus occidentalis.* I think it's around a hundred and ten. It could be around a hundred or a hundred and twenty."

"But we're in 2015 now. What did you have four years ago?"

He was clearly in agony. I knew he was hungry, but I kept flogging us forward, nixing his restaurant suggestions, unwilling to let anything interrupt the moment.

He sighed. "It's really hard to just number because there's a low number in each package. And I didn't count those packages, like how many packages and how many feathers. . . . I don't remember how many were sold. I think maybe I sold half of them, and then I had half the packages." I knew he had a number in mind, and that he was fighting like hell not to mention it.

Finally, after much prodding, he estimated the total number of loose feathers at between six hundred and eight hundred.

We stepped into Arakataka, an upscale Nordic restaurant a mile or so from the gallery. Under any other circumstances, eating at a place like this would have been a special occasion: how many chances does one get to have fried cod tongue or cabbage and razor clam? But Long was in the process of admitting something he'd never told a soul. And the act of telling me meant letting go of a narrative he'd been embracing for years: that the community of fly-tiers had unfairly maligned his reputation by accusing him of involvement with Edwin. He was coming to acknowledge the uncomfortable truth of what they said at last.

The waiter was walking away with our order when I leaned forward and asked, for maybe the twelfth time that weekend, how many skins Edwin had sent him to sell. For the first two days, he'd held firm at only three or four, but in the wake of the admission, I had to ask: "How many skins, Long? Was it ten? Or was it fifty?"

"It was between ten and twenty," his voice barely audible over the Norwegian pop music. "But definitely nothing like fifty skins."

I leaned back in the booth. Depending on the species, the value of twenty skins could be anywhere between $20,000 and $125,000. If the feathers had been plucked and sold retail, the number would only climb. The value of eight hundred Indian Crow feathers, presumably part of his payment from Edwin, could top $7,000.

His eyes were worriedly searching mine for some kind of reaction.

"Long, you know you have to show me them, right?"

"Yes." The weight of the admission pressed down upon us, dimming the world beyond our table. I looked up and saw tears streaking down his cheeks. Embarrassed, he excused himself and hurried off to the bathroom.

When he finally returned to the table, our waiter cheerfully appeared with our feast, placing a large crab with a pitiful hole cracked into its shell before me. Long stared down blankly at a plate of monkfish and hake. Neither of us had much of an appetite.

I thought back to Edwin's bravura performance in Düsseldorf, how he'd emphatically declared that Long was in no way involved but then grinned when he acknowledged that the case against his friend "looks bad." I remembered that Edwin had reached out to Long immediately after our interview, suggesting that he speak with me.

"What did Edwin tell you to say to me?" I asked. "Did he tell you to lie to me?"

"He said that you're not my friend, that we shouldn't become friends. He said 'We don't owe him anything,' and that I should get you to pay for all the food and everything."

I laughed. "Where did you hide the feathers before I came?"

"I just had them in a box."

We barely spoke on the train back out to Asker. While I was about to see what I'd spent years searching for, what I felt was not triumph but concern: what would happen to Long if I told Adele about his involvement? It was pitch-black when we got off at

Bondivann station. He dragged his feet as we made our way through the woods, as if I might change my mind, or a meteor might strike and relieve him of the need to show me the feathers.

Halfway up the path, I asked him how he felt. He stopped to catch his breath. He was in good shape, but in this moment he was exhausted. "I feel empty."

He emerged from his apartment with a small stamp album. It had a translucent gray cover with some Japanese writing on it. Our plan was to walk to a bar somewhere in Asker to look through it, but I couldn't wait.

Under a streetlamp just outside town, I opened it up to find feathers arrayed like stamps, five rows per page, with plastic sleeves protecting the plumes, which glittered like tiny orange, sapphire, and turquoise gems against the black background. The first page alone held over fifty Indian Crow and Blue Chatterer feathers.

I tried to mask my exhilaration as I pulled out my phone and took photos of each page, keeping a rough tally of the feathers. As I turned the pages, I thought of the chain of events that had led to this moment: hundreds of years of specimen collecting, a youthful love of fly-tying that had mutated into something disastrous, the meticulous plot and heist itself, the chance encounter with Spencer on a river in New Mexico. At the same time, I realized that I was looking at a minute fraction of what was still missing from the Tring—all together, they might have amounted to only one bird's worth of feathers.

I handed him the album.

As we headed off in search of a pint, I asked him how it felt to show them to me.

"I haven't felt this bad since my mom died," Long said after a lengthy silence. He said he didn't even feel comfortable looking at them and wanted to get rid of them.

He asked if I could take them with me and return them to the Tring. I smiled. I had hoped to leave Norway with a suitcase full of bird skins, with tags attached. As much as I would've enjoyed sending the album to the museum, I declined, saying that the decision was his to make.

"What will the museum do with them?" he asked hopefully.

"Probably nothing, honestly. They're going to put them in a drawer, and they'll sit there until long after we're gone."

24
MICHELANGELO VANISHES

Months after my return, Long wrote to say that his grades had plummeted. Since the interview, he felt as though his "life source had drained away," and he was ashamed that he had become so obsessed with something that had such a dark side. But when I asked if he'd sent the feathers back to the museum, he said he hadn't yet found the time. I was beginning to worry that he wouldn't break free from their pull. Even so, I wasn't going to notify Adele about my discovery. Long had made his share of mistakes, but it bothered me that he seemed to be suffering the consequences of the Tring heist more than Edwin himself.

Edwin had used him, setting him up as a fence, so that anyone digging into the crime would find a great big **X** marking someone else. Why else have Long make posts to the forum on his behalf? Why send feathers and skins to Norway for Long to ship them to his own customers? Why ask Long to handle payments through his own PayPal account, if not to set him up as the fall guy? There was no other way to interpret Edwin's actions than as creating a smoke-screen, implicating a friend who idolized him while he took the money and ran.

What kind of person would do this? In the aftermath of my interview with Long, with Edwin's actions seeming so transparently calculated, I was even more skeptical about the Asperger's diagnosis. Could he really have faked it?

My first attempt to speak about it with Dr. Simon Baron-Cohen fizzled quickly: he told me that, for obvious ethical reasons, he could not discuss details of the case without Edwin's permission. But when I asked him if, in theory, someone could fake Asperger's, he replied that the diagnosis ultimately relied on clinical judgment.

"There is no biological test of autism," he wrote. "This means, as with any psychiatric diagnosis, that in principle someone could fake it by providing false information in answer to a clinician's interview questions, but even then clinical judgment and experience (is the person lying?) comes into play."

Baron-Cohen was asking me to trust his judgment, but after reading a copy of his report to the court, which was leaked to me from someone close to Edwin, I found basic errors—that Edwin "had not been motivated by money" and that he didn't think he had "done anything bad in taking the stuffed birds." Baron-Cohen's misreading was perhaps the unavoidable consequence of a single evaluation. I'd spent years building a timeline of the crime; the Cambridge psychopathologist had met him for a couple hours.

Or perhaps it was an unavoidable consequence of the squishiness of the diagnosis process itself. In his report to the court, Baron-Cohen buttressed his diagnosis by citing Edwin's "scores" on the Adult Asperger's Assessment, but there was ample reason to doubt the validity of answers to questions like "I find it easy to work out what someone is thinking or feeling just by looking at their face." In a 2011 *Nature* article, Francesca Happé, a cognitive neuroscientist at King's College London, voiced her skepticism of Baron-Cohen's diagnostic tool: "Whether those self-perceptions, as with any of our self-perceptions, are accurate is questionable." Baron-Cohen's adviser, Uta Frith, echoed Happé: "Rigorous studies are still missing. . . . At the moment, he has people saying 'yes, I'm a person interested in details,' as opposed to actually observing them on tasks."

Two years after the diagnosis spared Edwin from prison, the American Psychiatric Association expunged the disorder from the fifth edition of the *Diagnostic and Statistical Manual of Mental Disorders*. The controversial shift—dropping Asperger's as a stand-alone disorder only nineteen years after it was included in the previous edition—happened "in large part because studies revealed little consistency in how the diagnosis was being applied," according to *The Atlantic*'s Hanna Rosin. After extensive review, the authors of an *Archives of General Psychiatry* report found that children with similar test scores were given different diagnoses: "Whether a child was labeled as having Asperger's or diagnosed instead with autism, or some other developmental disorder, depended mostly on the clinician's somewhat arbitrary interpretation."

In an op-ed about the decision to drop Asperger's from the *DSM-V*, Baron-Cohen wrote, "Psychiatric diagnoses are not set in stone. They are 'manmade,' and different generations of doctors sit around the committee table and change how we think about 'mental disorders.'"

———

I sensed that I was coming to the end of the road. Edwin was no longer replying to my e-mails, and the truth about Long had been revealed. But as thrilled as I was to lay my eyes on Long's album of feathers, I knew that I hadn't yet solved the mystery, and that the bulk of the Tring's missing birds were still out there. In a final search for clues, I combed through more than a thousand pages of transcripts of all the people I'd interviewed over the years, but I found that I couldn't stop thinking about the one person close to the story who had so far eluded me.

The Tring's curators told me their suspicions initially fell upon the Québécois tier Luc Couturier after discovering an e-mail from him, dated two years prior, asking whether the museum would be willing to sell a number of their Indian Crow skins. They declined, offering to sell a high-resolution photograph of the bird instead. It was an unusual enough request that they mentioned it to Adele in the early phase of her investigation, but she ruled him out as a suspect.

In Düsseldorf, Edwin had told me that his former mentor, whom he described as the Michelangelo of fly-tying, had not only been inside the Tring's bird vault at some point in the nineties—which the museum disputes—but had first encouraged him to visit the museum. At one point in the interview, Edwin said he'd sent Long some skins because he thought his friend "deserved them" for his flies. I wondered: had he also sent some to Couturier?

My suspicion mounted as I trawled through Couturier's inactive LinkedIn account and noticed that he was "connected" with Dr. Paul Sweet, the bird skins collection manager at the American Museum of Natural History in New York. I fired a note off to Sweet, who revealed that in April 2010, Couturier had asked to be granted access to the museum's collection of Birds of Paradise, Cotingas, and Indian Crows. When the curators asked for a reason, Couturier's response—"to refine my knowledge and test some of my hypotheses"—didn't pass scientific muster. He was denied entry.

I messaged Couturier in the forums, but his account hadn't been active for years. I pried an e-mail address from another tier but never heard back. I befriended other Couturiers on Facebook in search of him, but he seemed to have vanished.

The only other person I could think to ask was John McLain. When I reached him, he was holed up in his basement, dyeing feathers and sorting orders from across the globe. The last time he'd seen Couturier was the 2009 Somerset show, where he'd arranged for him to share a room with Bud Guidry, the administrator of ClassicFlyTying.com, who was hoping to keep travel costs down.

Couturier had a reputation for being erratic, so when Guidry reported that Couturier had stolen his credit card and run up a thousand dollars in charges that weekend, McLain cut ties with the French-Canadian.

To find him, McLain suggested I reach out to a friend of Couturier's named Robert Delisle. Before long, I was clicking through a massive Facebook album of exotic bird skin photos. In one, there were five Cotingas, all in perfect condition, arrayed like a fan on Delisle's tying bench. In another, a full Indian Crow skin with cotton eyes. In another were dozens of museum-quality skins.

I sent him a message, asking if he could connect me to Couturier, but Delisle told me he was no longer reachable. Couturier, he shared, lost his job in 2010. Over the past few years, Delisle had spent $40,000 buying up every last scrap of material from his hard-pressed friend. After selling off his rare skins and feathers, Couturier was no longer tying flies.

"Was there a lot of Indian Crow and Cotinga?" I asked eagerly, while Marie-Josée, who was born in Montreal, corrected my French.

The details appeared on the screen one line at a time: Couturier had "ten Indian Crows, five Western Tragopan, three Resplendent Quetzals, two Gymnogene Bustards, and all of the chatterers," referring to the seven species of Blue Chatterer, one of which is endangered.

"What about the Birds of Paradise?" I asked.

"Of course," he wrote, "I can't enumerate it all, but he had everything."

Heart thumping, I asked him if the skins still had tags on their feet. After a long pause, Delisle replied: "*Oui.*"

When I asked if I could see them, he told me he'd get back to me.

Instinctively, I returned to Delisle's Facebook page and pored over hundreds of photos of flies, hooks, and bird skins, in search of more evidence. I texted McLain an image of three full Indian Crow skins surrounded by eight severed and plucked breastplates: all that remained where the fiery orange feathers once shined was a leathery expanse of dried skin.

"That's a lot of empty shell casings," the detective texted back. "Must have been quite a gun fight."

Delisle didn't appear worried about raising suspicions when displaying his collection. There was a Superb Bird of Paradise patch in one photo. Another showed skins of all seven species of Blue Chatterer, next to feathers from Cock of the Rock, Western Tragopan, and two different subspecies of Indian Crow. All the plumes were neatly fanned out on a large patch of polar bear skin. If I could prove that the birds he'd purchased from Couturier were from the Tring, I could potentially cross twenty birds off the list of missing skins.

But I soon made the discouraging realization that Delisle had an eBay account. If these were Tring birds, they were already gone. Under the handle Bobfly2007, he sold Flame Bowerbird plumes for $19.99, Resplendent Quetzal for $43 a pop, Indian Crow feathers for $139, and a full skin of the endangered *Cotinga maculata* for $417.50.

Combing through over two thousand of his completed auctions, I logged $11,911.40 in feather sales, giving eBay a commission of over $1,300. As I read through his customer reviews—"Excellent to deal with and very personable service" and "THANK YOU FOR THE FAST SHIPPING"—I wondered how eBay could permit such flagrant violations of CITES and other wildlife trafficking laws.

But the Delisle sales were small potatoes compared to other feather vendors I started unearthing on the auction site. A simple search for Flame Bowerbird, the species hit the hardest by the Tring theft, brought me to Doug Millsap's auction page, which he ran under the handle lifeisgood.503: a pair of feathers were priced at $24. When I noticed a full skin in the background of one of the auction photos, I messaged him, feigning an interest in buying the whole skin. He said it was mine for $1,800. While the Flame Bowerbird is not a protected species, it was not a commonly available bird in the fly-tying world prior to the Tring heist. "Most of these are part of a collection from the 1920's Victorian era," Millsap wrote, encouraging bidders to "check out my other auctions for rare and hard to find materials."

Based in Ocean Park, Washington, Millsap manages a pizza parlor with his wife, but he advertised a surprising amount of rare bird skins and feathers. Between two separate eBay accounts, he had so many seller feedback ratings that I had to hire a research assistant to import the data into my spreadsheet. A "gorgeous vintage" Scarlet Macaw sold for $490, a Blue and Gold Macaw for $650, and a full Blue Chatterer skin for $1,675. As the species began to appear in row after row—Blue Chatterer, twelve-wire Bird of Paradise, Penguin, Banksian Cockatoos—the tally of revenue quickly cleared $80,000.

Though eBay's Wildlife and Animal Products policy advises its users to follow international treaties like CITES and domestic laws like the Migratory Bird Treaty Act, the company appeared to be doing little to preempt or monitor for illegal sales.

It wasn't as if Delisle and Millsap were using code words to describe the birds. Many listings used the bird's Latin names, which would make it easy for eBay's screeners to surface the posts, if such screeners existed. You won't find any rhino horn on the site, but type in the endangered *Cotinga maculata* or Resplendent Quetzal, the sale of which is prohibited by Appendix I of CITES, and you can check out with PayPal and have it rushed to your front door by the U.S. Postal Service with an eBay money-back guarantee.

I sent several inquiries to eBay, but the company never replied. It wasn't until I sent it a list of hyperlinks to current auctions of endangered bird species, and asked how I was meant to interpret the commission that eBay earned in facilitating those illegal sales, that they wrote back.

Ryan Moore, senior manager for Global Corporate Affairs at eBay, responded within a few hours, sending over a heap of corporate jargon that made me shudder with the memory of the kinds of watered-down statements I had to write as a junior public affairs officer at the U.S. Agency for International Development in Baghdad.

"eBay is committed to doing what it can to protect endangered species," Moore wrote. The extra words did a lot of lifting: it wasn't that eBay *was* doing what it could but that it was "committed" to doing what it could.

"eBay has demonstrated a commitment to prohibiting the sale of illegal wildlife products on its site," Moore continued. It wasn't that eBay *had prohibited* the sale of illegal wildlife products, but that it had "demonstrated a commitment" to doing so.

Moore stressed that eBay had over eight hundred million listings and provided "examples and links to resources with more details about state, federal and international wildlife laws." He added that the company "actively enforces this policy through a rules-based filtering system and reporting mechanisms available to eBay members and government agencies; and through removal of products and/or sellers as appropriate." When I asked how the filtering system worked, and whether he could provide statistics on the number of auctions that had been halted by eBay, he was unwilling to share.

I drew his attention to a listing of feathers from *Cotinga maculata*, an endangered and protected species. By listing it under its Latin name, the seller had made no effort to keep a low profile, making it clear that whatever filtering system eBay had in place wasn't populated with terms from the International Union for Conservation of Nature's Red List, the central database of threatened species. Moore promised to look into it. When I refreshed the Cotinga auction page, it was gone.

But this was obviously damage control. Instead of flagging something with a press officer, I was curious to see what happened when I used eBay's online form. I reported an illegal auction of a pair of Resplendent Quetzal feathers, but a week later, with no action by the company, they sold for thirty-nine dollars.

Delisle had gone silent.

After years of picking off names one by one, I decided to make one public post in the forum, challenging the entire community to help me find the remaining skins. If Edwin was truly just a bad apple in the cart, I argued, why not collectively work to undo the damage to their reputation?

"The black eye of greed has surfaced again," replied Aaron Ostoj, an Oregon-based feather dealer whose family motto is "God, Family, Feathers." I'd first seen his name when he joked about some Indian Crow patches being "stolen from a natural history museum and sold at 3000% profit" a full four months before Edwin's arrest.

Ostoj and others weren't thrilled to see the Tring heist rehashed. Several complained that I was just "stirring the pot." One member angrily suggested that if I cared so much, I should donate money from my book advance to the museum. Val Kropiwnicki called me an ambulance chaser, before asking: "Maybe I'm just sick of witch hunts? Maybe we are all poisoned by this?"

Bud Guidry, the administrator, was pissed. He said that despite his best efforts, the subject of the Tring heist could only "be buried as deep as the shovel handle." He announced that he would leave my post up until it "went south . . . then I'll sweep it under the rug again till it comes up again later."

Shortly thereafter he wrote that he was being bombarded with private messages from people asking him to remove it.

Why were they so troubled? I wondered. I had only asked for help in recovering stolen items to the museum. I had even arranged it so that birds could be returned to the Tring anonymously.

Only hours after it went up, Guidry declared that my post would be deleted: "The members of this community have spoken. I give you all my word: when another mention of this subject or those involved are posted here, it will immediately be deleted."

Guidry told me that forty-one members had privately begged him to delete my inquiry.

25
FEATHERS IN THE BLOODSTREAM

Weeks later, when Robert Delisle finally replied, his story had changed. He now said there were no tags. When I asked a question about Couturier, he said he didn't know him. Sensing I was losing him, I wrote, "I just wanted to know when you bought the skins from him." After fifteen minutes, he wrote "Good luck" and never replied to me again.

Were the birds Delisle bought off Couturier from the Tring?

I was desperate to find out but didn't even know if Couturier was still alive: Marie-Josée had found an obituary in French for someone with his name. Unless I was prepared to start searching through the homeless shelters, morgues, and cemeteries of Montreal, Couturier was lost to the story.

Marie-Josée, only a month away from our baby's due date, sensed my disappointment but asked a clarifying question: "What if he's still alive, and he admits that they were from Edwin? Then what? Aren't they all gone anyway?"

"I would know, I guess," I grumbled, suddenly aware of the diminishing returns of my obsession.

In the beginning, the mystery of the Tring heist had been little more than a puzzle to distract me from the pressures of my work with the List Project. I'd spent years trying to get people to care about tens of thousands of refugees fleeing a war they no longer cared about. My campaign for a dramatic, speedy solution—an airlift of our interpreters—had failed spectacularly, and I knew that I was staring at a lifetime of incremental gains, if I was lucky.

Now as I trawled the Web for some sign of Couturier, I realized I was stuck in another endless struggle. I had anointed myself the rescuer of the Tring's birds, even though the museum had long ago written them off as lost to science and wasn't searching for them. With a guilty plea and a closed case, the police were no longer investigating. The community of fly-tiers clearly wanted nothing to do with my quest.

The Tring's spreadsheet had been the fragment of a map that launched my expedition, but all I ever discovered were ruins. Of the sixty-four skins I set out to find, I knew that the remains of two were in South Africa with Ruhan Neethling. If Long helped Edwin sell twenty skins, that brought it down to forty-two. If Couturier's skins were from the Tring, and Delisle's count was right, then I was down to twenty-two.

But I was always too late. Long had already sold off whatever skins he had. Even if I could tie Couturier's birds to the Tring, Delisle had already auctioned them off. Ruhan was preparing for the Rapture and couldn't care less about my mission. If Edwin had played me and still had them locked away in some long-term storage unit in Düsseldorf, I'd never know—he never spoke to me again after our interview.

The only ones I ever laid eyes on were Long's feathers, and I was beginning to worry that they wouldn't be returned to the Tring.

Even worse, I had uncovered additional museum thefts by other fly-tiers. A few years prior to the Tring burglary, at least two German natural history museums—in Stuttgart and Frankfurt—had been robbed of dozens of Indian Crow and Blue Chatterer skins. The thief was believed to have been an older American fly-tier who moonlighted as a pest control expert: while spraying for bugs, he had allegedly taped the skins inside his white coveralls. Marie-Josée worriedly asked if I was now on the hunt for more missing skins.

As more and more museum curators shared stories of specimen thefts, I thought of the two currents of humanity running through the story of the Tring's birds. In one coursed Alfred Russel Wallace, Rick Prum, Spencer, Irish the undercover detective, the league of curators who had shielded the birds from Zeppelins and the Luftwaffe, and the scientists who probed each skin for insights, adding to our collective understanding of the world in tiny increments.

Here were humans bound across centuries by the faith-based belief that these birds were worth preserving. That they might help future generations, trusting that the march of scientific progress would forever present new ways of looking at the same ancient skins.

In the other current ran Edwin and the feather underground, and the centuries of men and women who looted the skies and forests for wealth and status, driven by greed and the desire to possess what others didn't.

In the war between knowledge and greed, it sure seemed as though greed were winning.

———

In the last trip I took before our baby was born, I paid a visit to the battleground of a similar war that had been waged a hundred years earlier: the feather district of New York.

The pigeons puttering around on the sidewalk on the section of Broadway that cuts through Greenwich Village barely made way for the humans pounding by in sneakers and heels. The city has evolved around them, mostly upward, but the buildings of the old feather merchants still cast the same cold shadows they did 120 years ago, when a hundred thousand New Yorkers fashioned the jewels of the sky into hats.

I wandered about, imagining great big vats of dye on the upper floors, bulk dealers ruffling through thousands of skins, haggling over the cost per kilo. Feather men wheeling new deliveries of birds bagged from the Malay Archipelago down side streets, shooing away stray dogs hoping for something feathery to chew on. French immigrants getting by on the tricks of the Parisian *plumassier* trade, dyeing and shaping feathers in the tenement house attics of the nearby Quartier français. Mothers and daughters fluttering down from the Upper West Side to peruse the latest plumed fashions.

I stopped in front of the ornate cast-iron pilasters of 625 Broadway, where Ph. Adelson & Bro once showcased the latest "lines of Aigrettes, Paradise and Ostrich feathers." Inside, a line of high schoolers waited to order burritos from Chipotle.

I'd unearthed the address in an 1899 issue of *The Millinery Trade Review*, whose editors railed against the mounting success of the Audubon Society and the conservationists fighting to topple their business, condemning them in the name of the free market for attempting "to dictate to American women what they shall wear and to American merchants what they shall buy or sell or what they shall import."

When the Lacey Act and other early conservation laws were passed at the turn of the century, the men who filled these storefronts with bird skins were beside themselves. "The foolish laws that now exist are obeyed to the letter by the millinery trade," snarled the editors: "any more of the kind, however, will be strenuously opposed."

Behrman & Colton. Max Herman & Company. Velleman & Co. A. Hochheimer's. Eventually all were claimed by the compounding pressures of changing fashions, new laws, and most powerfully, a societal recognition that people had taken their need to possess beautiful birds too far.

I crossed Bleecker and stopped in front of a twelve-story building that had once housed the New York Millinery and Supply Co., Aronson's Fine Headwear, and the Colonial Hat Company. I'd read about a seizure of a number of Bird of Paradise plumes here just after the First World War.

It is now a PetSmart. A large poster of a Parrot near the front entrance proclaims: EXOTIC PETS IN BACK.

In a dark and gloomy back corner, beyond the labyrinth of organic cat food and life preservers for dogs, were four knee-high cages. I squatted down to find twenty Parakeets, blue and green. CHOOSE A COLORFUL COMPANION, encouraged a nearby sign. On the floor of one cage, an orange-beaked Society Finch—$23.99 (or $21.99 with a PetPerks membership)—was standing a bit unsteadily on a pile of wood chips, staring blankly at an aisle of scratching posts.

My phone vibrated with a text from Long.

He'd recently told me he felt like Tony Stark from *Iron Man*. In the movie, Stark, an international arms dealer, is injured by one of his own missiles, leading him to change his ways and confront evildoers. Long was excitedly planning to launch a movement called Sustainable Fly-tying, throwing his master-tier status behind the use of common feathers, fighting against his community's destructive addiction to exotic and protected birds.

I was proud of him, but when he screwed up his courage and finally made the announcement on his Facebook page, his fellow fly-tiers scoffed. Jorge Maderal, a Spaniard in charge of a private Facebook group devoted to buying and selling rare feathers, was unmoved—he said he needed to "feel the real essence of the feathers" and "the history." On ClassicFlyTying.com, sales of feathers and skins continued. On eBay, it was as easy as ever to buy and sell feathers from protected species.

"It's really hard to convince people to quit using exotics!" Long texted. He was discouraged. "People just laugh at me and don't really take me seriously." I thought back to something Edwin had told me about his understanding of human nature: that there was an allure in what people knew to be taboo. When I'd asked Edwin why he didn't just use substitute feathers that had been dyed to resemble the real thing, he winced: "The knowledge of its falsity eats at you . . . and all these people have been eaten by it. Including me."

The allure was indeed powerful. I remembered the tale of Eddie Wolfer, a fly-tier known for owning a live Blue Chatterer. A couple of years earlier he had been rushed to the hospital to undergo surgery for a brain tumor. While he was getting a plate installed in his skull, two fly-tiers knocked on his front door and convinced his girlfriend to sell the bird, which they killed and sold at the next fly-tying show. "That bird was my pet," he lamented in a post to the forum. "Those 2 SOBs have more money than God. How greedy people can be. You know who you are. I thought you were my friends."

I texted Long to see if he'd returned the feathers to the Tring. "Soon!" he replied.

———

Years after it all began, I found myself back in the Rio Grande river valley with Spencer, searching for trout. The Blue-Winged Olive mayflies were hatching, floating to the surface to dry their wings, hoping to take flight before being gobbled up. My cast was out of form—I spent half my time unsnagging flies from the piñon and ricegrass on the riverbanks. Spencer, on the other hand, could cast through bramble like a slingshot: pinching the fly, he pointed the rod tip forward and shot the line through the tiniest of openings.

In the half-decade since he first said the name Edwin Rist, the war in Iraq had ended and another had taken its place. I had fallen in love with Marie-Josée, dismantled the List Project, and moved to

Los Angeles. We had a baby boy, happy and healthy, whose eyes light up at the hummingbirds flitting about the feeder by his nursery window. The middle name we share belonged to my grandfather but also to someone who has become special to our family: Wallace.

Spencer and I went for long stretches without needing to speak, hitting a pocket of water, drifting flies into deep pools, looking for a flash below the surface, studying the size of the emerging mayflies.

I told Spencer about the e-mail I'd just received from Wallace's great-grandson, Bill. He told me that his ninety-three-year-old father, Richard, had been invited to Tring a few years ago to see Wallace's Birds of Paradise. When one of the trays was pulled out, it was empty.

Spencer clucked. After seeing how the fly-tying community had reacted to my appeal for the missing skins, he told me he felt compelled to become a reformer. He was working on a book in the spirit of Kelson but that stripped each Victorian fly recipe of the exotic species that had cast such a dark spell over the community. He was certain that salmon flies could be just as beautiful using feathers that were common and cheap.

On the best of days on the river, the life of vibrating devices and glowing screens disappears, and all that matters is the temperature of the water, the speed of its flow, the skittishness of the fish, the accuracy of the fly, and the neatness of the cast. It all felt so pure, so untouched and hopeful.

Dr. Prum had assailed Victorian fly-tiers for desperately clinging to a world that no longer existed, calling them "historical fetishists" searching for meaning in the modern world, but as soon as he said it, I knew it also applied in some measure to me. The rivers I fished were dammed right and left. Many were choked with effluent and agricultural waste from industrial mines and farms. Even the brown trout we stalked weren't "natural"; they had been shipped from the Black Forest region of Baden-Württemberg in 1883 and introduced into our streams. For the right to cast my fake flies to them, I bought permits from state departments of fish and game, which manage hatcheries that raise and release trout into the water.

Spencer and I sloshed upstream, while a hawk circled high overhead. Smaller birds mobbed it, thrashing at its wing and tail, but it orbited patiently, biding its time.

"Got a call from Roger Plourde the other day," he said, knowing of Plourde's less-than-subtle threat years earlier at the fly-tying symposium.

"Yeah?"

"He had tons of Flame Bowerbird he was selling."

"Really?"

"But when I told him that I was about to go fishing with you, he hung up."

The bloodhound in me wanted to scurry up the riverbanks and hop on a flight to Plourde's front door, but I knew I was finished. Even if I sent the Tring a definitive list with five hundred names of those who'd bought the severed remains of their birds, nothing would happen. The museum had no reason to pursue scientifically useless feathers.

On we waded, scrambling over fallen trees, silently gesturing at unsuspecting trout. The chill of the water made our legs drowsy and our boots heavy, but we waded upstream beneath the piñon and ravens as though the river would never end, searching for darting golden flashes beneath the surface.

———

That fall the men of the Victorian salmon-fly-tying world boarded flights from across the globe for the 26th International Fly Tying Symposium, which would be held once again at the DoubleTree in Somerset, New Jersey.

Chuck Furimsky, the director and promoter-in-chief, described it as "the ultimate candy store for fly-tiers . . . more of everything— more fly shops, more displays . . . more fly-tying secrets." John McLain, Roger Plourde, and a hundred celebrity tiers would be there.

The theme of the show: "Never Enough."

There would be no Fish and Wildlife agents descending on Somerset. Instead, they were focused on headline-grabbing busts of rhino horn and elephant ivory. A Canadian college student who had recently been caught at the border with fifty-one turtles taped to his legs, intended for sale to Chinese turtle soup fanatics, was sentenced to prison for five years. In a statement to the court, he thanked the U.S. justice system for "stopping the darkness of my greed and ignorance."

But the men at the Never Enough symposium knew they were safe. Those who kept the skins Edwin stole had only to snip the tags off to remove the evidence and keep the law at bay. Those who bought patches or plucked feathers knew that nothing could tie their quarry back to the crime.

From the skins, they harvested wings and breastplates and capes.

From the fragments, they harvested individual feathers.

Miserly tiers stowed them away in mothballed drawers to treasure in private moments. Others, aware that the Tring and law enforcement weren't even looking for them anymore, openly traded and sold them back and forth until the bulk of the birds had dissolved into the bloodstream of the feather underground.

Before long, stealing birds from museums was once again a laughing matter on the forum. When a member posted a photo of himself in front of a stuffed Florican Bustard at the Natural History Museum in London, one user replied: "Thank goodness it was protected by a case of glass. I can see the look of fear in that bustard's eyes."

Another forum member uploaded photos of mounted birds that he had recently taken during a visit to the Academy of Natural

Sciences in Philadelphia—Blue Chatterers, Great Green Macaws, and the Birds of Paradise.

The subject line: "Paging: Secret Agent Edwin Rist."

————

In January 2016 snow crunched under boots as the postman cut across the parking lot with a delivery for Dr. Robert Prys-Jones. Nearby, kids tugged sleds up the shallow hills of Tring Park for another run, the exhalations of their parents' cheers visible in the January chill. Inside Walter Rothschild's museum, wide-eyed children pressed palms to glass, eyeballing the stuffed polar bear before sprinting off to see the rhinoceros.

The address on the envelope was written in neat block lettering. No return address. A Norwegian postage stamp.

When the staffer opened it, there was no letter. Just a Ziploc bag full of feathers, black and orange and crimson. After some discussion, a curator carried it down the long silent hallway to the vault, passing Victorian-era birds in spirit, tens of thousands of eggs and skeletons, the collection of endangered and extinct specimens, Darwin's finches, and the cabinets that once housed Wallace's birds, coming at last to a stop before the door marked PYRODERUS SCUTATUS.

A tray was pulled out, revealing a pile of crime-scene evidence bags. The Norwegian delivery was placed inside, and the cabinet doors closed with a quiet thump.

ACKNOWLEDGMENTS

It's customary to wait until the final sentences of the acknowledgments to thank one's spouse, but if Viking had permitted it, it would have been on the cover and in the header and footer of every page of this book. On our first date, I mentioned a book I dreamed of writing about a kid who stole dead birds from a museum in England. Amazingly, she agreed not only to a second date but to build a life with me. In an investigation that spanned years, she must have had flickers of doubt about my spiraling obsession, but she never let on. She believed in this project long before I had a book deal, and she supported me as I flew around the world on wild hunches about the missing skins. Six months after our wedding, she was in Düsseldorf for the interview with Edwin, working the audio recorder while a bodyguard hid outside.

She read every draft, perching pages on her pregnant tummy, while I rambled on excitedly about some new discovery. After our son, August, was born, she somehow managed to balance the demands of motherhood with a full-time job while still helping this book take shape. In the late stages of revisions, she did it all while our baby daughter grew inside her. She is the strongest person I've ever known, and *The Feather Thief* would never have happened without her.

If Katherine Flynn told me to hop on one leg for a month, I would do so unhesitatingly, so complete is my faith in her counsel. Beyond being a superagent, she is brilliant, funny, wise, and a true friend.

My deep thanks to Kathryn Court for believing in this book and giving it a home at Viking. Lindsey Schwoeri, Jocasta Hamilton, Sarah Rigby, Gretchen Schmid, and Beena Kamlani provided illuminating feedback, pushback, and patient support throughout many revisions: I am lucky to have them in the trenches with me.

Thanks, too, to Hope Denekamp, Ike Williams, and Paul Sennott at Kneerim and Williams; to Danny and Heather Baror of Baror International, Inc., for coordinating foreign rights; and to Jocasta Hamilton of Hutchinson in Britain, Marijke Wempe of Atlas Contact in Holland, Hans-Peter Uebleis of Droemer in Germany, and Lena Pallin of Brombergs in Sweden.

Sylvie Rabineau, whom I met on my second day in Los Angeles, has been a force of nature, believing in and promoting my work and offering sage guidance.

A very special note of gratitude to Spencer Seim in Taos, New Mexico. Had we not gone fishing that fall day in 2011, I would have never heard the name Edwin Rist. In the years since, he has helped this project along, patiently taking my calls, sounding out theories about the missing skins, and teaching me about fly-tying and its history. In the process, we have become dear friends. Anyone who wants to spend a day fly-fishing with the best guide in the country should visit ZiaFly.com, where they can also buy his gorgeous salmon flies (tied using legal, ethically sourced feathers).

I am very grateful to the staff at the Natural History Museum in Tring (and London) for putting up with several years' worth of questions about an unpleasant chapter in their institution's history.

To their great credit, they were always forthcoming and shared whatever they could: what happened to them wasn't their fault, but I do hope that funding for the protection of specimens in the UK (and throughout the world) is increased by host governments. Particular gratitude goes to Dr. Robert Prys-Jones, Mark Adams, and Dr. Richard Lane, as well as Chloe and Sophie in the press shop.

One of the pleasures of this investigation was getting to know Adele Hopkin of the Hertfordshire Constabulary, who was always generous with her time as she fielded questions large and small about the fate of the missing skins. Thanks to the Constabulary's Hannah Georgiou and Rachel Hyde for assistance with photos. Elsewhere in the UK justice system, thanks to David Chrimes and Tapashi Nadarajah with the Crown Prosecution Service, and to the St. Albans Crown Court for approving my request for the release of the sentencing hearing transcripts.

Dr. Rick Prum is one of the most colorful, brilliant, and thoughtful people I've ever met. My thanks to him for sharing so much of his time, for illuminating the lives of these birds, for explaining the modern curatorial mission, and for sharing an early copy of what will surely become known as a seminal work, *The Evolution of Beauty*.

The AVECOL and eBEAC listservs of ornithologists were very helpful in the late stages of my research. Thanks to Dr. James Remsen, Mark Adams, and Douglas Russell for facilitating my requests for information and to all the curators who responded.

Dr. John Bates at the Field Museum in Chicago was a great resource, as was Dr. Paul Sweet at the American Museum of Natural History in New York. So was Dr. Kirk Johnson (what a strange interview that was!) at the Smithsonian National Museum of Natural History.

Sir David Attenborough probably can't appreciate just how thrilling it is to receive letters from him in the mail—his first letter came at an uncertain time, before this book had a publisher. I am forever grateful that he made himself available by phone to discuss the Tring heist, his beloved Birds of Paradise, and Alfred Russel Wallace.

Thanks, too, to Bill Wallace, great-grandson of Alfred Russel, for sharing the story about his father's trip to the Natural History Museum.

Long Nguyen opened up his home and life in Norway to me for what must have been an incredibly challenging interview. Of all the interviews I conducted, his was the most honest and searching.

I'd also like to thank Edwin Rist for agreeing to tell me his story. Over some eight hours, there were plenty of opportunities for him to walk out the door, but he admirably answered any question I put to him. While I never met his father, Curtis, I want to thank him for the efforts he took—at considerable financial pain—to recover birds for the museum.

While many in the fly-tying community were wary of this project, I am grateful to everyone who spoke with me, including John McLain, Ed Muzeroll, Jens Pilgaard, Robert Verkerk, Marvin Nolte, Tony Smith, Dave Carne, Mike Townend, Bud Guidry, Jim Goggans, Terry, Phil Castleman, Stuart Hardy, Gary Litman, Paul Davis, Shawn Mitchell, Ruhan Neethling, T. J. Hall, Robert Delisle, Flemming Sejer Andersen, Irish, Andrew Herd, Mortimer, Ryan Houston, and Paul Rossman. Thanks also to everyone who spoke with me on background or off the record.

Tom Whiting of Whiting Farms not only opened up his doors but picked me up at the airport: thanks for introducing me to the wild world of genetic poultry hackle.

Thanks to George Beccaloni, director of the Wallace Correspondence Project, for his helpful comments on the Wallace chapter.

Ever since my good friend Judge Mark Wolf introduced us, Geoff Cowan has been an endless source of encouragement and assistance. I am honored to be a senior fellow at the USC Annenberg Center on Communication Leadership & Policy, and am grateful to its team, particularly Ev Boyle and Susan Goelz.

The idea for this book took root during a residence at the Helene G. Wurlitzer Foundation in New Mexico. A substantial amount of historical research occurred during a residence at the unforgettable Delta Omicron studio at the MacDowell Colony in New Hampshire (my special thanks to David Macy and Cheryl Young).

Thanks to Tim and Neda Disney for their support and for letting me work on an early version of the book proposal at their Joshua Tree escape.

I'm lucky to have George Packer as a mentor and friend. Better than most, he understood the bind the Iraq War had put me in, and offered nothing but wise counsel and encouragement as I started to consider a life beyond the List Project.

Nancy Updike also listened to recordings of my earliest interviews, taught me the ropes of working a Marantz, and sensed the worthiness of this strange story before almost anyone.

John Wray, Michael Lerner, and Max Weiss all took considerable time to read and provide invaluable comment on early, baggy drafts. This book was dramatically improved by their feedback.

Thanks to the Hoekstra brothers: Tim, for his guidance in plumbing public records, and Misha, for his help translating Danish e-mails about illicit bird transactions.

I am forever grateful for friendships that keep me sane and happy: Max Weiss, Tom and Christen Hadfield, Peter and Lisa Noah, Jakke and Maria Erixson, Sarah Uslan and Ian Duncan, Mélanie Joly, Henrik and Victoria Björklund, Loubna El-Amine, Jonathan and Tara Tucker, Amélie Cantin, Julie Schlosser and Rajiv Chandrasekaran, Kevin and Annie Jacobsen, Tim Hoekstra and Fatimah Rony, John Wray, Lizzy and Shawn Peterson, Yanic Truesdale, Ezra Strausberg and Enrique Gutierrez, Philip Wareborn and Hanna Helgegren, Jon Staff, Meena and Liaquat Ahamed, Gahl Burt, Arie Toporovsky, Eddie Patel, Justin Sadauskas, Kevin Brewer, Tim Martin, Andy Rafter, Jesse Dailey, Maxim Roy, Sherine Hamdy, Alyshia and Lee Knaz, Anthony Chase and Sofia Gruskin,

Maryse and Jérôme, Dennis Spiegel, Azar Nafisi, Tim and Annette Nelson, Janine Cantin, Deb and Hannah VanDerMolen, Bev, Ken, and Jennie Paigen, Usman and Nadia Khan, Tona Rashad, Yaghdan and Ghada Hameid, Serim Çetin, Jordan and Lauren Goldenberg, Mohammed and Atiaf al-Rawi, Matt King and Sarah Cunningham, Lela and Mark Smrecek, Sally Hutchinson and John Cartwright. Rest in peace, Uncle Luke.

As always, I have the great fortune to have been born into the Johnson clan. My dad lovingly read every draft of the manuscript, while my mom eagerly filled our house (and dressed my wife) with feather-themed paraphernalia. My brothers, Soren and Derek, are my best friends. They, along with Carolyn, Ever, and my late aunt Betty—the original birder in the family—all provided brilliant feedback on early versions of the book. My *belle-maman*, Suzanne Ladouceur, even got in on the bird frenzy, celebrating our marriage and children's births with a collection of brass swans from Nepal.

With endless love for August, Isidora, and Marie-Josée, the source of all that is good and beautiful and wise in my life.

NOTES

PROLOGUE

2 *Wait a minute!:* Edwin Rist, interview by author, May 26, 2015.

3 **Engrossed in a soccer match:** Ibid.

4 **as few as 250 mature individuals:** "Cotinga maculata," IUCN Red List of Threatened Species (2017), http://dx.doi.org/10.2305/IUCN.UK.2017-1 .RLTS.T22700886A110781901.en.

1. THE TRIALS OF ALFRED RUSSEL WALLACE

13 **seven hundred miles off the coast:** Alfred Russel Wallace, "Letter Concerning the Fire on the *Helen*," *Zoologist* (November 1852).

14 **the skins of nearly ten thousand birds:** Ross A. Slotten, *The Heretic in Darwin's Court: The Life of Alfred Russel Wallace* (New York: Columbia University Press, 2004), p. 83.

15 **thousands of miles of tracks:** Christian Wolmar, *Fire & Steam: How the Railways Transformed Britain* (London: Atlantic, 2008).

15 **vanished species like belemnites:** Alfred Russel Wallace, *My Life: A Record of Events and Opinions* (London: Chapman & Hall, 1905), p. 1:109.

15 **It wasn't until the arrival of the trains:** Lynn L. Merrill, *The Romance of Victorian Natural History* (New York: Oxford University Press, 1989), p. 7.

15 **the ideal form of recreation:** Ibid., p. 8.

16 **Hats were designed:** Ibid., p. 45.

16 **the French led the way with conchlyomania:** Ibid., p. 80.

16 Pteridomania followed, as the British: Sarah Whittingham, *The Victorian Fern Craze* (Oxford: Shire, 2009).

16 "regarded as one of the essential furnishings": David Elliston Allen, *The Naturalist in Britain: A Social History* (Princeton, N.J.: Princeton University Press, 1994), p. 26.

16 When young Wallace: Wallace, *My Life,* p. 110.

16 "that there was any kind of": Ibid., p. 111.

17 "I should like to take some one family": Ibid., pp. 256–67.

17 "Promising indeed to lovers of the marvelous": William H. Edwards, *A Voyage up the River Amazon: Including a Residence at Pará* (New York: D. Appleton, 1847), p. 11.

18 They ate alligators, monkeys: Michael Shermer, *In Darwin's Shadow: The Life and Science of Alfred Russel Wallace: A Biographical Study on the Psychology of History* (Oxford: Oxford University Press, 2002), p. 72.

18 "at every step I almost expected to feel": Alfred Russel Wallace, *A Narrative of Travels on the Amazon and Rio Negro, with an Account of the Native Tribes, and Observations on the Climate, Geology, and Natural History of the Amazon Valley* (London: Reeve, 1853), p. 171.

18 "While in that apathetic state": Ibid., p. 226.

18 He loaded the canoe: Slotten, *Heretic in Darwin's Court,* p. 83.

18 He paid a small fortune to liberate them: Wallace, *Narrative of Travels,* p. 382.

19 the smoke was so thick: Ibid., p. 392.

19 "now suffocatingly hot": Ibid., p. 393.

19 "a kind of apathy": Ibid.

19 huddled on the bowsprit: Ibid., p. 395.

19 "a magnificent and awful sight": Alfred Russel Wallace to Richard Spruce (written aboard the *Jordeson*), September 19, 1852, http://www.nhm.ac.uk/research-curation/scientific-resources/collections/library-collections/wallace-letters-online/349/5294/S/details.html.

20 "It was now, when the danger appeared past": Alfred Russel Wallace, quoted in "The President's Address," *Transactions of the Entomological Society of London* (London, 1853), p. 2:146.

20 dangerously overloaded and underprovisioned: *The Annual Register, Or, A view of the History and Politics of the Year 1852* (London: F. & J. Rivington, 1852), p. 183.

21 a £200 insurance policy: Shermer, *In Darwin's Shadow,* p. 74.

21 **Darwin's Cambridge professor:** J. S. Henslow to C. Darwin, August 24, 1831, quoted in *The Correspondence of Charles Darwin: 1821–1836* (Cambridge: Cambridge University Press, 1985), pp. 1:128–29, https://www .darwinproject.ac.uk/letter/?docId=letters/DCP-LETT-105.xml;query= Henslow%201831;brand=default.

21 **Only five weeks after his return:** Alfred Russel Wallace, "On the Habits of the Butterflies of the Amazon Valley," *Transactions of the Entomological Society of London* (n.s.) 2 (1854): 253–64.

22 **The "great divisions":** Slotten, *Heretic in Darwin's Court*, p. 95.

22 **"In the various works on natural history":** Alfred Russel Wallace, "On the Monkeys of the Amazon," *Proceedings of the Zoological Society of London* 20 (December 14, 1852): 109.

22 **"a new world":** Samuel G. Goodrich, *History of All Nations, from the Earliest Periods to the Present . . .* (Auburn, N.Y.: Miller, Orton and Mulligan, 1854), p. 1192.

22 **In June 1853:** Wallace, *My Life*, p. 327.

23 **Wallace frequented the insect and bird rooms:** Ibid.

23 **The first skins:** Michael Shrubb, *Feasting, Fowling and Feathers: A History of the Exploitation of Wild Birds* (London: T & AD Poyser, 2013), p. 201.

23 **They thought females laid their eggs:** David Attenborough and Errol Fuller, *Drawn from Paradise: The Natural History, Art and Discovery of the Birds of Paradise* (New York: Harper Design, 2012), p. 47.

23 **called them *manuk dewata*:** Alfred Russel Wallace, *The Annotated Malay Archipelago*, ed. John van Wyhe (Singapore: National University of Singapore Press, 2015), p. 705.

23 **Young King Charles I:** Attenborough and Fuller, *Drawn from Paradise*, p. 50.

23 **Rembrandt, Rubens, and Bruegel:** Ibid., p. 47.

24 **"richly wooded shores":** Wallace, *My Life*, p. 335.

24 **Within a month of arriving:** Slotten, *Heretic in Darwin's Court*, p. 106.

24 **Each morning he was up at five-thirty:** Ibid., p. 106.

24 **"night work may be very well for amateurs":** Alfred Russel Wallace to Samuel Stevens, September 2, 1858, http://www.nhm.ac.uk/research-curation /scientific-resources/collections/library-collections/wallace-letters-online /4274/4391/T/details.html#2.

24 **Small black ants routinely "took possession":** Wallace, *Annotated Malay Archipelago*, p. 663.

25 **"it was sure to be carried off":** Ibid., p. 612.

25 **the best method to preserve birds:** Charles Waterton, *Wanderings in South America* (London: B. Fellowes, 1825), p. 295.

25 **knock a wounded and aggressive Heron:** James Boyd Davies, *The Practical Naturalist's Guide: Containing Instructions for Collecting, Preparing and Preserving Specimens in All Departments of Zoology, Intended for the Use of Students, Amateurs and Travellers* (Edinburgh: MacLachlan & Stewart, 1858), p. 16.

25 **To help with the quotidian tasks:** Kees Rookmaaker and John van Wyhe, "In Alfred Russel Wallace's Shadow: His Forgotten Assistant, Charles Allen (1839–1892)," *Journal of the Malaysian Branch of the Royal Asiatic Society* 85, pt. 2 (2012): 17–54.

26 **"can now shoot pretty well":** Alfred Russel Wallace to Mary Ann Wallace, July 2, 1854, http://www.nhm.ac.uk/research-curation/scientific-resources /collections/library-collections/wallace-letters-online/355/5901/S/details .html#S1.

26 **"I could not be troubled with another":** Alfred Russel Wallace to Frances Sims, June 25, 1855, http://www.nhm.ac.uk/research-curation/scientific -resources/collections/library-collections/wallace-letters-online/359/5905 /S/details.html.

26 **The Peninsular & Oriental's "Overland" route:** John van Wyhe and Gerrell M. Drawhorn, "'I am Ali Wallace': The Malay Assistant of Alfred Russel Wallace," *Journal of the Malaysian Branch of the Royal Asiatic Society* 88, no. 1 (2015): 3–31.

26 **In December 1856:** Wallace, *Annotated Malay Archipelago*, p. 544.

27 **As the prow inched east:** Ibid.

27 **One hundred forty million years ago:** Gavan Daws and Marty Fujita, *Archipelago: The Islands of Indonesia: From the Nineteenth-Century Discoveries of Alfred Russel Wallace to the Fate of Forests and Reefs in the Twenty-first Century* (Berkeley: University of California Press, 1999), p. 84.

27 **For eighty million years:** Bird-of-Paradise Project, Cornell Lab of Ornithology, http://www.birdsofparadiseproject.org/content.php?page=113.

28 **There were no civets or cats:** *Birds of the Gods,* narrated by David Attenborough, PBS, January 22, 2011.

28 **the river channels veining the islands:** Wallace, *Annotated Malay Archipelago*, p. 579.

28 **a room in a crude hut:** Ibid., p. 584.

29 **revenge, he joked:** Slotten, *Heretic in Darwin's Court*, p. 132.

29 **"To be kept prisoner":** Wallace, *Annotated Malay Archipelago*, p. 607.

29 **"intense cinnabar red":** Ibid., p. 586.

29 "I thought of the long ages of the past": Ibid., p. 588.

29 "It seems sad": Ibid.

30 thrumming "golden glory": Ibid., p. 608.

30 Wallace became the first naturalist: Tim Laman, and Edwin Scholes, *Birds of Paradise: Revealing the World's Most Extraordinary Birds* (National Geographic Books, 2012), p. 26.

30 He had set up a home base: Wallace, *Annotated Malay Archipelago*, p. 428.

31 Despite the 90-degree heat: Slotten, *Heretic in Darwin's Court*, p. 144.

31 "Vaguely thinking over the enormous": Wallace, *My Life*, p. 190.

31 "it suddenly flashed upon me": Ibid.

32 "found the long-sought-for law of nature": Ibid., p. 191.

32 Wallace waited anxiously: Ibid., p. 362.

32 "I wrote a letter": Ibid., p. 363.

32 "interrupted by letter from AR Wallace": Quoted in Slotten, *Heretic in Darwin's Court,* p. 153.

32 "I never saw a more striking coincidence": Charles Darwin to Charles Lyell, June 18, 1858, https://www.darwinproject.ac.uk/letter/?docId=letters/DCP-LETT-2285.xml.

32 "So all my originality": Ibid.

32 "These gentlemen, having, independently": J. D. Hooker and Charles Lyell to the Linnean Society, June 30, 1858, https://www.darwinproject.ac.uk/letter/DCP-LETT-2299.xml.

33 "I have received letters from Mr. Darwin": Wallace, *My Life,* p. 365.

33 Over an eight-year period, he had boxed up 310: Wallace, *Annotated Malay Archipelago*, p. 53.

33 By his own estimate: Ibid.

34 he would deposit the worried bird: Ibid., p. 687.

34 "endless trouble & great anxiety": Alfred Russel Wallace to P. L. Sclater, March 31, 1862, http://www.nhm.ac.uk/research-curation/scientific-resources/collections/library-collections/wallace-letters-online/1723/1606/T/details.html.

34 forcing him to slip into the storeroom: Wallace, *My Life*, p. 383.

34 "I have great pleasure in announcing": Alfred Russel Wallace to P. L. Sclater, March 31, 1862, http://www.nhm.ac.uk/research-curation/scientific-resources/collections/library-collections/wallace-letters-online/1723/1606/T/details.html.

35 "Once in a generation, a Wallace may be": Thomas Henry Huxley, *Evidence as to Man's Place in Nature* (New York: D. Appleton, 1863), p. 36.

35 John Gould, England's most renowned: Slotten, *Heretic in Darwin's Court*, p. 136.

35 summoned a carpenter: Wallace, *My Life*, p. 386.

35 "as a token of personal esteem": Wallace, *Annotated Malay Archipelago*, p. 46.

35 "what strikes me most about Mr. Wallace": Charles Darwin to H. W. Bates, December 3, 1861, https://www.darwinproject.ac.uk/letter/?docId= letters/DCP-LETT-3338.xml.

36 "the individual letters": Alfred Russel Wallace, "On the Physical Geography of the Malay Archipelago," *Journal of the Royal Geographical Society* 33 (1863): 217–34.

36 "If this is not done": Ibid.

37 German Zeppelins drifting silently: Jasper Copping, "Rare Charts Show WW1 German Air Raids on Britain," *Telegraph*, November 7, 2013.

37 The British Museum was hit: Karolyn Shindler, "Natural History Museum: A Natural Wartime Effort That Bugged Owners of Period Homes," *Telegraph*, September 28, 2010.

37 To protect them from Hitler's bombers: Ibid.

2. LORD ROTHSCHILD'S MUSEUM

38 the richest family in human history: Niall Ferguson, *The House of Rothschild* (New York: Viking, 1998), pp. xxiii, 2.

38 "Mama, Papa. I am going to make a Museum": Miriam Rothschild, *Walter Rothschild: The Man, the Museum and the Menagerie* (London: Natural History Museum, 2008), p. 1.

39 By fourteen, he had: Ibid., p. 62.

39 He arrived at the University of Cambridge: Ibid., p. 73.

39 By twenty he'd accumulated: Richard Conniff, *The Species Seekers: Heroes, Fools, and the Mad Pursuit of Life on Earth* (New York: W. W. Norton, 2011), p. 323.

39 The museum soon attracted: Rothschild, *Walter Rothschild*, p. 101.

40 "a grand piano on castors": Michael A. Salmon, Peter Marren, and Basil Harley, *The Aurelian Legacy: British Butterflies and Their Collectors* (Berkeley: University of California Press, 240), p. 206.

40 For years, he carelessly: Conniff, *Species Seekers*, p. 322.

40 After two live bear cubs: Virginia Cowles, *The Rothschilds: A Family of Fortune* (New York: Alfred A. Knopf, 1973), Kindle loc. 3423.

40 "My father was absolutely right": Rothschild, *Walter Rothschild*, p. 86.

40 In 1931 his collection of 280,000 skins: Ibid., p. 302.

40 "He was as jubilant over it": Ibid., p. 303.

41 "Walter seemed to shrink visibly": Ibid., p. 304.

41 "Ask of the beasts": Jacob Mikanowski, "A Natural History of Walter Rothschild," *Awl*, April 11, 2016.

41 Before it all came to ruin: "The Rothschild Collection," Natural History Museum.

41 The collectors he employed: Conniff, *Species Seekers*, p. 334.

41 "the world with a severe attack": Rothschild, *Walter Rothschild*, p. 155.

41 "I can't agree with you in thinking": Alfred Newton to Walter Rothschild, December 16, 1891, http://discovermagazine.com/2004/jun/reviews.

42 the Age of Extermination: Robin W. Doughty, *Feather Fashions and Bird Preservation: A Study in Nature Protection* (Berkeley: University of California Press, 1975), p. 156.

42 the greatest direct slaughter: Barbara Mearns and Richard Mearns, *The Bird Collectors* (San Diego: Academic, 1998), p. 12.

3. THE FEATHER FEVER

43 In 1775 she took: Émile Langlade, *Rose Bertin, the Creator of Fashion at the Court of Marie-Antoinette* (London: J. Long, 1913), p. 48.

43 new rotary printing presses: Robin W. Doughty, *Feather Fashions and Bird Preservation: A Study in Nature Protection* (Berkeley: University of California Press, 1975), p. 14.

43 Within a century of Marie-Antoinette's death: Ibid., p. 15.

43 "elegant assortment of Paris Millinery": *Vogue*, December 17, 1892, p. vii.

44 "Stiff wings are in high vogue": "Millinery," *Delineator* LI.1 (January 1898): p. 70.

44 "A large fraction of our time": Cynthia Asquith, quoted in Karen Bowman, *Corsets and Codpieces: A History of Outrageous Fashion, from Roman Times to the Modern Era* (New York: Skyhorse, 2015), p. 204.

44 entire bird skins were mounted: Doughty, *Feather Fashions*, p. 1.

45 He counted seven hundred ladies: Ibid., p. 16.

45 one merchant peddled a shawl: Michael Shrubb, *Feasting, Fowling and Feathers: A History of the Exploitation of Wild Birds* (London: T & AD Poyser, 2013), p. 201.

45 "plume merchants purchased stock": Doughty, *Feather Fashions*, p. 73.

45 Only two hundred: Ibid., p. 74.

45 By 1862 there were 120: Edmond Lefèvre, *Le commerce et l'industrie de la plume pour parure* (Paris, 1914), pp. 226–28.

45 Union of Raw Feather Merchants: Ibid.

45 nearly one hundred million pounds: Doughty, *Feather Fashions*, p. 25.

45 155,000 Birds of Paradise: Ibid., p. 30.

45 part of a $2.8 billion industry: Shrubb, *Feasting, Fowling and Feathers*, p. 197.

45 One dealer reported selling: Barbara Mearns and Richard Mearns, *The Bird Collectors* (San Diego: Academic, 1998), p. 11.

46 By 1900 eighty-three thousand: Doughty, *Feather Fashions*, p. 23.

46 A kilo of Egret feathers: Ibid., p. 74.

46 farmers blinded the birds: Ibid., p. 78–79.

46 when the *Titanic* went down: Thor Hanson, *Feathers: The Evolution of a Natural Miracle* (New York: Basic Books, 2011), p. 176.

46 salmon ran in such great numbers: Charles F. Waterman, *History of Angling* (Tulsa, Okla.: Winchester, 1981), p. 26.

46 eclipsing horde of Passenger Pigeons: John J. Audubon, "Passenger Pigeon," Plate 62 of *The Birds of America* (New York and London, 1827–38), Audubon.org.

47 The plains rumbled with bison herds: Jed Portman, *The Great American Bison*, PBS, 2011.

47 hurtling exponentially toward 1.6 billion: "Historical Estimates of World Population," U.S. Census Bureau, http://www.census.gov/population/international/data/worldpop/table_history.php.

47 "insensible to the wonders": Alexis de Tocqueville, *Democracy in America*, trans. Henry Reeve (London: Saunders and Otley, 1840), p. 3:152.

47 sixty million American bison: "Timeline of the American Bison," U.S. Fish and Wildlife Service, https://www.fws.gov/bisonrange/timeline.htm.

47 loaded their decks: Harriet Beecher Stowe, quoted in Jim Robison, "Hunters Turned Osceola Riverbanks into Bloody Killing Fields for Wildlife," *Orlando Sentinel*, January 23, 1995.

47 "an orgy of noise": Mark Derr, *Some Kind of Paradise: A Chronicle of Man and the Land in Florida* (New York: William Morrow, 1989).

47 The 1890 census: Jedediah Purdy, *After Nature: A Politics for the Anthropocene* (Cambridge, Mass.: Harvard University Press, 2015), p. 31.

47 Between 1883 and 1898: Doughty, *Feather Fashions*, p. 82.

48 **In 1914, Martha:** Elizabeth Kolbert, "They Covered the Sky, and Then . . . ," *New York Review of Books,* January 9, 2014.

48 **Four years later:** "The Last Carolina Parakeet," John James Audubon Center at Mill Grove, http://johnjames.audubon.org/last-carolina-parakeet.

4. BIRTH OF A MOVEMENT

49 **"would shrink from inflicting":** Mary Thatcher, "The Slaughter of the Innocents," *Harper's Bazaar,* May 22, 1875, p. 338.

49 **"Our fashions as you all know":** Elizabeth Cady Stanton, "Our Girls," Winter 1880, http://voicesofdemocracy.umd.edu/stanton-our-girls-speech-text/.

50 **In 1889 Emily Williamson:** "Our History," Royal Society for the Protection of Birds, https://ww2.rspb.org.uk/about-the-rspb/about-us/our-history/.

50 **In 1896 a Bostonian Brahmin:** "History of Audubon and Science-based Bird Conservation," Audubon, http://www.audubon.org/about/history -audubon-and-waterbird-conservation.

50 **"The Badge of Cruelty!":** "Our History," Royal Society for the Protection of Birds, https://ww2.rspb.org.uk/about-the-rspb/about-us/our-history/.

50 **"This beautiful bird":** "Urgent Plea for Birds," *New York Times,* December 3, 1897.

51 A BIRD OF PREY: Linley Sambourne, "A Bird of Prey," *Punch, or the London Charivari* 102 (May 14, 1892), p. 231.

51 **"it really seems as though":** Robin W. Doughty, *Feather Fashions and Bird Preservation: A Study in Nature Protection* (Berkeley: University of California Press, 1975), p. 22.

51 **"The next time you buy":** "What Women Are Heedlessly Doing," *Ladies' Home Journal* 25 (November 1908), p. 25.

51 **"and will certainly do all":** Queen Alexandra to Royal Society for the Protection of Birds, in "The Use of Bird Plumage for Personal Adornment," *Victorian Naturalist* 23 (1907): 54–55.

51 **"faddists and sickly sentimental":** "The Audubon Society Against the Fancy Feather Trade," *Millinery Trade Review* 31 (1906): 61.

51 **"there is no alternative":** Ibid., p. 57.

52 **Lobbyists representing groups:** Doughty, *Feather Fashions,* p. 61.

52 **"The feather men are fighting":** Ernest Ingersoll, "Specious Arguments Veil Feather Trade's Real Purpose" (letter), *New York Times,* March 25, 1914.

52 **The arrival of the automobile:** Doughty, *Feather Fashions,* p. 155.

53 **In 1905 poachers murdered:** Stuart B. McIver, *Death in the Everglades: The Murder of Guy Bradley, America's First Martyr to Environmentalism* (Gainesville: University of Florida Press, 2003).

53 **dead Black-Footed Albatrosses:** Jeffrey V. Wells, *Birder's Conservation Handbook: 100 North American Birds at Risk* (Princeton, N.J.: Princeton University Press, 2010), p. 92.

53 **In 1921 a passenger:** "$100,000 Loot Seized in Smuggling Arrest: Drugs, Jewels, Feathers and Rum Found in Baggage," *New York Times*, March 3, 1921.

53 **"On one occasion":** "Fine Feathers No More: How New Law Bars Birds of Paradise and Other Plumage from Importation," *New York Times*, April 2, 1922.

53 **An Italian cook:** Doughty, *Feather Fashions,* p. 146.

53 **Two Frenchmen were busted:** Ibid., p. 143.

53 **An international Bird of Paradise smuggling ring:** "Plume Smugglers in Organized Band," *New York Times*, August 8, 1920.

53 **Officials in Laredo:** Doughty, *Feather Fashions,* p. 146.

53 **high-speed boat chases:** Daniel Mizzi, "Bird Smuggler Who Led Police, Army on Land and Sea Chase Jailed," *Malta Today*, August 7, 2014.

53 **to buy "parrot sausages":** John Nichol, *Animal Smugglers* (New York: Facts on File, 1987), p. 3.

54 **Often described as the Magna Carta:** Robert Boardman, *International Organization and the Conservation of Nature* (Bloomington: Indiana University Press, 1981).

5. THE VICTORIAN BROTHERHOOD OF FLY-TIERS

55 **Inside, Dr. Eric Gardner:** Andrew Herd, *The Fly* (Ellesmere, U.K.: Medlar Press, 2003), p. 51.

55 **"welcome change in the diet":** Frederick Buller, "The Macedonian Fly," *American Fly Fisher* 22, no. 4 (1996), p. 4.

56 **"crimson red wool":** Ælianus quoted in Herd, *Fly,* p. 25.

56 **"blackest drake" mallard:** Juliana B. Berners and Wynkyn de Worde, *A Treatyse of Fysshynge wyth an Angle* (1496; reprint London: Elliot Stock, 1880).

56 **"the most stately fish":** Ibid.

57 **"Rivers and the inhabitants":** Izaak Walton, *The Compleat Angler* (London: John Lane, 1653), p. 43.

58 **Working-class anglers:** Herd, *Fly,* p. 168.

58 **"very little water left":** Ibid.

58 "rapidly accumulated a burden": Ibid., p. 247.

58 "egged on by local tackle": Ibid., p. 155.

59 "They will be found most killing": William Blacker, *Blacker's Art of Fly-making: Comprising Angling & Dyeing of Colours, with Engravings of Salmon & Trout Flies* (1842; reprint London: George Nichols, 1855), p. 104.

59 Blacker was an expert: Herd, *Fly*, p. 208.

60 "Exactitude is needed": George M. Kelson, *The Salmon Fly: How to Dress It and How to Use It* (London: Wyman & Sons, 1895), p. 4.

60 So exact was his craft: Herd, *Fly*, p. 265.

60 "so low down in the scale": Kelson, *Salmon Fly*, p. 9.

60 Kelson admitted in his book: Ibid., p. 18.

60 "At times salmon will take anything": Ibid., p. 24.

61 "mental and moral discipline": Ibid., p. 10.

61 "We have here a well-bred hobby": Ibid.

61 "The greatest find": Ibid., p. 58.

62 "however well hackles may be dyed": Ibid., p. 44.

62 as "narrow-minded enthusiasts": George M. Kelson, *Tips* (London: Published by the author, 1901), p. 47.

62 "If Donald Trump continues having trouble": Robert H. Boyle, "Flies That are Tied for Art, not Fish," *Sports Illustrated*, December 17, 1990.

6. THE FUTURE OF FLY-TYING

65 In 1705, just outside: Richard Conniff, "Mammoths and Mastodons: All American Monsters," *Smithsonian*, April 2010.

65 another hundred species: "What We've Lost: Species Extinction Time Line," *National Geographic*, n.d., http://www.nationalgeographic.com/deextinction/selected-species-extinctions-since-1600/.

66 the mere sight of red ants: Edwin Rist, interview by author, May 26, 2015.

66 "Now *that* is what I want": Curtis Rist, "Santa Barbara's Splendid Beaches," *ABC News*, June 3, 2017.

69 ten thousand colors of wool: Edwin Rist and Anton Rist to Ronn Lucas, Sr., http://www.ronnlucassr.com/rists.htm, accessed May 23, 2016, page no longer exists.

69 sixty-eight trout flies in an hour: "Danbury Show," ClassicFlyTying.com, November 14, 2005, http://www.classicflytying.com/?showtopic=12531.

70 The man who'd created them: Edward Muzeroll, interview by author, April 6, 2017.

70 **"Tying with exotic materials"**: Morgan Lyle, "Tying with Exotic Materials: Avoiding the Long Arm of the Law," *Fly Tyer*, Winter 2003, p. 6.

71 **The Durham Ranger**: "The Durham Ranger," BestClassicSalmonFlies .com, n.d., http://www.bestclassicsalmonflies.com/durham_ranger.html.

73 **When he asked**: Muzeroll interview.

73 **"I only wish I possessed such a friend!"**: T. E. Pryce-Tannatt, *How to Dress Salmon Flies: A Handbook for Amateurs* (London: Adam and Charles Black, 1914), p. 53.

73 **"*This* is what it's all about"**: Muzeroll interview.

74 **the Fly Boys**: "Teen Brothers Make Exotic Art with 'Flies,'" *Columbia-Greene Community College: News & Class Schedule*, Fall 2006, p. 3, https://www.sunycgcc.edu/Forms_Publications/CGCCNewsletters/2006 -10_cgcc_mininews06.pdf.

74 **There were disasters**: Rick Clemenson, "Teenage Brothers Create Salmon Fly Art," *Albany Times Union*, September 6, 2006.

74 **"They would spend all day out"**: "Teen Brothers Make Exotic Art."

75 **"There is something"**: "Cotinga on eBay," ClassicFlyTying.com, October 29, 2007, http://www.classicflytying.com/index.php?showtopic= 29391.

75 **"If you're going to tie good flies"**: "Materials for Sale," FeathersMc .com, screenshot of page as it existed on August 12, 2004, https://web .archive.org/web/20041009151910/http://www.feathersmc.com/home.php, accessed May 23, 2016.

76 **"to ensure everybody that wants"**: Ibid.

76 **"Do your parents know you're"**: John McLain, interview by author, November 20, 2011.

76 **He called up the Bronx Zoo**: "Teen Brothers Make Exotic Art."

77 **"the master of infinite elaboration"**: George M. Kelson, in Anonymous, ed., *Fishing, Fish Culture & the Aquarium* (1886; reprint Nabu Press, 2012), p. 185.

78 **what he called "thematical flies"**: "Luc Couturier," FeathersMc.com, screenshot of page as it existed in 2008, https://web.archive.org/web/2008080120 1429/http://www.feathersmc.com:80/friends/show/12.

78 **When Edwin first saw**: "Friends," EdwinRist.com, screenshots on Kirkw johnson.com/screenshots.

78 **When Couturier replied**: Ibid.

78 **"Fly-tying is not merely a hobby"**: Edwin Rist and Anton Rist to Ronn Lucas, Sr., http://www.ronnlucassr.com/rists.htm, accessed May 23, 2016, page no longer exists.

78 **"Good grief, Edwin!":** "Blacker Celebration Fly," ClassicFlyTying.com, January 17, 2006, http://www.classicflytying.com/index.php?showtopic= 13892&hl=cites#entry129465.

79 **Curtis thought it'd be fun:** Curtis Rist, "Dogged Determination," *Robb Report Worth,* October 2004, http://www.hudsondoodles.com/pages/IN THENEWS.htm.

79 **"fly looks a little droopy":** "Blue Boyne," ClassicFlyTying.com, March 2, 2006, http://www.classicflytying.com/?showtopic=15111.

80 **"They are two of the finest young":** Quoted in "Anton & Edwin Rist," FeathersMc.com, screenshot of page as it existed on May 15, 2008, accessed May 23, 2016, https://web.archive.org/web/20080515060043/http://feath ersmc.com/friends/show/38.

80 **"All they need to remember":** Quoted in "Ed Muzzy Muzeroll," Feath ersMc.com, screenshot of page as it existed on May 15, 2008, accessed June 17 2017, https://web.archive.org/web/20080515055338/http://www .feathersmc.com:80/friends/show/14.

80 **"I'm toying with the idea":** Quoted in "Anton & Edwin Rist," Feath ersMc.com, screenshot.

81 **He dreamed of becoming:** Rist interview.

7. FEATHERLESS IN LONDON

85 **He was no stranger:** Edwin Rist, interview by author, May 26, 2015.

86 **"Unfortunately I'm not tying":** "British Fly Fair," ClassicFlyTying.com, Octo- ber 16, 2007, http://www.classicflytying.com/index.php?showtopic=29028.

87 **"I will eat absolutely anything":** Edwin Rist to Terry, January 28, 2008. In possession of the author.

87 **"Life without tying":** Edwin Rist to Terry, January 14, 2008. Ibid.

88 **On February 9, 2008:** Mark Adams and Dr. Robert Prys-Jones, interview by author, January 21, 2015.

88 **Edwin created a fake e-mail:** Ibid.

89 **"He is the BEST":** Terry to author, February 14, 2008.

89 **"I look forward to coming back":** Rist to author, February 16, 2008.

90 **the guard smiled:** Rist interview.

90 **On November 5, 2008:** Adams and Prys-Jones interview.

91 **"let him know when you're done":** Rist interview.

91 **In 2008 ten Riflebird:** "Buying Magnificent Riflebird," ClassicFlyTying .com, December 19, 2008, http://www.classicflytying.com/index.php?show topic=35774.

91 Standing inside the Tring: Ibid.

92 "the head, throat": Alfred Russel Wallace, *The Annotated Malay Archipelago*, ed. John van Wyhe (Singapore: National University of Singapore Press, 2015), p. 715.

93 He knew Couturier: Rist interview.

8. PLAN FOR MUSEUM INVASION.DOC

94 *It won't be easy:* Edwin Rist, interview by author, May 26, 2015.

94 At first it was a game: Ibid.

94 If he owned these birds: Ibid.

95 But his desire to possess the birds: Ibid.

95 a $20,000 golden flute: Curtis Rist to Terry, December 6, 2010. In the author's possession.

95 the birds would be an inoculation: Rist interview.

95 Maybe, he thought, if: Ibid.

96 "PLAN FOR MUSEUM INVASION": *Regina v. Edwin Rist,* St. Albans Crown Court, April 8, 2011, transcript, p. 3.

96 a list of tools: Rist interview.

96 *This is ridiculous!:* Ibid.

96 *If you're going to do it:* Ibid.

96 *I'm gonna need a pair:* Ibid.

96 On June 11, 2009: "Fluteplayer 1988: Seller Feedback," eBay.com.

97 he ordered a box of fifty mothballs: "Information from Police from Interview with Edwin Rist," copy provided to author.

99 a kind of limbic motor movement: Rist interview.

100 By his estimation: Ibid.

100 adrenaline shuddered through him: Ibid.

101 Hoping not to wake: Ibid.

101 he felt it was the greatest day: Curtis Rist to Terry, December 6, 2010.

9. THE CASE OF THE BROKEN WINDOW

102 "Extinct and Endangered Bird Collections: J. H. Cooper and M. P. Adams, "Extinct and Endangered Bird Collections: Managing the Risk," *Zoologische Mededelingen* 79, no. 3 (2005): 123–30.

103 **Asked by police for an estimate:** Sergeant Adele Hopkin of Hertfordshire Constabulary, interview by author, January 20, 2015.

103 **$11.5 million at auction:** Scott Reyburn, "'Birds of America' Book Fetches Record $11.5 Million," *Bloomberg News*, December 7, 2010.

104 **relieved that nothing appeared to be missing:** Mark Adams and Dr. Robert Prys-Jones, interview by author, January 21, 2015.

104 **consumed with paranoia and guilt:** Curtis Rist to Terry, December 6, 2010.

105 **"Fly Tier of the Year":** "2008 FTOTY Overall Winners," ClassicFlyTying .com, February 27, 2009, http://www.classicflytying.com/index.php?show topic=36532.

105 **He opened up a blank file:** Edwin Rist, interview by author, May 26, 2015.

107 **Using tweezers, he began:** Ibid.

107 **When he was younger:** Curtis Rist to Terry.

107 **Edwin packed the birds:** Rist interview.

10. "A VERY UNUSUAL CRIME"

108 *Pyroderus scutatus is here:* Mark Adams and Dr. Robert Prys-Jones, interview by author, January 21, 2015.

109 **Only the dull-colored females:** Ibid.

109 **they were beginning to sense:** Ibid.

110 **"It's about four miles of nothing":** Sergeant Adele Hopkin of Hertfordshire Constabulary, interview by author, January 20, 2015.

110 **Had the birds been taken:** Ibid.

110 **Initially, Adele wondered:** Ibid.

111 **"The museum took pity on him":** M. P. Walters, "My Life with Eggs," *Zoologische Mededelingen* 79, no. 3 (2005): 5–18.

111 **the "incalculable damage":** "'Irreparable Damage' to National Heritage by Museum Eggs Theft," article from unknown publication hanging on the foyer wall of the Tring Police Station, photographed by author on January 20, 2015.

112 **the rest of his career:** Walters, "My Life with Eggs."

112 **Colonel Richard Meinertzhagen:** Brian Garfield, *The Meinertzhagen Mystery: The Life and Legend of a Colossal Fraud* (Washington, D.C.: Potomac, 2007).

112 **a depressing amount of time:** Pamela C. Rasmussen and Robert P. Prys-Jones, "History vs. Mystery: The Reliability of Museum Specimen Data," *Bulletin of the British Ornithologists' Club* 1232.A (2003): 66–94.

112 **Between 1998 and 2003:** Jennifer Cooke, "Museum Thief Jailed," *Sydney Morning Herald,* April 20, 2007.

113 **"Why Museums Matter":** "Why Museums Matter: Avian Archives in an Age of Extinction," papers from a conference at Green Park, Aston Clinton, and workshops at the Natural History Museum, Tring, November 12–15, 1999, *Bulletin of the British Ornithologists' Club* 1232.A (2003): 1–360.

114 **"It is very distressing":** Andy Bloxham, "Hundreds of Priceless Tropical Bird Skins Stolen from Natural History Museum," *Telegraph,* August 13, 2009.

11. HOT BIRDS ON A COLD TRAIL

115 **"Somebody stole birds from a museum!":** Edwin Rist, interview by author, May 26, 2015.

115 **"We would ask any collectors":** Arthur Martin, "Priceless Tropical Birds 'Stolen to Decorate Dresses' from Natural History Museum," *Daily Mail,* August 13, 2009.

115 **"gang of thieves":** Sam Jones, "Fears National History Museum Birds Will Be Used as Fishing Lures," *Guardian,* August 13, 2009.

115 **"We keep an open mind":** Chris Greenwood, "Bird Specimens Stolen from National Collection," *Independent,* August 13, 2009.

115 **Edwin knew that it was too late:** Rist interview.

116 **Edwin purchased eleven hundred small Ziploc:** "Fluteplayer 1988: Seller Feedback," eBay.com.

116 **On November 12:** "Indian Crow Feathers for Sale, Buying New Flute!" ClassicFlyTying.com, November 12, 2009, now deleted from website, scan at Kirkwjohnson.com/screenshots.

116 **The following day:** "Fluteplayer 1988: Seller Feedback," eBay.com.

116 **"so if you still want some":** "Crow Feathers," ClassicFlyTying.com, November 12, 2009, now deleted from website, scan at Kirkwjohnson .com/screenshots.

116 **On November 28:** "Blue Chatter," ClassicFlyTying.com, November 29, 2009. http://www.classicflytying.com/index.php?showtopic=38760.

117 **She was skeptical:** Sergeant Adele Hopkin of Hertfordshire Constabulary, interview by author, January 20, 2015.

117 **a dedicated CITES team:** "Wildlife Crime in the United Kingdom," Directorate-General for Internal Policies, Policy Department A: Economic

and Scientific Policy, April 2016, p. 16, http://www.europarl.europa.eu
/RegData/etudes/IDAN/2016/578963/IPOL_IDA(2016)578963_EN.pdf.

117 **Adele asked them to be on the lookout:** Hopkin interview.

118 **Edwin didn't seem particularly concerned:** Mortimer to author, May 11, 2016.

118 **Mortimer, unsure of their legality:** Mortimer to author, May 2, 2016.

118 **Shortly after Edwin started selling:** Phil Castleman, interview by author, April 9, 2012.

118 **Edwin found that his buyers:** Rist interview.

119 **Two initial suspects emerged:** Natural History Museum at Tring to author, February 17, 2016.

119 **they had privately come to the conclusion:** Unpublished account of the scientific impact of the theft by the Tring's curators, provided to the author January 14, 2015.

120 **On March 6, he packed:** Rist interview.

120 **Dave Carne, who had recently sent:** Dave Carne to author, May 13, 2012.

120 **At the show, Carne saw Edwin:** Ibid.

121 **"Why are you selling this?!":** Jens Pilgaard, interview by author, April 16, 2017.

121 **The bill came to about $6,000:** Jens Pilgaard to author, September 22, 2013.

121 **he had recently started taking Japanese:** EdwinRist.com, screenshots at Kirkwjohnson.com/screenshots.

121 **he sent a follow-up note to Jens:** Edwin Rist to Jens Pilgaard, April 18, 2010.

12. FLUTEPLAYER 1988

122 **Massive salmon steaks:** Spezi, "DUTCH FLY FAIR 2010, the World of Fly Fishing," *Teutona.de*, August 3, 2010.

123 **To keep sane in those dark times:** Irish to author, September 13, 2016.

123 **Irish wandered through the tent:** Ibid.

123 **To Irish, it didn't look:** Ibid.

123 **"Some kid in England named Edwin Rist":** Ibid.

123 **"Flame Bowerbird male full skin":** "Flame Bowerbird Male Full Skin," ClassicFlyTying.com, May 7, 2010, http://www.classicflytying.com/index .php?showtopic=40163.

124 **Her department didn't have:** Sergeant Adele Hopkin of Hertfordshire Constabulary, interview by author, January 20, 2015.

125 September 2010 offerings: "Talented Fly Tier Turns Thief," FlyFishing .co.uk, November 18, 2010.

125 A few weeks later: Edwin Rist to Jens Pilgaard, April 18, 2010.

125 "A Mix pack for sale": "Classic Fly Tying—Trading Floor," ClassicFlyTying .co.uk, https://web.archive.org/web/20101129081054/http://www.classic flytying.com/index.php?showforum=9, screenshot of trading floor activity in 2010.

125 That night Edwin: Edwin Rist, interview by author, May 26, 2015.

125 He already had an invitation: Curtis Rist to Terry, December 6, 2010.

125 Early in the morning: Hopkin interview.

126 He was awake: Rist interview.

126 "Is something wrong?": Ibid.

13. BEHIND BARS

127 Edwin confessed immediately: Edwin Rist, interview by author, May 26, 2015.

127 He led them to his room: Ibid.

127 "I was having some psychological problems": Regina v. Edwin Rist, St. Albans Crown Court, April 8, 2011, transcript, p. 2.

127 He pointed out a flatscreen TV: Sergeant Adele Hopkin of Hertfordshire Constabulary, interview by author, January 20, 2015.

128 As the bars locked shut: Rist interview.

128 Adele called up the Tring: Hopkin interview.

129 Thinking that if he cooperated: Rist interview

129 He didn't feel particularly bad: Ibid.

130 "Oh my god! Is that a fly?!": Hopkin interview.

130 I could just leave!: Rist interview.

14. ROT IN HELL

131 Confessing to her was worse: Edwin Rist, interview by author, May 26, 2015.

131 When Anton, who was headed: Ibid.

131 His father also wanted to locate: Ibid.

132 The morning after his arrest: Ibid.

132 At his first court appearance: Ibid.

132 But Edwin's prosecutors: Ibid.

133 "extremely childish fantasies": "Exotic Bird Pelts 'Worth Millions' Stolen from Natural History Museum by Musician Acting Out 'James Bond' Fantasy," *Daily Mail*, November 27, 2010.

133 "Flute player admits": "Flute Player Admits Theft of 299 Rare Bird Skins," *BBC.com*, November 26, 2010.

133 "Exotic bird pelts": "Exotic Bird Pelts . . . ," *Daily Mail*, November 27, 2010.

133 "RARE FEATHER THIEF BUSTED": "Rare Feather Thief Busted . . . and He's One of Us. SHOCKING," FlyTyingForum.com, November 23, 2010, http://www.flytyingforum.com/index.php?showtopic=55614.

133 "I hope Rist, if found guilty": "Talented Fly Tier Turns Thief," FlyFishing.co.uk, November 18, 2010.

134 Before it was deleted: "Classic Fly Tying—The Lodge," ClassicFlyTying.com, https://web.archive.org/web/20101129081749/http://www.classicfly tying.com/index.php?showforum=10, screenshot of Lodge activity, November 29, 2010.

134 described as "irresponsible accusations": Ibid.

134 On November 29, 2010: "Stolen Bird Post," ClassicFlyTying.com, November 29, 2010, http://www.classicflytying.com/index.php?showtopic= 41583.

134 "There is no way to condone": "Welcome to FeathersMc.com," FeathersMc .com, screenshot of page as it appeared on December 1, 2010, https://web .archive.org/web/20101215041809/http://feathersmc.com/.

135 rot in hell: Rist interview.

135 The Honorable Judge Stephen Gullick: *Regina v. Edwin Rist*, St. Albans Crown Court, January 14, 2011, transcript, p. 1.

135 "Are you going to invite": Ibid.

15. THE DIAGNOSIS

137 "I prefer to do things": Simon Baron-Cohen, Sally Wheelwright, Janine Robinson, and Marc Woodbury-Smith, "The Adult Asperger Assessment (AAA): A Diagnostic Method," *Journal of Autism and Developmental Disorders* 35, no. 6 (2005): 807–19.

137 "Sorry, am I making you uncomfortable?": Edwin Rist, interview by author, May 26, 2015.

138 **His diagnosis of:** David Kushner, "The Autistic Hacker," *IEEE Spectrum*, June 27, 2011, http://spectrum.ieee.org/telecom/internet/the-autistic-hacker.

138 **to the term** *Asperger's Defense*: "Did Asperger's Make Him Do It?" NPR, August 24, 2011.

138 **Because of the way Edwin had spoken:** Rist interview.

138 **After Edwin filled out the questionnaire:** Ibid.

138 **"taken fly-tying to the highest level":** Simon Baron-Cohen, *Re Edwin Rist* (report), January 30, 2011.

138 **"I am persuaded that the shock of being arrested":** Ibid.

138 **armed with a diagnosis:** Rist interview.

16. THE ASPERGER'S DEFENSE

141 **To him, Edwin seemed fully aware:** *Regina v. Edwin Rist,* St. Albans Crown Court, April 8, 2011, transcript, p. 1.

141 **"offence was committed for financial gain":** Ibid.

142 **"explained that he used the money":** Ibid., p. 3.

142 **"a catastrophic event":** Ibid.

142 **"stealing knowledge from humanity":** Dr. Richard Lane, interview by author, January 20, 2015.

143 **"things didn't always go as":** Ibid.

143 **The prosecution was making him:** Edwin Rist, interview by author, May 26, 2015.

143 **"There's one TIC to be put":** *Regina v. Edwin Rist,* St. Albans Crown Court, April 8, 2011, transcript, p. 4.

145 **The door was secured:** *Regina v. Simon James Gibson, Maxine Ann Burridge, Jack Barnaby Anderson,* Court of Appeal, Royal Courts of Justice, Strand, March 6, 2001, transcript.

145 **They had meant only to look around:** Ibid.

145 **"offensive to the public":** "Posing with the Dead," News24.com, December 16, 2000.

146 **"a chocoholic being let loose":** *Regina v. Simon James Gibson, Maxine Ann Burridge, Jack Barnaby Anderson,* Court of Appeal, Royal Courts of Justice, Strand, March 6, 2001, transcript.

146 **"Edwin Rist, you may sit":** *Regina v. Edwin Rist,* St. Albans Crown Court, April 8, 2011, transcript, p. 11.

146 **"All that can be done is to try to support":** Ibid., p. 15.

17. THE MISSING SKINS

148 "Asperger's as a defence???": Anonymous to author, May 29, 2013.

148 "he certainly did not display": "Talented Fly Tier Turns Thief," Flyfishing
.co.uk, November 18, 2010, https://www.flyfishing.co.uk/fly-fishing-news
/107611-talented-fly-tier-turns-thief.html.

149 "available to pay": *Regina v. Edwin Rist,* St. Albans Crown Court, July 29,
2011, transcript p. 1.

149 "to lose his piccolo and flute": Ibid.

149 "Should he come into more money": "Natural History Museum Thief Ordered to Pay Thousands," BBC.com, July 30, 2011.

150 He asked Adele: Jens Pilgaard to Adele Hopkin, December 14, 2010.

150 "If you can give me a full accounting": Curtis Rist to Jens Pilgaard, December 28, 2010.

150 "out of the blue": Dave Carne to author, May 13, 2012.

150 "get raided by the police": Ibid.

151 "The Fly-Tying Crime Report": Morgan Lyle, "The Case of the Purloined
Pelts," *Fly Tyer,* Spring 2011, pp. 10–12.

151 She was proud that she'd arrested: Sergeant Adele Hopkin, interview by
author, July 28, 2015.

151 "Had there not been such a report": David Chrimes to author, May 18,
2012.

151 "The whole thing was a complete kick": Mark Adams and Dr. Robert Prys-
Jones, interview by author, January 21, 2015.

152 "We are pleased the matter has been": "Man Sentenced for Stealing Rare
Bird Skins from Natural History Museum," Natural History Museum at
Tring, April 8, 2011.

18. THE 21ST INTERNATIONAL FLY TYING SYMPOSIUM

156 searched for "Edwin": "Indian Crow Feathers for Sale, Buying new flute!"
ClassicFlyTying.com, November 12, 2009, now deleted from website, scan
at Kirkwjohnson.com/screenshots.

156 I mentioned an article: "Natural History Museum Thief Ordered to Pay
Thousands," *BBC News,* July 30, 2011.

158 To commemorate the departed: Michael D. Radencich, *Classic Salmon Fly
Pattern: Over 1700 Patterns from the Golden Age of Tying* (Mechanicsburg, Penn.: Stackpole, 2011), p. 300.

160 "What the hell": John McLain, interview by author, November 20, 2011.

19. THE LOST MEMORY OF THE OCEAN

164 the events of August 27: "Tring Museum Replica Rhino Horn Theft: Man Charged," *BBC News*, January 17, 2012.

164 With only six left in existence: Edward O. Wilson, *Half-Earth: Our Planet's Fight for Life* (New York: W. W. Norton, 2016), p. 29.

164 Vietnamese clubgoers, who: Nicky Reeves, "What Drives the Demand for Rhino Horns?" *Guardian*, March 3, 2017.

164 Months earlier, after Europol: Europol Public Information, "Involvement of an Irish Mobile OCG in the Illegal Trade in Rhino Horn," OC-SCAN Policy Brief for Threat Notice: 009-2001, June 2011.

164 Darren Bennett was sentenced: "Rhino Horn Thief Who Stole Fakes from Natural History Museum Jailed," *Telegraph*, December 7, 2013.

166 "The United Kingdom doesn't spend": Mark Adams and Dr. Robert Prys-Jones, interview by author, January 21, 2015.

166 In the middle of the twentieth century: "Scientific Impact of the Bird Specimen Theft from NHM Museum Tring 2009," courtesy curators at Tring.

166 feather samples from 150 years' worth: Ibid.

166 "memory of the ocean": Todd Datz, "Mercury on the Rise in Endangered Pacific Seabirds," Harvard School of Public Health, April 18, 2011.

167 Scientists can now pluck a feather: Dr. Richard O. Prum, interview by author, April 18, 2013.

167 Specimens in the collection: "Scientific Impact of the Bird Specimen Theft."

171 191 skins had been recovered: "Natural History Museum Thief Ordered to Pay Thousands," *BBC News*, July 30, 2011.

170 In one article: "Student, 22, Ordered to Pay Back £125,000 He Made from Theft of 299 Rare Bird Skins," *Daily Mail*, July 31, 2011.

172 "couple of weeks": "Exotic Bird Pelts 'Worth Millions' Stolen from Natural History Museum by Musician Acting Out 'James Bond' Fantasy," *Daily Mail*, November 27, 2010.

173 "I looked you up, suspicious copper": Sergeant Adele Hopkin, interview by author, January 20, 2015.

20. CHASING LEADS IN A TIME MACHINE

179 **In his first year, 2009, he tied:** Gordon van der Spuy, "Our Own Major Traherne," *African Angler,* June–July 2014, pp. 10–15.

179 **Elvis Has Left the Building:** Ibid.

179 **the Blue Uncharmed:** Ibid.

179 **"No no no no no":** Ruhan Neethling, interview by author, January 19, 2016.

182 **until he forwarded proof:** Mark Adams to Flemming Sejer Andersen, December 6, 2010.

183 **a post from July 26, 2010:** Bud Guidry, "It's Found a New Home," Clas sicFlyTying.com, July 26, 2010.

184 **On four separate dates:** "Classic Fly Tying—Trading Floor," ClassicFlyTying .com, https://web.archive.org/web/20101129081054/http://www.classicfly tying.com/index.php?showforum=9, screenshot of page as it existed in 2010.

184 **There was a listing for a full Blue Chatterer:** Ibid.

185 **"We do it to ourselves":** "Crow Anyone?" ClassicFlyTying.com, April 21, 2010.

185 **"Have a friend in need":** "Classic Fly Tying—Trading Floor," ClassicFly Tying.com, https://web.archive.org/web/20101129081054/http://www.classic flytying.com/index.php?showforum=9, screenshot of page as it existed in 2010.

185 **On October 6, 2010:** "Blue Chatter for Sale, Cotinga Cayana," ClassicFly Tying.com, October 19, 2010, now deleted from website, scan at Kirkwjohnson.com/screenshots.

186 **On November 11:** "Classic Fly Tying—Trading Floor," ClassicFlyTying.com, https://web.archive.org/web/20101129081054/http://www.classicflytying .com/index.php?showforum=9, screenshot of page as it appeared in 2010.

21. DR. PRUM'S THUMB DRIVE

188 **"I was trying to get Fish and Wildlife":** Dr. Richard O. Prum, interview by author, April 18, 2013.

189 **"Nine or ten vendors were displaying":** Richard O. Prum, "Notes on Fly Tying International Symposium," November 20, 2010.

190 **"Exotic Materials Photo Album and Sale Page":** "Exotic Materials Photo Album and Sale Page," EdwinRist.com; no longer on website, screenshots at Kirkwjohnson.com/screenshots.

190 **"the Masoni subspecies":** Ibid.

191 **"had not been motivated by money":** Simon Baron-Cohen, *Re Edwin Rist,* January 30, 2011.

191 **"I am currently working on a book":** "About," EdwinRist.com; no longer on website, screenshots at Kirkwjohnson.com/screenshots.

192 **"Oi! lonngu sama!!":** Facebook post, December 9, 2009, screenshot.

192 **"Flame bowerbird, male, full skin":** "Flame Bowerbird Male Full Skin— Trading Floor," ClassicFlyTying.com, May 7, 2010, http://www.classicfly tying.com/index.php?showtopic=40163.

193 **"I know this happened back in 2010":** "Cotinga—Classic Salmon Flies," Facebook group discussion, August 27, 2013, screenshot.

194 **a post entitled "Long Nguyen":** Edwin Rist, "Long Nguyen," ClassicFlyTying .com, March 7, 2015, http://www.classicflytying.com/index.php?show topic=54555.

195 **"I hope you understand":** Edwin Rist to author, February 15, 2012.

22. "I'M NOT A THIEF"

200 **"We could be done in two hours":** Edwin Rist, interview by author, May 26, 2015.

201 **419-million-year-old bacterial DNA:** J. S. Park et al., "Haloarchaeal Diversity in 23, 121 and 419 MYA Salts," *Geobiology* 7, no. 5 (2009): 515–23.

203 **a "marked impairment":** Simon Baron-Cohen, Sally Wheelwright, Janine Robinson, and Marc Woodbury-Smith, "The Adult Asperger Assessment (AAA): A Diagnostic Method," *Journal of Autism and Developmental Disorders* 35, no. 6 (2005): 807–19.

203 **lack of "theory of mind":** Simon Baron-Cohen, Alan M. Leslie, and Uta Frith, "Does the Autistic Child Have a 'Theory of Mind'?" *Cognition* 21 (1985): 37–46.

210 **"Hi Kirk. Got words from Edwin":** Long Nguyen to author, May 27, 2015.

23. THREE DAYS IN NORWAY

214 **"basically a millionaire":** Edwin Rist, interview by author, May 26, 2015.

215 **He'd said online that it had been:** Facebook album, December 8, 2009, screenshot.

215 **"I guess you'll want to see":** Long Nguyen, interview by author, October 9, 2015.

220 **"What should I feel?":** Ibid.

222 **thanks to Walter Palmer:** "Cecil the Lion: No Charges for Walter Palmer, Says Zimbabwe," *BBC News*, October 12, 2015.

224 **Twenty-one years earlier:** "Greatest Heists in Art History," *BBC News*, August 23, 2004.

227 **the case against his friend "looks bad":** Rist interview.

24. MICHELANGELO VANISHES

230 **"life source had drained away":** Long Nguyen to author, January 11, 2016.

231 **My first attempt to speak about it:** Simon Baron-Cohen to author, May 27, 2013.

231 **"There is no biological test of autism":** Simon Baron-Cohen to author, October 27, 2015.

231 **"Whether those self-perceptions":** Lizzie Buchen, "Scientists and Autism: When Geeks Meet," *Nature*, November 2, 2011.

232 **the American Psychiatric Association:** Hanna Rosin, "Letting Go of Asperger's," *The Atlantic*, March 2014.

232 **"Whether a child was labeled":** Catherine Lord et al., "A Multisite Study of the Clinical Diagnosis of Different Autism Spectrum Disorders," *Archives of General Psychiatry* 69, no. 3 (2012): 306.

232 **"Psychiatric diagnoses are not":** Simon Baron-Cohen, "The Short Life of a Diagnosis," *New York Times*, November 9, 2009.

233 **his friend "deserved them":** Edwin Rist, interview by author, May 26, 2015.

233 **"to refine my knowledge":** Paul Sweet to author, April 20, 2017.

234 **Delisle told me he was no longer:** Robert Delisle to author, January 13, 2016.

234 **"ten Indian Crows":** Ibid.

235 **Under the handle Bobfly2007:** "Feedback Profile: Bobfly 2007," eBay.com, http://feedback.ebay.com/ws/eBayISAPI.dll?ViewFeedback2, accessed May 26, 2016, page no longer exists.

235 **A simple search for Flame Bowerbird:** "Feedback Profile: Lifeisgood.503," eBay.com, http://feedback.ebay.com/ws/eBayISAPI.dll?ViewFeedback2, accessed May 26, 2016, page no longer exists.

237 **"eBay is committed to doing":** Ryan Moore to author, May 3, 2016.

238 **"The black eye of greed":** "The Tring's Missing Birds," ClassicFlyTying .com, March 29, 2016, printout of now-deleted post.

25. FEATHERS IN THE BLOODSTREAM

239 **"Good luck"**: Robert Delisle to author, February 12, 2016.

242 **"lines of Aigrettes, Paradise and Ostrich"**: "Ph. Adelson & Bro.," *Illustrated Milliner* 9 (January 1908), p. 51.

242 **"to dictate to American women"**: "Notes and Comments," *Millinery Trade Review* 33 (1899), p. 40.

242 **"The foolish laws that now exist"**: Ibid.

244 **"It's really hard to convince people"**: Long Nguyen to author, October 25, 2015.

244 **"The knowledge of its falsity"**: Edwin Rist, interview by author, May 26, 2015.

244 **the tale of Eddie Wolfer**: Eddie Wolfer, "Dear Friends and Forum Members," ClassicFlyTying.com, December 7, 2014, printout of now-deleted post.

245 **his ninety-three-year-old father**: Bill Wallace to author, April 24, 2017.

246 **shipped from the Black Forest region**: Robert M. Poole, "Native Trout Are Returning to America's Rivers," *Smithsonian*, August 2017.

247 **"the ultimate candy store"**: Chuck Furimsky, "A Note from the Director," InternationalFlyTyingSymposium.com, June 19, 2017.

247 **"stopping the darkness of my greed"**: "Man Who Tried Smuggling 51 Turtles in His Pants Gets 5 Years in Prison," *Associated Press*, April 12, 2016.

247 **"Thank goodness it was protected"**: "Whats that daddy and why the big smile," ClassicFlyTying.com, October 18, 2012.

248 **"Paging: Secret Agent Edwin Rist"**: Charlie Jenkem, "Paging: Secret Agent Edwin Rist," *Drake*, March 1, 2013.

A NOTE ON SOURCES

This book draws extensively upon primary sources, including court transcripts, statements to the police, private correspondence and e-mails, an unpublished museum account of the theft, and character reference letters and other reports prepared for the Crown Court. Some of these were obtained through a Freedom of Information request; others were shared directly by the participants. In some cases, sources were granted anonymity and a pseudonym: their names appear in quotes in the first instance.

I have benefited enormously from hundreds of hours of interviews with dozens of fly-tiers, ornithologists, evolutionary biologists, historians, curators, prosecutors in the Crown Prosecution Service, members of the Hertfordshire Constabulary, feather dealers, agents from the U.S. Fish and Wildlife Service, and the characters at the heart of this story.

Before writing this book, I shared the assumption with many that something posted online can rarely be removed, but it became painfully clear to me just how naïve I was: this investigation was constantly racing against time or, more precisely, against the delete key. I have hundreds of screenshots of Facebook and forum posts related to the Tring heist that were deleted shortly after I took them.

The Internet Archive's Wayback Machine was helpful with exhuming a number of posts that had been wiped before I began the investigation. Additional screenshots were sent to me by sources who were concerned about the content.

Where an individual's remarks appear in quotations, I am drawing directly from transcripts of a recorded conversation, the original e-mail, court document, forum post, phone text, or Facebook comment. In some instances, particularly with forum and Facebook posts, spelling and grammar have been lightly edited for ease of reading.

To reconstruct Wallace's story, I am particularly indebted to the work of John van Wyhe, Michael Shermer, Ross Slotten, and Peter Raby, but nothing beats reading this brilliant writer in his own words. I have drawn heavily on the original notebooks and letters of Alfred Russel Wallace, helpfully digitized as part of the Wallace Correspondence Project and the Linnean Society.

For Victorian-era history, Lynn Merrill, Richard Conniff, Miriam Rothschild, D. E. Allen, Michael Shrubb, and Ann Colley's scholarship was critical.

For feather fashion history, Robin Doughty's *Feather Fashions and Bird Preservation* was of paramount importance. Barbara and Richard Mearns's *The Bird Collectors* was also helpful, as was the twenty-seven-volume *Catalogue of the Birds in the British Museum* (1874–98). Thor Hanson was generous with his time: *Feathers* was a joy to read. Other archival material was made available through the libraries at the University of Southern California.

The fly-fishing and fly-tying writings of Andrew Herd and Morgan Lyle were immensely valuable to me.

I have outlined many crucial sources in the bibliography, and have also credited key insights in the notes section.

BIBLIOGRAPHY

Allen, David Elliston. *The Naturalist in Britain: A Social History.* Princeton, N.J.: Princeton University Press, 1994.

Attenborough, David. *Alfred Russel Wallace and the Birds of Paradise.* Centenary Lecture, Bristol University, September 24, 2009.

Attenborough, David, and Errol Fuller. *Drawn from Paradise: The Discovery, Art and Natural History of the Birds of Paradise.* New York: Harper Design, 2012.

Audubon, John J. *Birds of America.* New York and London: 1827–1838.

Baron-Cohen, Simon. *Autism and Asperger Syndrome.* Oxford: Oxford University Press, 2008.

———. *Mindblindness: An Essay on Autism and Theory of Mind.* Cambridge, Mass.: MIT Press, 1995.

———. "Two New Theories of Autism: Hyper-systemising and Assortative Mating." *Archives of Disease in Childhood* 91, no. 1 (2006): 2–5.

Baron-Cohen, Simon, Sally Wheelwright, Janine Robinson, and Marc Woodbury-Smith. "The Adult Asperger Assessment (AAA): A Diagnostic Method." *Journal of Autism and Developmental Disorders* 35, no. 6 (2005): 807–19.

Berners, Juliana B., and Wynkyn de Worde. *A Treatyse of Fysshynge wyth an Angle.* 1496; reprint by London: Elliot Stock, 1880.

Blacker, William. *Blacker's Art of Fly Making, &c. Comprising Angling, & Dyeing of Colours: With Engravings of Salmon & Trout Flies Showing the Process of the Gentle Craft as Taught in the Pages: With Descriptions of Flies for the Season.* 1842; reprint London: George Nichols, 1855.

Bowman, Karen. *Corsets and Codpieces: A History of Outrageous Fashion, from Roman Times to the Modern Era.* New York: Skyhorse, 2015.

Brackman, Arnold C. *A Delicate Arrangement: The Strange Case of Charles Darwin and Alfred Russel Wallace.* New York: Times, 1980.

Catalogue of the Birds in the British Museum. London: Printed by Order of the Trustees, 1877.

Cocker, Mark, David Tipling, Jonathan Elphick, and John Fanshawe. *Birds and People.* New York: Random House, 2013.

Colley, Ann C. *Wild Animal Skins in Victorian Britain: Zoos, Collections, Portraits, and Maps.* London: Routledge, 2014.

Conniff, Richard. *The Species Seekers: Heroes, Fools, and the Mad Pursuit of Life on Earth.* New York: W. W. Norton, 2011.

Cooper, J. H., and M. P. Adams. "Extinct and Endangered Bird Collections: Managing the Risk." *Zoologische Mededelingen* 79, no. 3 (2005): 123–30.

Cowles, Virginia. *The Rothschilds: A Family of Fortune.* New York: Alfred A. Knopf, 1973.

Cronin, Helena. *The Ant and the Peacock: Altruism and Sexual Selection from Darwin to Today.* New York: Cambridge University Press, 1991.

Darwin, Charles. *The Descent of Man: And Selection in Relation to Sex.* New York: D. Appleton, 1871.

Darwin, Charles, Robert Jastrow, and Kenneth Korey. *The Essential Darwin.* Boston: Little, Brown, 1984.

Davies, James Boyd. *The Practical Naturalist's Guide: Containing Instructions for Collecting, Preparing and Preserving Specimens in All Departments of Zoology, Intended for the Use of Students, Amateurs and Travellers.* Edinburgh: MacLachlan & Stewart, 1858.

Daws, Gavan, and Marty Fujita. *Archipelago: The Islands of Indonesia: From the Nineteenth-Century Discoveries of Alfred Russel Wallace to the Fate of Forests and Reefs in the Twenty-first Century.* Berkeley: University of California Press, 1999.

Desmond, Adrian J., and James R. Moore. *Darwin*. New York: W. W. Norton, 1991.

Doughty, Robin W. *Feather Fashions and Bird Preservation: A Study in Nature Protection*. Berkeley: University of California Press, 1975.

Douglas, Marjory Stoneman. *The Everglades: River of Grass*. New York: Rinehart, 1947.

Edwards, William H. *A Voyage Up the River Amazon: Including a Residence at Pará*. New York: D. Appleton, 1847.

Ferguson, Niall. *The House of Rothschild*. New York: Viking, 1998.

Fuller, Errol. *Voodoo Salon: Taxidermy*. London: Stacey, 2014.

Garfield, Brian. *The Meinertzhagen Mystery: The Life and Legend of a Colossal Fraud*. Washington, D.C.: Potomac, 2007.

Goodrich, Samuel G. *History of All Nations, from the Earliest Periods to the Present*. Auburn, N.Y.: Miller, Orton and Mulligan, 1854.

Greenberg, Joel. *A Feathered River Across the Sky: The Passenger Pigeon's Flight to Extinction*. New York: Bloomsbury, 2014.

Greene, W. T. *Birds of the British Empire*. London: Imperial Press, 1898.

Hanson, Thor. *Feathers: The Evolution of a Natural Miracle*. New York: Basic Books, 2011.

Hartert, Ernst. *Types of Birds in the Tring Museum*. Tring, U.K.: Zoological Museum, 1918.

Herd, Andrew. *The Fly*. Ellesmere, U.K.: Medlar Press, 2003.

Hornaday, William T. *Our Vanishing Wildlife: Its Extermination and Preservation*. New York: Charles Scribner's, 1913.

———. *Thirty Years War for Wildlife: Gains and Losses in the Thankless Task*. New York: Charles Scribner's, 1931.

Huffstodt, Jim. *Everglades Lawmen: True Stories of Danger and Adventure in the Glades*. Sarasota, Fla.: Pineapple, 2000.

Hume, Julian P., and Michael Walters. *Extinct Birds*. London: Bloomsbury, 2012.

Huxley, Thomas Henry. *Evidence as to Man's Place in Nature*. New York: D. Appleton, 1863.

Kelson, George M. *The Salmon Fly: How to Dress It and How to Use It*. London: Wyman & Sons, 1895.

———. *Tips*. London: Published by the Author, 1901.

Kolbert, Elizabeth. *The Sixth Extinction: An Unnatural History.* New York: Henry Holt, 2014.

Kushner, David. "The Autistic Hacker." *IEEE Spectrum,* June 27, 2011.

Laman, Tim, and Edwin Scholes. *Birds of Paradise: Revealing the World's Most Extraordinary Birds.* Washington, D.C.: National Geographic Books, 2012.

Langlade, Émile. *Rose Bertin, the Creator of Fashion at the Court of Marie-Antoinette.* London: J. Long, 1913.

Lefèvre, Edmond. *Le Commerce et l'industrie de la plume pour parure.* Paris: Chez l'auteur, 1914.

Lord, Catherine, et al. "A Multisite Study of the Clinical Diagnosis of Different Autism Spectrum Disorders." *Archives of General Psychiatry* 69, no. 3 (2012): 306.

Lyle, Morgan. *Simple Flies.* Mechanicsburg, Penn.: Stackpole, 2015.

McClane, A. J. *Fishing with McClane.* Upper Saddle River, N.J.: Prentice Hall, 1975.

McIver, Stuart B. *Death in the Everglades: The Murder of Guy Bradley, America's First Martyr to Environmentalism.* Gainesville: University of Florida Press, 2003.

Mearns, Barbara, and Richard Mearns. *The Bird Collectors.* San Diego: Academic Press, 1998.

Merrill, Lynn L. *The Romance of Victorian Natural History.* New York: Oxford University Press, 1989.

Nichol, John. *Animal Smugglers.* New York: Facts on File, 1987.

Pearson, Thomas G. *Adventures in Bird Protection: An Autobiography.* New York: D. Appleton-Century, 1937.

Prum, Richard O. "Aesthetic Evolution by Mate Choice: Darwin's Really Dangerous Idea." *Philosophical Transactions of the Royal Society B* 367, no. 1600 (2012).

——. *The Evolution of Beauty.* New York: Doubleday, 2017.

Prum, Richard O., and Ann E. Johnson. "Display Behavior, Foraging Ecology, and Systematics of the Golden-Winged Manakin (*Masius chrysopterus*)." *Wilson Bulletin* 99, no. 4 (1987): 521–39.

Prum, Richard O., and Vololontiana R. Razafindratsita. "Lek Behavior and Natural History of the Velvet Asity (*Philepitra castanea*: Eurylaimidae). *Wilson Bulletin* 109, no. 3 (1997): 371–92.

Prum, Richard O., et al. "Mechanism of Carotenoid Coloration in the Brightly Colored Plumages of Broadbills (Eurylaimidae)." *Journal of Comparative Physiology B* 184, no. 5 (2014): 651–72.

Pryce-Tannatt, Thomas Edwin. *How to Dress Salmon Flies: A Handbook for Amateurs.* London: Adam & Charles Black, 1914.

Purdy, Jedediah. *After Nature: A Politics for the Anthropocene.* Cambridge: Harvard University Press, 2015.

Raby, Peter. *Alfred Russel Wallace: A Life.* Princeton, N.J.: Princeton University Press, 2001.

Radencich, Michael D. *Classic Salmon Fly Patterns: Over 1700 Patterns from the Golden Age of Tying.* Mechanicsburg, Penn.: Stackpole, 2011.

Rasmussen, Pamela C., and Robert P. Prys-Jones. "History vs. Mystery: The Reliability of Museum Specimen Data." *Bulletin of the British Ornithologists' Club* 1232.A (2003): 66–94.

Ronalds, Alfred. *The Fly-Fisher's Entomology.* 1839; reprinted Secaucus, N.J.: Wellfleet Press, 1990.

Rookmaaker, Kees, and John van Wyhe. "In Alfred Russel Wallace's Shadow: His Forgotten Assistant, Charles Allen (1839–1892)." *Journal of the Malaysian Branch of the Royal Asiatic Society* 85, pt. 2 (2012): 17–54.

Rothschild, Miriam. *Walter Rothschild: The Man, the Museum and the Menagerie.* London: Natural History Museum, 2008.

Rothschild, Walter. *Extinct Birds: An Attempt to Unite in One Volume a Short Account of those Birds Which Have Become Extinct in Historical Times.* London: Hutchinson, 1907.

Royal Society for the Protection of Birds. *Feathers and Facts: A Reply to the Feather-Trade, and Review of Facts with Reference to the Persecution of Birds for their Plumage.* London: Withersby & Co., 1911.

Salmon, Michael A., Peter Marren, and Basil Harley. *The Aurelian Legacy: British Butterflies and Their Collectors.* Berkeley: University of California Press, 2000.

Schmookler, Paul, and Ingrid V. Sils. *Rare and Unusual Fly Tying Materials: A Natural History Treating Both Standard and Rare Materials, Their Sources and Geography, as Used in Classic, Contemporary, and*

Artistic Trout and Salmon Flies. Millis, Mass.: Complete Sportsman, 1994.

Schmookler, Paul M., Ingrid V. Sils, and J. David Zincavage. *The Salmon Flies of Major John Popkin Traherne (1826–1901): Their Descriptions and Variations.* Millis, Mass.: Complete Sportsman, 1993.

Shermer, Michael. *In Darwin's Shadow: The Life and Science of Alfred Russel Wallace: A Biographical Study on the Psychology of History.* Oxford: Oxford University Press, 2002.

Shrubb, Michael. *Feasting, Fowling and Feathers: A History of the Exploitation of Wild Birds.* London: T & AD Poyser, 2013.

Silberman, Steve. *NeuroTribes: The Legacy of Autism and the Future of Neurodiversity.* New York: Avery, 2015.

Slotten, Ross A. *The Heretic in Darwin's Court: The Life of Alfred Russel Wallace.* New York: Columbia University Press, 2004.

Smith, Harold H. *Aigrettes and Birdskins: The Truth About Their Collection & Export.* London: "Tropical Life" Publishing Department, John Bale, Sons & Danielsson, 1910.

Stein, Sarah A. *Plumes: Ostrich Feathers, Jews, and a Lost World of Global Commerce.* New Haven, Conn.: Yale University Press, 2010.

Tocqueville, Alexis de. *Democracy in America.* Translated by Henry Reeve. London: Saunders and Otley, 1840.

Van Kleeck, Mary. *A Seasonal Industry: A Study of the Millinery Trade in New York.* New York: Russell Sage Foundation, 1917.

Wallace, Alfred Russel. *The Annotated Malay Archipelago.* Edited by John van Wyhe. Singapore: National University of Singapore Press, 2015.

———. "Letter Concerning the Fire on the *Helen.*" *Zoologist.* November 1852.

———. *Letters and Reminiscences.* Edited by James Marchant. 1916; reprint New York: Arno Press, 1975.

———. *Letters from the Malay Archipelago.* Edited by John van Wyhe, and L. C. Rookmaaker. New York: Oxford University Press, 2013.

———. "Museums for the People." *Macmillan's Magazine* 19 (1869): 244–50.

———. *My Life; A Record of Events and Opinions.* London: Chapman & Hall, 1905.

———. "Narrative of Search after Birds of Paradise." *Proceedings of the Zoological Society of London* (1862): 153–61.

———. *A Narrative of Travels on the Amazon and Rio Negro, with an Account of the Native Tribes, and Observations on the Climate, Geology, and Natural History of the Amazon Valley.* London: Reeve, 1853.

———. "On the Habits of the Butterflies of the Amazon Valley." *Transactions of the Entomological Society of London* (n.s.) 2 (1854): 253–64.

———. "On the Monkeys of the Amazon." *Proceedings of the Zoological Society of London* 20 (December 14, 1852): 107–10.

———. "On the Physical Geography of the Malay Archipelago." *Journal of the Royal Geographical Society* 33 (1863): 217–34.

Walters, M. P. "My Life with Eggs." *Zoologische Mededelingen* 79, no. 3 (2005): 5–18.

Waterman, Charles F. *History of Angling.* Tulsa, Okla.: Winchester, 1981.

Waterton, Charles. *Wanderings in South America.* London: B. Fellowes, 1825.

Wells, Jeffrey V. *Birder's Conservation Handbook: 100 North American Birds at Risk.* Princeton, N.J.: Princeton University Press, 2010.

Whittingham, Sarah. *The Victorian Fern Craze.* Oxford: Shire, 2009.

Whitelaw, Ian. *The History of Fly-Fishing in Fifty Flies.* New York: Stewart Tabori & Chang, 2015.

Why Museums Matter: Avian Archives in an Age of Extinction. Papers from a conference of this title held at Green Park, Aston Clinton, and workshops at the Natural History Museum, Tring, November 12–15, 1999. *Bulletin of the British Ornithologists' Club* 123A (2003).

Wilson, Edward O. *The Future of Life.* New York: Alfred A. Knopf, 2002.

———. *Half-Earth: Our Planet's Fight for Life.* W. W. Norton, 2016.

Wolmar, Christian. *Fire & Steam: How the Railways Transformed Britain.* London: Atlantic, 2008.

Wyhe, John Van, and Gerrell M. Drawhorn. "'I am Ali Wallace': The Malay Assistant of Alfred Russel Wallace." *Journal of the Malaysian Branch of the Royal Asiatic Society* 88, no. 1 (2015): 3–31.

INDEX